The Universal Kitchen

The
Universal
Kitchen

by Elisabeth Rozin

Viking

VIKING
Published by the Penguin Group
Penguin Books USA Inc., 375 Hudson Street,
New York, New York 10014, U.S.A.
Penguin Books Ltd, 27 Wrights Lane,
London W8 5TZ, England
Penguin Books Australia Ltd, Ringwood,
Victoria, Australia
Penguin Books Canada Ltd, 10 Alcorn Avenue,
Toronto, Ontario, Canada M4V 3B2
Penguin Books (N.Z.) Ltd, 182–190 Wairau Road,
Auckland 10, New Zealand

Penguin Books Ltd, Registered Offices:
Harmondsworth, Middlesex, England

First published in 1996 by Viking Penguin,
a division of Penguin Books USA Inc.

1   3   5   7   9   10   8   6   4   2

Excerpt from Ishi in Two Worlds: A Biography of the
Last Wild Indian in North America by Theodora Kroeber
(University of California Press, 1961). Used by permission.

Rozin, Elisabeth
The universal kitchen / Elisabeth Rozin.
p.   cm.
Includes bibliographical references and index.
ISBN 0-670-85404-2
1. Cookery, International.   I. Title.
TX725.A1R686   1996
641.59—dc20   96-11115

Printed in the United States of America
Set in New Baskerville
Designed by LiLi Yen

To all the cooks

who didn't write books.

Salud!

Acknowledgments

As always, I am deeply grateful for the love, support, and encouragement of my family and friends, who sampled endlessly and critiqued mercilessly.

Many thanks and an extra helping of dessert to my son Lex, whose passion for food is exceeded only by his passion for music, and who in many lively discussions has helped me to a better understanding of both.

Kudos to those generous friends and colleagues who tested the recipes and gave unsparingly of their time, their enthusiasm, and their skill: Rick Bell, Reid Bodek, Marion Briefer, Lynn Buono, Fifi Epstein, Alyne Freed, Linda Gellman, Norma Gottlieb, Jon Jividen, Ruth Loewen, Arden Neisser, Marci Pelchat, Irene Pleasure, Patricia Pliner, Rosalie Rivera, Lex Rozin, Lillian Rozin, Phyllis Stein-Novack, Judy Stern, Marcy Stricker.

And, finally, a grateful acknowledgment to my editor, Dawn Drzal, who did her job with savvy and intelligence, suffered my crotchets with good grace, and kept me (mostly) honest.

Contents

Introduction

One of the marvelous things about America's great cities is the opportunity they offer to sample what seems to be an almost un- limited number of ethnic cuisines. If we ignore for the moment the dollar's ever-shrinking capacity to satisfy one's desires, it is always possible to engage in the pleasant debate about what kind of food to eat. "Shall we go Indian tonight?" we ask one another, conjuring up visions of succulent chicken korma braised in a richly spiced sauce, and crisp little samosas filled with flavorful vegetables. Or should we try one of the new little Vietnamese restaurants that specialize in caramel pork, slow-simmered to aromatic perfection in a clay pot, and cha gio, the delicate fried rice-paper spring rolls stuffed with crabmeat and beansprouts? Or perhaps we might think of sampling a Polish bigos, that robust stew of mixed meats and sauerkraut, served with our favorite pierogi, tender dumplings filled with mashed potato and slathered with sour cream.

Implicit in this imaginary gastronomic odyssey is the assumption that we have some understanding of what these cuisines are about, what makes them different and distinguishable from one another. We can experience in our minds as well as in our mouths the variety of sensations that are likely to be provided by an Indian or a Vietnamese or a Polish meal, and describe in mouthwatering detail the textures, the flavors, the aromas that each dish offers. And so we make a choice of what to eat, a decision based on describable differences, on the characteristics that make all cuisines unique and distinctive.

This is the close-up view, a way of looking at cuisine that we as cooks and consumers find useful and informative. But what if we were to reverse the lens, as it were, and look at cuisine from the long view? What new perspectives may occur if we step back from the details of individual cuisines and scan the wide panorama of world cookery? What happens is an interesting new way of seeing things, for as the details fade out, larger patterns begin to emerge, and it is these larger patterns that give us some insight into the universal activity we call cooking. This is the view that shows us how profoundly similar our food habits are, how much we share of kitchen practice, how deeply alike we really all are.

Remember the three meals we contemplated. Certainly Indian, Vietnamese, and Polish are very separate and distinct traditions, in terms of culture, geography, and food. But look once again. The chicken korma, the caramel pork, the bigos are simply three different versions of meat slowly cooked in a savory liquid. The samosas, the spring rolls, the pierogi are really all the same thing, an envelope of dough filled with a savory stuffing and served with a condiment or sauce. And these three are just a few examples of a product that is so widespread that it can be called universal, including such familiar favorites as ravioli from Italy, pot-stickers from China, empanadas from Cuba, knishes from Eastern Europe.

What we see, through this wide-angle culinary lens, is a pervasive commonality in kitchen practice, across cultures and throughout time. There are, indeed, a good number of such familiar forms and practices, extraordinary parallels in the preparation and presentation of food, that make clear that no matter who we are or where we come from, we are all doing the same thing. We all make tasty and nourishing broths from the bones of animals; we all simmer meats and vegetables in pots of seasoned liquids; we all devise piquant condiments and savory sauces to give zest and excitement to our food. And, yes, we all stuff envelopes of dough with savory fillings. And, what's more, we seem to experience these products in very much the same way, as festive delicacies, special treats, fun food.

It is fascinating to speculate about these striking similarities of technique, of form, of food preference, which seem as a common human experience to have their origins in a long-distant past. Are our contemporary practices genuinely comparable to those of some paleolithic housewife, grinding seeds in a stone mortar or stewing chunks of mastodon in a pot made of animal intestine? Indeed they are, because despite enormous advances in technology, the basic techniques and the basic tastes remain very much the same. Heat is heat and meat is meat. We have gas grills and electronic burners and microwave ovens, but they perform the same function that the hearth fire performed. We may favor rack of lamb over mastodon, but both foods fulfill the nearly universal desire for red meat.

Of course, the food has changed through the generations, becoming ever more elaborate and complex. Like other traditions, cuisines evolve—adapting, enlarging, innovating, according to the needs of people and the constraints of the environment, responding to new choices of ingredients and technologies with ever-expanding sets of products and practices. Yet, for all the changes and the choices made by so many different people in so many different places, our cuisines have evolved along remarkably similar lines, eloquent testimony to the universality of the human food experience.

One of our cherished myths in America is that of the melting pot, the coming together of many diverse traditions to meld into an undistinguishable mush. From the long view of culinary history, however, it may be quite the opposite: we humans undertook our destiny as the cooking animal with a fairly uniform set of techniques and tastes, which then elaborated and branched into a wide variety of individual forms, the multitude of ethnic cuisines we know today. But what was created in the beginning by who we were then is still there for who we are now. The kitchen may truly be one of the few places where we can celebrate commonality as well as diversity, for we all trace the roots of what we eat back to the ancestral melting pot and to those among us who first put fire and salt to meat.

Talking Recipes

In a desire to document as fully as possible the premise of this book—that despite vast differences in geography and culture we are all doing very much the same things with our food—I would have liked to provide recipes for every category from every possible cuisine. But since my publisher had not contracted for a lifetime project or a twenty-volume set, I was (wisely) kept in check and forced to select a subset of samples from a variety of cuisines to illustrate each product or technique. I had some clear goals: first, to present recipes for food that would be appealing and interesting; second, to present, overall, examples from as many different cuisines as possible; and, third, to choose wherever possible recipes and cuisines that are not so familiar or so frequently covered in our cookbook repertoire.

As for the recipes themselves, I have tried, as always, to keep them as simple and as easy to prepare as possible, without sacrificing their basic authenticity. There is of course a real sense in which any food prepared outside its home environment can never be wholly authentic, but I have exercised care over the ingredients, the techniques, the basic feel and flavor of the food. The global village provides many of us with a vast assortment of ethnic ingredients that were once very difficult to obtain, but wherever I could I have suggested alternatives. To explore fully the varied delights of ethnic cooking, you should get to know your ethnic neighborhoods, groceries, and restaurants. Taste, smell, read labels, ask questions; you'll discover that most shopkeepers and restauranteurs are flattered by your interest and eager to help.

And so to the cooking itself. It cannot be said too often: always read the recipe through before you start, so that you know where you're headed, how long it will take, and what you need to do to get there.

Where preheating is critical, as in baked goods and some casseroles, I have placed instructions in the body of the recipe; otherwise, they occur at the end of the recipe, as in ". . . bake in a preheated 350° oven."

Use eggs that are graded large, unless otherwise specified.

Lemon and lime juice should always be fresh—use bottled for emergencies only.

Herbs are always better fresh, with the following qualifications: fresh oregano is sometimes flat and sometimes bitter; unless you have a reliable supply, the dried is fine (and remember that the Mexican is somewhat more pungent than the Greek). Dried mint sometimes works better in sauces and stews; I use it when the original traditions themselves call for it. Dried parsley and dried coriander leaf (cilantro) are utterly useless; don't waste your money on them. Coriander leaf is so named in Old World recipes; in New World (i.e., Mexican and Carribbean) recipes it is called cilantro. Fresh lemon grass sometimes has an unpleasant strawlike texture in a soup or sauce; the dried powder provides good flavor and you don't have to strain it out at the end.

Spices should be bought in small quantities and stored in tightly covered containers. A small, inexpensive coffee grinder to use exclusively as a spice grinder is useful for Indian food, in which toasted freshly ground spices are a must. Curry powders are useful, particularly for cuisines that use them as ready-made spice blends—those of Africa, the Caribbean, Southeast Asia. Keep several different varieties on hand.

Brown sugar is always dark brown unless otherwise specified.

Fresh chiles can vary greatly in pungency, even from pepper to pepper of the same type and batch. If the unique flavor of a specific chile is called for, try to use it, but for simple hotness cayenne, crushed dried hot chiles, and liquid hot-pepper sauce are the most reliable and constant sources of pungency.

Fresh tomatoes are always a problem, wonderful to cook with if they are fully ripe and flavorful but not good for much if they are not—and many are not, especially out of season. There are many good brands of canned sauce, puree, crushed tomatoes, and whole tomatoes, and an excellent Italian boxed variety—taste around and find the ones that work for you.

Our taste for salt has in general declined markedly in the last couple of decades, and individual preference varies widely. A heavy salter myself, I have tried to keep salt levels at the lower edge. Always taste the food and adjust the seasoning to suit your own palate.

Above all, take satisfaction in the cooking and joy in the eating. If cooking is no more than time-consuming drudgery and eating nothing better than fear, denial, and the observation of dietary guidelines, then we subvert and deny one of the great pleasures of our kind. Enjoy!

The Universal Kitchen

Chapter One

Meat on a Stick

It may seem a little odd to begin a cookbook with a chapter on grilled meat, rather than the more customary appetizers or soup. But in terms of the human food story, meat on a stick is an obvious place to start: cooked over an open fire, it is likely to have been our very first real culinary accomplishment, the act that started us on the long and ever-branching road to the complex and elaborate behavior we call cooking. Although the roasting of meat in or over a fire is in principle a very simple technique, it seems to have been the starting point, the literal spark that ignited our imaginations and fueled our desire for food that looked, tasted, smelled, and chewed better than anything we had previously consumed raw.

The discovery of roasted meat was almost certainly an accident, an event that must have occurred thousands of times before a creature came along who was capable of understanding and appreciating it, and who had as well the ability and the resources to reproduce it. It may have been the fortuitous find of an animal slowly cooking on the burning stubble of a grass fire, for this was surely a time before man's mastery and control of fire. And though the discovery of roasted meat was no small event itself, it may also have contributed to the deliberate acquisition of fire for other crucial purposes—warmth, light, and protection against wild predators.

Those long-distant ancestors who first reveled in the savory delight of a sizzling, juicy, fire-singed hunk of meat may well have been attracted initially not by the sight or the flavor but by the aroma, for the odor of roasting meat seems to be a powerful and unprecedented stimulus in the human experience. The aromatic compounds produced by the browning of fat and muscle tissue are extraordinarily attractive, and prefigure the complex and appealing flavors that roasted meat provides, as well as the desirable characteristics of heightened tenderness and juiciness. Indeed, the delicious aroma is surely one of the crucial factors in the widespread use of roasted meat as a sacrificial offering to our gods; it is, as the Old Testament tells us, "an odor that is pleasing to the Lord."

Though the first roasted meat consumed by ancient humans was no doubt whole unbutchered carcasses, people would quickly have figured out that cutting or chopping their prey into smaller, more manageable pieces had distinct advantages: meat could be more quickly cooked, in amounts necessary for the number of eaters, and for a length of time appropriate to achieve the desired effects of a meal neither underdone nor burned to an unpleasant char. For this increased control, utensils were required, implements that were handily fashioned from items found in the natural environment. Twigs, branches, rigid stems, and spiny plant parts served as skewers on which hunks of meat were impaled, held by a cook who could then control the timing and the amount of exposure to the flames. And if those sticks were green and juicy rather than dead and dried out, they could withstand the heat of the fire for a long enough time to cook the meat.

This earliest of culinary scenarios is not very different from the hundreds of barbecues and grills that are enacted today in cultures throughout the world. We have in the course of our history developed a number of tools and utensils that make the cooking of meat over an open fire easier to regulate and more subject to our control—grates, grills, spits, metal skewers, tongs, and long-handled forks. But the principle of the technique and the nature of the finished product remain remarkably constant and universally well loved. Whether fish, fowl, or flesh, whole or in serving-size pieces, as chunky kabobs or bite-sized morsels, fire-roasted meat has a widespread and tenacious appeal. Is this an expression of the collective unconscious—a tangible evocation of our ancient origins, when we discovered ourselves as *Homo culinarius,* the creature who cooks his food? Or is it the delight we take in the uniquely human realm of the aesthetic, the pleasure we derive from the unparalleled aroma and flavor and texture of crusted, browned meat dripping with fat and savory juices?

However much we have come to control our world and the food we eat, however our individual culinary traditions have evolved as an expression of where we live and what we believe, we all seem to have held on to this common ancestral food, and to enjoy it in a way that transcends cultural barriers. When we squat in front of a campfire, listening to the sizzle of a freshly caught trout, or watching a hot dog charring on a stick—whether we call it barbecue or satay or shish kabob—we are participating in a common human experience, smelling and tasting our way back to a simpler time and the beginning of a story.

RECIPES

Armenian Shish Kabob
Korean-Style Barbecued Lamb
Singapore Beef Satay
Asian Grilled Beef Rolls (Vietnamese)
Steak and Potato Kabobs (Franco-American)
Indonesian Pork Satay
Spareribs with Tamarind Peanut Sauce (Malaysian)
Chicken Souvlakia (Greek)
Chicken Tikka (Indian)
Hot and Smoky Jerked Chicken (Jamaican)
Mayan Turkey Kabobs
Salt-Grilled Mackerel (Japanese)
Grilled Tuna Provençal
Chile-Grilled Salmon Kabobs (Mexican)
Fresh Salmon Teriyaki (Japanese)
Turkish Swordfish Kabobs
Rosemary-Grilled Shrimp (Provençal)
Chile-Ginger Barbecued Shrimp (Chinese)
Creole Barbecued Oysters

Armenian Shish Kabob

Although the Turkish language has given us the widely accepted name for the archetype of meat on a stick, the claim for its origin must be shared by all the people of Central Asia, for whom it is an ancient and traditional dish. The meat is almost always lamb, cut in fairly large chunks, marinated with a variety of herbs and spices, and cooked only until it is nicely browned on the outside but still somewhat rare on the inside. Separate skewers of onion, peppers, mushrooms, and cherry tomatoes can be lightly brushed with oil and grilled to serve along with the kabobs.

3 tablespoons olive oil

2 tablespoons fresh lemon juice

1 medium onion, finely chopped

2 cloves garlic, crushed

2 teaspoons ground cumin

1 teaspoon ground allspice

1/4 teaspoon freshly ground black pepper

1 1/2–2 pounds lean boneless lamb, cut from the leg, in
    1 1/4-inch chunks

Salt to taste

1. Combine the oil, the lemon juice, the onion, the garlic, the spices, and the pepper. Whisk to blend thoroughly.

2. Pour the marinade over the lamb chunks and mix well. Let stand, covered, in the refrigerator for 6–8 hours.

3. Thread the lamb on metal skewers and grill over hot charcoal, turning once, about 4 minutes each side. Salt to taste after cooking.

Serves 4–6

Words to Grill By

Many of our familiar grilled-meat dishes have their origin in the Middle East and Central Asia, and involve meat, usually lamb, marinated in oil and spices, then spitted and cooked over hot coals. "Shish kabob" comes from the Turkish; *shish (sis)* means "skewer" and *kabob (kebab, kebap)* means a chunk of meat. In Russian the dish is called "shashlik," in Greek "souvlakia." From Persian comes the word *kofta,* which means pounded, minced, or ground meat, seasoned and formed into balls, croquettes, or sausage-shaped kabobs. In India, spitted grilled foods are frequently designated as "tandoori," because they are cooked over hot coals in the clay ovens called "tandoors." Tandoori cooking is characteristic of northern India, and probably also had its origins in the Aryan culture of Central Asia. In all these traditions, the *shish,* or skewer, is usually made of metal and is thought to derive from the swords of ancient Asian horsemen. In Southeast Asia, on the other hand, skewers are almost always fashioned from the thin, rigid spines of bamboo, which, used green, contain enough moisture to withstand the heat of the open fire; the wood or bamboo skewers we buy packaged should be thoroughly soaked in water for several hours before cooking. In the realm of the bamboo skewer, grilled food is most often known as "satay" (saté), a Malay term that has been adopted throughout Southeast Asia to designate skewered pieces of meat grilled over fire, and to refer as well to the savory sauces with which they are typically served.

It is interesting that both "grill" and "skewer" have entered our contemporary vocabulary as unabashedly aggressive metaphors: to "grill" someone means to question relentlessly, to subject him to the heat; to "skewer" means to puncture, to defeat, to nail someone to the wall.

Korean-Style Barbecued Lamb

Korean cuisine has a strong popular tradition of meats marinated in spicy sauces and grilled over charcoal. Lamb, though much less frequently used than beef or pork, is splendidly enhanced by the forthright flavors of garlic, sesame, and chile that characterize Korean sauces. As in other Asian barbecue traditions, the meat is cut into small pieces or thin slices; the savory marinade permeates the meat, which cooks very quickly.

> 2 tablespoons soy sauce
> 2 teaspoons brown sugar
> 4 large cloves garlic, crushed
> 1 tablespoon Asian sesame oil
> 1 teaspoon crushed dried hot peppers
> 1 pound lean boneless lamb, cut in very thin slices
> Lightly crushed toasted sesame seeds, for garnish (optional)

1. Combine the soy sauce, sugar, garlic, oil, and hot peppers. Mix thoroughly, then pour over the sliced lamb and mix well. Let stand, covered, in the refrigerator for 2–4 hours.

2. Thread the lamb, ribbon-style, on soaked bamboo skewers. Grill over hot charcoal, turning once, until brown and crispy, about 2–3 minutes each side. Garnish with sesame seeds, if desired.

Serves 4, more if used as an appetizer

Singapore Beef Satay

Though most satays are marinated in complex mixtures of spices and seasoning ingredients and are richly flavored on their own, they are almost always served with savory peanut dipping sauces; indeed, it is the peanut, as a component of both the marinade and the condimental sauce, that in large part defines the satay.

2 shallots or 1 small onion, chopped
2 cloves garlic
2 teaspoons minced gingerroot
2 tablespoons peanut oil
1 tablespoon soy sauce
1 teaspoon lemon-grass powder or 2 teaspoons finely
    chopped lemon grass
1 teaspoon ground cumin
1 teaspoon ground coriander
1/4–1/2 teaspoon crushed dried hot peppers
1 teaspoon sugar
3 tablespoons roasted peanuts
1 pound lean beef, cut into small cubes (thumbnail size)
Peanut Dipping Sauce (page 10)

1. In a food processor, combine the shallots, the garlic, the gingerroot, the oil, the soy sauce, the spices, and the sugar. Process until smooth.

2. Add the peanuts and process into a paste.

3. Combine the seasoning paste with the beef cubes and mix thoroughly. Let stand, covered, in the refrigerator for 4–6 hours.

4. Thread the meat on skewers and broil over hot coals for 2–3 minutes each side, turning once. Serve the satay with Peanut Dipping Sauce.

Serves 3–4

Asian Grilled Beef Rolls

So great is the Southeast Asian love of wrapped and rolled foods that they turn up on the grill as well as in the form of dumplings and other dough-wrapped preparations. These delicate little beef rolls show the Vietnamese taste for beef, subtly flavored with traditional ingredients. Because the meat is sliced so thin, they need only a very quick cooking.

1 tablespoon Asian sesame oil
2 tablespoons fish sauce
½ teaspoon powdered lemon grass or 1 teaspoon finely
    chopped lemon grass
1 pound braciole (boneless beef cut paper-thin for stuffing
    and rolling), cut in 3–4-inch squares
2 tablespoons finely chopped roasted peanuts
Small bunch fresh coriander
Additional sesame oil
Additional chopped peanuts, for garnish

1. In a small cup, combine the oil, the fish sauce, and the lemon grass. Mix well with a fork.

2. Brush each square of meat generously with the sauce. Sprinkle on about ½ teaspoon of chopped peanuts, then a layer of coriander leaves. Roll up and secure with a toothpick. Similarly make rolls of all the meat squares. Brush the filled rolls lightly with sesame oil.

3. Grill the rolls over hot charcoal, turning once, about 2–3 minutes each side. Garnish the rolls with additional coriander leaf and chopped peanuts, and serve with a sweet-and-sour cucumber salad and rice or noodles.

Makes about 12 rolls (serves 4)

Steak and Potato Kabobs

Here the American taste for meat and potatoes refashions a French classic, steak au poivre, into a festive recipe for the backyard barbecue—tender, juicy steak and tiny new potatoes, spread with tangy mustard-and-pepper sauce and grilled to crusty perfection.

12 1–1½-inch new potatoes
2 pounds boneless sirloin or beef tenderloin, cut in 1-inch cubes
1 tablespoon olive oil
2 cloves garlic, crushed
2 tablespoons red wine vinegar
2 tablespoons Dijon mustard
½ teaspoon coarsely cracked black pepper
Salt to taste

1. Cook the potatoes in boiling water for about 5 minutes, until just tender when pierced with a sharp knife; drain and set aside to cool.
2. Combine the beef cubes and the cooled potatoes in a bowl.
3. In a small bowl, combine the oil, garlic, vinegar, mustard, and pepper. Whisk to blend thoroughly. Pour the dressing over the beef and potatoes and mix well.
4. Thread the beef and the potatoes on sturdy wood or metal skewers. Grill the kabobs over hot coals, turning once, about 3 minutes each side for medium rare. Baste with any remaining sauce while cooking. Salt to taste.

Serves 6

Indonesian Pork Satay

The island nation of Indonesia is famous for its skewer-grilled meats, marinated in spices and served with savory peanut sauces. The many different satays are a popular street food and are also served as appetizers or as part of the rijstafel. The marinade for this pork satay works equally well with chicken or beef, and the Peanut Dipping Sauce can be used with any variety of satay.

2 tablespoons soy sauce
1 tablespoon fresh lemon juice
1 tablespoon brown sugar
3 cloves garlic, crushed
1/2 teaspoon ground coriander
1 pound lean boneless pork, cut in 1/2-inch cubes

1. Combine the soy sauce, lemon juice, sugar, garlic, and coriander. Blend thoroughly, then pour over the pork cubes and mix well. Let stand, covered, in the refrigerator for 3–4 hours.
2. Thread the pork on soaked bamboo skewers and grill over hot charcoal, turning once, for 3–4 minutes each side. Serve with Peanut Dipping Sauce.

Serves 3–4

Peanut Dipping Sauce
1 large shallot, or 1 small onion, minced
2 large cloves garlic, minced
1/2 teaspoon crushed dried hot peppers
1 tablespoon peanut oil
2 tablespoons soy sauce
2 tablespoons fresh lemon juice
1 tablespoon brown sugar
1/2 cup peanut butter
1/2 cup unsweetened coconut milk

1. In a small saucepan, cook the shallot, the garlic, and the hot peppers in the oil over moderate heat, stirring, until the mixture starts to turn golden and becomes aromatic.

2. Add the soy sauce, the lemon juice, and the sugar, and mix well. Add the peanut butter and stir in until it is well blended.

3. Add the coconut milk and cook, stirring, until the sauce just comes to the simmer and is smooth and well blended. Remove from the heat and serve either warm or at room temperature.

Makes about 1½ cups

NOTE: The sauce will keep for weeks, tightly covered, in the refrigerator.

Spareribs with Tamarind Peanut Sauce

In China, with its avoidance of calcium-rich dairy foods, the traditional gift to new mothers was spareribs with sweet-and-sour sauce; it is said that the vinegar in the marinade and sauce liberates some of the calcium in the pork bones, making available a supply of this important mineral to lactating women. Vinegar provides gastronomic benefits as well: it allows the slowly grilled or roasted ribs to become tender, juicy, and richly browned. In this Malaysian recipe, the vinegar reinforces the fruity acid flavor of the tamarind sauce.

  1 lump tamarind, the size of a large walnut
  ½ cup hot water
  2 shallots, minced
  1 tablespoon finely minced gingerroot
  ½ teaspoon crushed dried hot peppers
  1 tablespoon peanut oil
  2 tablespoons regular soy sauce
  1 tablespoon black soy sauce
  2 tablespoons brown sugar
  ¼ cup peanut butter
  3–4-pound rack spareribs
  Cider vinegar
  Salt to taste

1. In a small bowl, combine the tamarind and the hot water. With the back of a spoon or your fingers, mash the tamarind into a coarse pulp. Let the mixture stand for ½ hour.

2. In a small saucepan, cook the shallots, the gingerroot, and the hot peppers in the oil, stirring, for a couple of minutes, until the mixture becomes aromatic.

3. Strain the tamarind liquid into the pot, discarding the pulp. Add the soy sauces and the sugar, then cook, stirring, over moderate heat until the mixture comes to the simmer.

4. Add the peanut butter and stir until the mixture becomes smooth and thick. Remove from the heat.

5. Brush the spareribs generously on both sides with vinegar and

let stand, at room temperature, for 1–2 hours. Place the ribs on a rack over a roasting pan, brush again generously with vinegar, then salt lightly. Roast the ribs in a 350° F. oven for about 1 hour and 15 minutes. After about ½ hour of cooking, lightly baste the ribs with some of the sauce. After another ½ hour, turn the ribs over and baste the other side. Or grill the ribs on a rack over the cool side of the grill, basting with vinegar and sauce as directed, for 1½–2 hours.

6. When the ribs are done, cut them into individual pieces and serve with the remaining sauce.

Serves 4–6 (makes 1 cup sauce)

Chicken Souvlakia

The combination of olive oil, lemon, and oregano is characteristic of much Greek cooking, particularly the spitted, grilled meats and roasted animals that endure in Greek consciousness as an expression of ancient ritual sacrifice to the gods. The tradition persists as a public, festive, and restaurant form of cookery that most frequently involves lamb and organ meats; chicken is a less common but delicious alternative.

2 tablespoons olive oil
2 tablespoons fresh lemon juice
1 tablespoon crumbled dried oregano (preferably Greek)
Plenty of freshly ground black pepper
1½ pounds boneless chicken, cut into 1-inch cubes
1 large onion, quartered, then separated into leaves
1–2 green peppers, seeded and cut into 1-inch pieces
Salt to taste
Lemon wedges, for garnish

1. Combine the oil, the lemon juice, the oregano, and the black pepper. Whisk to blend thoroughly.

(continued)

2. In a bowl, combine the chicken, the onion, and the green pepper. Pour the marinade over and mix well. Let stand, covered, in the refrigerator for 2–3 hours.

3. Thread the chicken on skewers alternately with pieces of onion and pepper. Grill over hot charcoal, turning once, about 3–4 minutes each side. Salt to taste after cooking. Serve with lemon wedges.

Serves 4–6

Chicken Tikka

"Tikka" is another term in Indian cuisine for grilled skewered chunks of meat, usually chicken or liver. The marinade for these kabobs—made from yogurt, lime, and aromatics—is full of lively flavor, and a little different from the more familiar curry-spice mixtures.

    1 medium onion, coarsely chopped
    1 tablespoon gingerroot, chopped
    1 tablespoon fresh lime juice
    3 tablespoons plain yogurt
    ½ teaspoon salt
    Several good grinds black pepper
    Good pinch crushed dried hot peppers
    Small handful fresh coriander leaves
    1 bay leaf
    1 pound boneless chicken, cut into 1-inch chunks
    Sprigs of fresh mint or coriander, for garnish

1. In a food processor or blender, combine the onion, gingerroot, lime juice, yogurt, salt, peppers, coriander, and bay leaf. Process the mixture into a paste.

2. Spoon the marinade over the chicken and mix thoroughly. Let stand, covered, in the refrigerator for 1–2 hours, stirring once or twice.

3. Thread the chicken on skewers, keeping as much of the marinade on the meat as possible. Grill over hot coals, turning once, about 3–4 minutes each side. Garnish the kabobs with sprigs of mint or coriander.

Serves 4

Hot and Smoky Jerked Chicken

The Caribbean "jerk" refers not only to meat grilled over hot coals, but, perhaps more important, to its marination in a highly seasoned, frequently fiery sauce characterized by two indigenous ingredients— Jamaican allspice and the Habañero chile, one of the world's hottest. There has developed in recent years a fascinating multitude of jerk sauces and rubs, some of them hot enough to blow your head off, so experiment with the chiles to find a level of pungency that suits your palate. Pork is the traditional jerked meat, but fish, game, and poultry can also be used. I like boneless chicken thighs, which, slowly grilled, get a nice crust from the marinade and stay tender and juicy on the inside.

1 chipotle (smoked dried jalapeño)
1 medium onion, chopped
2 Habañero chiles (or Scotch bonnets), seeded
4 cloves garlic
1/4 cup soy sauce
2 tablespoons fresh lime juice
2 tablespoons vegetable oil
2 teaspoons ground allspice
1 teaspoon dried thyme
1 teaspoon paprika
1/2 teaspoon cinnamon
1 tablespoon chopped fresh gingerroot
2 pounds boneless, skinless chicken thighs

(continued)

1. With a small sharp knife, open the chipotle and scrape out the seeds.

2. In a food processor, combine the chipotle and all the remaining ingredients except the chicken. Process into a smooth paste.

3. Pour the marinade over the chicken, mix well, then let stand, covered, in the refrigerator for 4–6 hours, turning the chicken in the marinade from time to time.

4. Grill the chicken slowly, at least 6 inches above the coals or on the cool side of the grill, for 30–40 minutes, until crusted and tender. Spoon any remaining marinade over the chicken as it cooks. (Or bake the chicken in a 350° F. oven for about 1–1½ hours, until well crusted and tender.)

Serves 4–6

Mayan Turkey Kabobs

This recipe is an adaptation, using the ancient domestic meat of Mexico—turkey—with a seasoning paste, called "adobo," characteristic of Yucatec cooking. The kabobs have a fine rich flavor; be careful not to overcook them or they will become dry.

1 ancho chile
1 small onion, coarsely chopped
3 cloves garlic
1 tablespoon fresh orange juice
1 tablespoon fresh lemon juice
1 teaspoon ground achiote
¼ teaspoon salt
1 teaspoon dried oregano
1 tablespoon olive oil
1–1½ pounds boneless turkey, cut into 1-inch chunks
Sweet-and-sour onions, for garnish (page 286)
Warm corn tortillas and cooked black beans

1. Remove the stem end of the ancho, then open the chile and shake or scrape out the seeds and discard. Cover the chile with lukewarm water and let stand for ½ hour.

2. In a food processor, combine the drained ancho, the onion, the garlic, the juices, the achiote, the salt, and the oregano. Process into a paste.

3. Add the oil to the paste and mix well, then spoon the paste over the turkey chunks and mix thoroughly. Let stand, covered, in the refrigerator for 6–8 hours.

4. Thread the kabobs on skewers, keeping as much of the marinade on as possible. Grill over hot coals, turning once, about 3–4 minutes each side.

5. Garnish the kabobs with sweet-and-sour onions and serve with warm corn tortillas and black beans.

Serves 4–6

Salt-Grilled Mackerel

One of the simplest of grilled dishes is the Japanese *shioyaki*, which translates as "salt-roasted" or "salt-broiled." Full-flavored fish like mackerel is sprinkled with salt half an hour before cooking; the salt lightly penetrates and coats the flesh, and this most basic of seasonings enhances the fine flavor of fresh fish. Of course, the fish must be the freshest possible, and the salt should be coarse or freshly grated sea salt. The fish fillets can be spitted, using two parallel bamboo skewers, and grilled over charcoal; they are also good broiled in the oven.

1–1½ pounds fresh mackerel fillets
1–2 tablespoons coarse (kosher) salt or coarsely grated
    sea salt
Lemon wedges, for garnish

1. One half hour before cooking, place the fish fillets in a single layer on a baking tray. Sprinkle each fillet with about ½ teaspoon of salt.

(continued)

2. Skewer the fillets, if desired, on soaked bamboo skewers. Grill over hot charcoal, turning once, about 3–4 minutes each side. (Cooking time will depend on the thickness of the fish.) Or broil the fillets in the oven for 2–3 minutes each side.

3. Serve the fish with lemon wedges for garnish.

Serves 4–6

Grilled Tuna Provençal

Fresh tuna, long a Mediterranean favorite, has until only recently been something of a rarity in many of our markets. With its mild flavor and firm meaty texture, it is an ideal fish for grilling, and can serve as a delicious main course or as a component of hearty salads like the Salade Niçoise (page 228).

¼ cup olive oil
2 shallots, minced
3 cloves garlic, crushed
1 tablespoon chopped fresh rosemary, or 1 teaspoon
    crumbled dried
1 tablespoon chopped fresh thyme, or 1 teaspoon crumbled
    dried
¼ teaspoon freshly cracked black pepper
1 pound boneless fresh tuna, cut into 1-inch cubes
Salt to taste
Lemon wedges, for garnish

1. In a shallow casserole or pan, combine the oil, shallots, garlic, herbs, and pepper; blend thoroughly. Add the tuna chunks and mix well. Refrigerate, covered, for 4–6 hours. Turn the fish in the marinade occasionally.

2. Skewer the fish, then grill over hot charcoal, brushing generously with the remaining marinade, about 4–6 minutes each side.
3. Salt lightly to taste, then serve with lemon wedges.

Serves 4

NOTE: This tuna is excellent served with the Saffron and Tomato Ali-Oli (page 254). It can also be prepared unskewered in the form of steaks cut 1 inch thick.

Chile-Grilled Salmon Kabobs

Seasoning pastes, made from a variety of chiles pounded together with other flavoring ingredients, are a common feature of traditional Mexican cookery and are excellent with grilled meat, poultry, or fish. The pastes can be used as well on broiled or baked fish fillets.

1 ancho chile
1 chipotle chile (smoked jalapeño)
1 tablespoon olive oil
1 tablespoon fresh lemon juice
1 tablespoon fresh lime juice
2 cloves garlic
1/2 teaspoon dried oregano
1/4 teaspoon ground cumin
1/4 teaspoon salt
1 small onion, coarsely chopped
1 1/2 pounds boneless fresh salmon, cut into 3/4–1-inch chunks
Lemon wedges or lime wedges and sprigs of cilantro, for
    garnish
Guacamole
Warm corn tortillas

(continued)

1. With a sharp knife, remove the stem ends from the chiles; open the chiles and scrape or shake out the seeds. Soak the chiles in lukewarm water to cover for ½ hour. Drain the chiles thoroughly.

2. In a food processor, combine the soaked chiles with the oil, the juices, the garlic, the seasonings, and the onion. Process into a paste.

3. Combine the paste with the salmon chunks, mix well, then let stand, covered, in the refrigerator for 1–2 hours.

4. Thread the salmon on skewers and grill over hot charcoal about 4–5 minutes each side, turning once, until the kabobs are just cooked through.

5. Garnish the kabobs with lemon or lime wedges and sprigs of fresh cilantro, and serve with guacamole and warm corn tortillas.

Serves 4–6

Fresh Salmon Teriyaki

"Teriyaki" is the Japanese term for meat, poultry, or seafood marinated and grilled over hot coals. The gingery soy marinade works particularly well with fresh salmon, which can be cut into kabobs and skewered, or cooked as steaks or fillets. As in so much Japanese food, the ingredients and the preparation are extremely simple and the results very good.

1½ pounds boneless, skinless salmon, cut into 1-inch chunks
½ cup soy sauce
½ cup sake
¼ cup sugar
1 tablespoon grated fresh gingerroot
Slivered scallions, pickled gingerroot, sliced cucumber,
    for garnish

1. Place the salmon chunks in a bowl or a shallow pan.

2. Combine the soy sauce, sake, sugar, and gingerroot and mix thoroughly. Pour the marinade over the fish, then let stand, covered, in the refrigerator for at least 30 minutes but no longer than 2 hours.

3. Thread the salmon on soaked bamboo skewers. Grill over hot charcoal, turning once, about 4 minutes each side. Baste the fish lightly with the marinade while grilling.

4. Heat any of the remaining marinade in a small pot and serve as additional sauce with the teriyaki. Garnish the salmon with slivered scallions, and serve with pickled gingerroot and sliced cucumber.

Serves 4–6

Turkish Swordfish Kabobs

With its chunky, meatlike texture, swordfish makes an excellent choice for grilled kabobs. It is much favored in Turkey, where its fresh mild flavor is enhanced with olive oil, lemon, and herbs. This grilled fish is a popular *shish* dish, from the cuisine that gave us the name, and an ancient tradition, of skewered charbroiled foods.

2 tablespoons olive oil
2 tablespoons fresh lemon juice
2 bay leaves, finely crumbled
1/2 teaspoon crushed dried thyme
Several good grinds black pepper
1 pound boneless swordfish, cut into 1-inch chunks
1 medium onion, cut into quarters and separated into leaves
Salt to taste
Lemon wedges, for garnish

1. Combine the oil, lemon juice, bay leaves, thyme, and pepper. Whisk to blend thoroughly.

2. Pour the dressing over the fish chunks and onion leaves and mix well. Let stand in the refrigerator for 1–2 hours, turning once or twice in the marinade.

(continued)

3. Thread the fish alternately with the onion leaves onto skewers. Grill over hot coals, turning once, about 3–4 minutes each side. Salt lightly to taste after cooking. Serve with lemon wedges for garnish.

Serves 4

Rosemary-Grilled Shrimp

In Provence, rosemary flourishes as a perennial throughout the countryside, perfuming the air as well as the food. Dried rosemary branches scent the fires for grilling and are sometimes used to skewer meat and seafood, imparting a rich herbal aroma and flavor. If you don't have rosemary branches, use this simple marinade, which gives much the same flavor. And for a special accompanying treat, wrap heads of garlic in foil and roast them in the hot coals for 20–30 minutes. Serve the shrimp with good crusty bread and squeeze the roasted garlic over both.

2 tablespoons olive oil (or a rosemary-infused olive oil)
1 teaspoon grated lemon zest
Several good grinds black pepper
2 tablespoons chopped fresh rosemary
1 pound large shrimp or prawns, peeled and deveined
Salt to taste
2–3 heads roasted garlic (optional)

1. Combine the oil, the lemon zest, the pepper, and the rosemary and whisk to blend thoroughly. Pour the mixture over the shrimp, mix well, then let stand in the refrigerator for 3–4 hours.
2. Skewer the shrimp, then grill over hot coals for just a couple of minutes. As soon as one side just becomes pink, turn the skewer and cook until the other side just becomes pink. Salt the shrimp lightly to taste after cooking.
3. Serve the shrimp with good bread and roasted garlic, if desired.

Serves 4

Chile-Ginger Barbecued Shrimp

Unlike some Asian cuisines, such as those of Korea and Indonesia, that of China is not particularly noted for the grilling of food over open fire. Chinese cooking has developed nonetheless a whole complex of barbecue sauces, sweet and spicy, that are used for broiled or oven-roasted foods, like the traditional roast pork. These delicious shrimp make a nice appetizer or cocktail nibble, and are equally good baked in a very hot oven or spitted and grilled. In either case, cook them very briefly, just until they turn pink.

1/4 cup chili sauce (the American tomato variety)
1 tablespoon hoisin sauce
1 tablespoon grated gingerroot
1/2–1 teaspoon Chinese chile paste with garlic
2 teaspoons Asian sesame oil
1 pound large shrimp, peeled and deveined
Small handful fresh coriander leaves, for garnish

1. In a small bowl, combine the chili sauce, the hoisin sauce, the gingerroot, the chile paste, and the oil. Mix to blend well.
2. Mix the sauce thoroughly with the shrimp, then let stand for 1/2–1 hour in the refrigerator.
3. Thread the shrimp on skewers, or place in a single layer on a foil-lined baking tray. Grill over hot coals or bake in a very hot (450–500° F.) oven for 3–4 minutes. Baste with any remaining sauce. Serve warm or at room temperature, garnished with some fresh coriander.

Serves 4–6 as an appetizer or with other foods

To Spit or Not to Spit

On these shores, the word for grilled food is "barbecue," a term whose origin is unclear. Some attribute it to the French *de la barbe à la queue,* "from the beard to the tail," meaning the cooking of a whole animal. A more likely derivation is the word *barbacoa,* adopted by the Spanish from the name of a tribe of Ecuadorian Indians who cooked animals over fires on frames made of green saplings, a technique similar to that used by the native people of the northwestern coast to smoke their harvest of salmon. In contemporary usage, "barbecue" can refer to a social event, to a kind of cooking (usually out of doors and over an open fire or hot coals), and to a way of saucing or seasoning food. In Mexican tradition, "barbecue" frequently refers to meat wrapped in protective vegetation (agave or banana leaves) and steamed in pits lined with red-hot stones; the *pibil* cookery of the Yucatán is marinated and wrapped meat cooked in the *pib,* or fire pit. Mexican cuisine also offers the *barbacoa de olla,* or pot barbecue, in which meat is slowly stewed in a savory sauce. Another New World term is "jerk," used in Jamaica and the West Indies to designate meat marinated in a spicy sauce or rub and grilled over hot coals. It probably derives from the Peruvian *charqui,* a word that evolved into our "jerky," referring to meat that is seasoned and air-dried for preservative purposes. The barbecue of the Americas is obviously a complex tradition, including a number of cooking techniques, a variety of forms—whole animals, animal parts, and spitted chunks—and an impressive range of spiced savory sauces, marinades, and seasonings that reflect our regional and ethnic diversity.

Creole Barbecued Oysters

A thoroughly American dish from New Orleans, a city that has made the most of ethnic diversity in its kitchens and at its tables. The ketchup-based barbecue sauce is frequently used as well for shrimp, which are traditionally baked in their shells in the oven. Whether you broil the oysters or grill them on skewers over charcoal, you must watch them like a hawk and remove them from the heat as soon as the edges curl. They make a terrific hors d'oeuvre or appetizer, served on their skewers or with toothpicks to dip them in the hot sauce.

4 tablespoons butter
4 large cloves garlic, minced
1/2 cup ketchup
2 tablespoons Worcestershire sauce
1 tablespoon fresh lemon juice
Several good grinds black pepper
1/4 teaspoon cayenne pepper
16 ounces shucked large oysters, drained

1. In a small saucepan, heat the butter over moderate heat. Add the garlic and cook, stirring, for a few minutes, until the garlic wilts.

2. Add the ketchup, the Worcestershire, the lemon juice, the black pepper, and the cayenne, and cook, stirring, until the mixture comes to the simmer. Cook, stirring, for a few more minutes, until the mixture becomes smooth and well blended.

3. Thread 2 or 3 oysters on each soaked bamboo skewer or place the oysters on a baking tray. Brush the oysters lightly with the sauce. Grill the oysters over hot charcoal, turning once, just until the edges curl, or broil for a few minutes until the edges curl.

4. Heat the remaining sauce and serve as a dip with the grilled oysters.

Serves 6 as an appetizer or hors d'oeuvre

Dry Rubs

In addition to oil or liquid-based sauces and semi-liquid pastes, barbecued meats can be marinated and seasoned with dry spice mixtures, called "rubs." These are particularly well suited to slow-roasted or grilled foods; they produce a crisp, spicy crust without burning, which many liquid sauces, especially those containing sugar, frequently do. This rub is a good all-purpose mixture with a Southwestern flair; like any dry spice, it can be stored in the pantry in a tightly covered jar. It is particularly good with lamb or chicken.

2 tablespoons coarse (kosher) salt
2 tablespoons sweet paprika (preferably Hungarian)
2 tablespoons ground cumin
4 teaspoons dried oregano
2 teaspoons ground coriander
4 teaspoons granulated dry garlic
1/2 teaspoon black pepper
1 teaspoon cinnamon
1/2 teaspoon ground cloves
1/2 teaspoon (more or less to taste) cayenne pepper

Combine all the ingredients and mix thoroughly.

Chapter Two
The Primal Soup

Of the many different kinds of cooked food that people have designed throughout their history, perhaps none is so well loved as soup. There is a Spanish proverb that says, "Of love and soup, soup is the better," and that may be because soup *is* love, perceived as an edible offering of caring and comfort. What is it about this steaming liquid food that is so appealing to so many of us?

One possibility is that soup recaptures, in a more complex and grown-up form, the warm nourishing fluid that is our first food. Mother's milk is sweet rather than savory, of course, but research has shown that it may contain many of the flavors that characterize the mother's diet and may thus be the means by which infants first learn about the foods and flavors of their home and culture. An even more far-reaching view would connect soup with the warm nutrient-filled seas from which all life arose; this "primordial soup" that was the quickening medium for all living things finds its parallel in the warm salty liquids that course through our bodies, bringing vital nourishment to every cell.

Whatever the interpretation, the evidence is clear: we all love soup, and we all seem to value it for the same reasons. The question is, how did soup first get made? For, after all, soup is liquid, a form of food very different from an animal roasting in a fire or chunks of meat spitted on sticks and cooked over an open flame.

The momentous discovery of cooking by fire was crucial to our kind not only in and of itself but because it led ultimately to the realization that it was not necessarily the direct flames themselves but *heat* that was the significant agent of change. Fire applies heat directly and sometimes, as we know only too sadly when we contemplate the blackened, inedible remains of a gooey marshmallow, with adverse effects. Once early people learned to control fire, they must have quickly understood that under certain circumstances it would be advantageous to apply heat without exposing food to direct flames. The ingenious human made good use of objects found in the natural environment: flat stones that served as griddles when placed over glowing coals, or rocks or slabs of clay built over the fire or coals in structures that concentrated heat while protecting the food from the direct flame, a concept from which the modern oven would ultimately evolve.

But these griddles and primitive ovens used dry heat to cook food; liquid-based foods like soup, stews, or beverages required some kind of pot or waterproof container in a time long before the invention of pottery or ceramic or metal. Anthropologists speculate that these early pots took the form of baskets fashioned from tightly woven reeds or fronds, or containers made from animal hide or the watertight intestinal paunches recovered from butchered animals. Such pots were waterproof but not fireproof, and so could not be exposed to direct flame; their liquid contents were heated with "pot-boilers," small rocks heated red-hot in the fire. When dropped into the basket or paunch, they caused the liquid to boil, and hence the soup or stew to cook. These stones, of a characteristic kind and shape, have been found at the hearths of ancient people and were used into the twentieth century by traditional cultures that did not possess metal or pottery cookware.

Once discovered, the processes and the equipment necessary for cooking in liquid led to a wide variety of techniques—stewing, simmering, steaming—and a bounty of dishes that have become universally popular, including not only soups and stews but a wealth of medicinal teas, infusions, and stimulant beverages. Cooking in liquid—particularly long, slow cooking—is an extractive process: whatever qualities the ingredients contain, whether nutrients, medicinal agents, or flavors, are pulled into the liquid, which then becomes the medium through which those valuable substances are consumed.

Though almost every edible substance on the face of the earth seems ultimately to find its way into a soup pot somewhere, the use of animal bones and flesh is nearly universal in the production of rich, fortifying, substantial soups. Bones are a source of much flavor and of valuable minerals like calcium. When slowly cooked in liquid, they release a natural gelatin that provides considerable body and textural richness to the stock. It is for these reasons that the French consider a good homemade stock to be the essential foundation of all soups and sauces, well worth the time and the effort necessary to coax a balanced and full-flavored liquid from bones, meat, vegetables, and seasonings. There are of course shortcuts available, commercially prepared bouillons, powders, canned broths, and pastes that vary widely in quality. Check their ingredients carefully and try to pick ones that are not based primarily on salt, monosodium glutamate, or artificial coloring.

Although soup is made from a staggering variety of ingredients, I have chosen to focus on two basic kinds: soups based on chicken stock, because they are so versatile and so widely popular, and fish and seafood soups, because they are likely to have been the earliest of our liquid foods. Indeed, the scenario for the first oyster stew is not very hard to imagine: A giant mollusk is accidentally dropped into the hearth fire. The shell provides a natural fire-resistant container that, when steamed open by the heat, reveals the succulent oyster simmering in its own delicate briny juices. And the taste of the sea is primal, evoking the origin of life itself.

Whatever the ingredients or the form, whether a clear ungarnished broth or a thick, chunky, or pureed mixture, soup is the great leveler, appealing to all of us, no matter our age or gender or condition in life. The savory steaming bowl seems to provide an extra measure of ease and familiarity, of comfort and well-being, nourishing the spirit as well as the body.

RECIPES

Fish Stock
Seafood Stock
Japanese Oyster Consommé
Spanish Bread and Garlic Soup with Shrimp
Mussel Soup Avgolemono (Greek)
New Orleans Bouillabaisse
Down East Fish Chowder (American)
Summer Salmon Chowder (American)
Thai Catfish, Corn, and Coconut Soup
Veracruz Snapper Soup (Mexican)
Creamy Bisque of Smoked Herring and Potato (Northern European)
Chicken Stock
Yugoslav Chicken and Red Pepper Soup
Thai "Monkey Ball" Chicken Soup
Vietnamese Chicken Noodle Soup
Italian Escarole Soup
Sopa de Tortilla (Mexican Chicken and Vegetable Soup)
Cock-a-Leekie with Vegetables and Barley (Scottish)
Sesame Chicken and Asparagus Soup (Chinese)
Indonesian Coconut Vegetable Soup
Bulgarian Leek, Cabbage, and Potato Soup
Egyptian Lentil and Chickpea Soup
Curried Cream of Plantain Soup (Caribbean)
Provençal Soup of Pureed White Beans with Rosemary and Roasted
  Garlic

Fish Stock

To make a good fish stock, it is useful to cultivate the acquaintance of your local fishmonger or the manager of your supermarket's fish department. The highest flavor-yielding parts of the fish—the heads, the bones, and the trimmings—are frequently thrown away, and most fish dealers will be happy to save them for you free or at a very low cost. Fish stock is generally lighter and more delicate than meat or poultry stock, and there is usually no preliminary browning of the vegetables or the fish.

2–3 pounds fish trimmings—heads, bones, etc.
1 large onion, coarsely chopped
1 large leek, coarsely chopped
2 carrots, sliced
2 ribs celery, with leaves, chopped
12 black peppercorns
1 bay leaf
1 lemon, sliced
3 quarts cold water
Salt

1. In a large pot, combine all the ingredients except the salt. Bring to the simmer, then cook, uncovered, over moderate heat for about 1 hour.
2. Strain the stock, pressing as much liquid from the cooked ingredients as possible. Measure the stock, then add salt, using about 1 teaspoon of salt per 1 quart liquid.

Makes about 2 quarts

Seafood Stock

Natives of Italy's Ligurian coast are said to have brewed a "stone" soup—not really a stone at all but formations of calcified crustaceans which, when boiled in water, yielded the sharp briny flavor of the sea. The same effect can be had from shrimp, crab, or lobster shells. Have your local fish dealer save shells for you, and keep a plastic bag in the freezer to store the shells from your own cooking.

2 tablespoons butter or oil
1 onion, coarsely chopped
2 carrots, sliced
At least 4 cups shrimp shells plus crab and/or lobster shells,
    if available
8–10 black peppercorns
3 quarts cold water

1. In a large pot, heat the butter or oil over moderate heat. Add the onion and the carrots, and sauté, stirring, until the onions become limp and translucent.

2. Add the shrimp shells and other shells, if available, and continue to cook, stirring, until the shells turn pink.

3. Add the peppercorns and the water, bring to the boil, then cook, uncovered, over moderate heat for 30–40 minutes.

4. Strain the stock, pressing as much liquid from the shells as possible. Measure the stock, then add salt, using about 1 teaspoon of salt per 1 quart liquid.

Makes about 2 quarts

Japanese Oyster Consommé

Nowhere is the flavor of the sea so valued as it is in Japan, which has long and fully exploited the rich complexity of the ocean harvest. Dashi, the classic stock of the Japanese kitchen, is made not from animal bones or poultry but from dried bonito and konbu, giant kelp. These ingredients are available in Japanese groceries so that you can make your own dashi, but you can also purchase, as do many Japanese nowadays, small packets of instant dashi that dissolve in hot water. The following is a very simple but elegant soup—clear, light, and rich in flavor.

4 cups water
4 envelopes instant dashi
3 large slices fresh gingerroot
3 scallions, coarsely chopped
2 tablespoons mirin (sweet rice wine for cooking)
1 tablespoon soy sauce
8 ounces shucked oysters, with their liquor
2–3 scallions, cut into 2-inch pieces and slivered

1. In a medium saucepan, combine the water, the dashi, the gingerroot, the chopped scallions, the mirin, and the soy sauce. Bring to the simmer, then cook, uncovered, over low heat for 10–15 minutes.

2. With a slotted spoon, strain out the gingerroot and scallion pieces and discard.

3. Bring the stock to the simmer again, then add the oysters with their liquor. Cook for a few minutes, just long enough for the edges of the oysters to curl.

4. Spoon the hot broth and 2–3 oysters into small Oriental soup bowls. Garnish each bowl with some slivers of scallion.

Serves 4–6

A Sip of Soup for Supper

If that seems like a mouthful, it is! All three words derive from a single basic concept of a liquid food, or a food cooked in liquid, traditionally served at the evening meal. In many European languages both "sip" and "sup" are old words that may originally have been coined to describe the sound made by sucking hot liquid off a spoon. Another related word is "sop," which referred to the hard crackers or stale crusts of bread that were added to the liquid to soften them and in so doing to thicken the soup. This is the meaning still retained by the French *soupe*, which generally designates thick peasant soups containing bread or other farinaceous foods. The French now prefer *potage* as a general term for soup, a word related to the Old English "pottage," a potful of soft liquid-cooked food. Soups usually fall into two categories: thick or thickened, and clear. Clear soup, known in French as consommé, is made from strained and clarified stock, with no thickening from starch or legumes or liaisons from eggs and cream. Such soups may have ingredients added to them, but they remain clear and unthickened. "Bouillon," like the English word "broth," comes from the French *bouilli*, "boiled," and refers to the liquid produced when meat, bones, vegetables, and seasonings are boiled in water. The first bouillon cube, or instant bouillon, was produced by a Swiss food manufacturer named Maggi, who designed it as a nutritional boost to the meat-poor diets of the lower classes in the latter decades of the nineteenth century. His well-intentioned product has had extraordinary success as a shortcut for lazy cooks the world over.

Spanish Bread and Garlic Soup with Shrimp

Here is a true "soup," made with cubes of stale bread that add body and substance. Poor folk would make the soup from nothing more than water, garlic, and bread, but the addition of stock and shrimp makes it richer and more complex, the bits of firm, chewy shrimp providing an excellent textural foil for the soft, soppy bread, all of it bathed in an aromatic garlicky broth.

½ pound shrimp
3 tablespoons olive oil
2 cups water
¼ teaspoon salt
Freshly ground black pepper
3–4 cups chicken stock or fish stock
6 large cloves garlic, finely minced (about ¼ cup minced)
2 cups stale French bread cubes
½ teaspoon paprika
Finely chopped parsley, for garnish

1. Shell and devein the shrimp, reserving the shells.
2. In a medium saucepan, sauté the shrimp shells in 1 tablespoon of the oil over moderate heat, stirring, until the shells turn pink.
3. Add the water, the salt, and several good grinds of pepper. Bring to the simmer, then cook, uncovered, over low heat for about ½ hour. Strain the liquid and discard the shells. To the strained liquid add enough chicken or fish stock to measure 5 cups.
4. In the same saucepan, sauté the garlic in the remaining 2 tablespoons of oil, stirring, for a few minutes. Add the bread cubes (and all crumbs) and cook over moderate heat, stirring, until the bread and the garlic begin to turn golden.
5. Stir in the paprika and several good grinds of pepper. Add the stock, then bring to the simmer and cook, uncovered, over low heat for about 15–20 minutes, stirring from time to time. Taste for salt.

(continued)

6. Cut the shrimp into coarse pieces. Add the shrimp to the soup and cook for a few minutes, just until the shrimp turn pink and opaque.

7. Serve the soup garnished with some chopped parsley.

Serves 4–6

Mussel Soup Avgolemono

Plump, flavorful mussels are enjoyed throughout the Mediterranean; in this rich soup all the flavors of those sun-drenched lands come together—olive oil, garlic, saffron, tomatoes, plus the dill and creamy egg-lemon sauce of Greek tradition.

2 pounds fresh mussels
1 cup bottled clam juice
3 tablespoons fresh lemon juice
3 large cloves garlic, smashed
1 medium onion, finely chopped
2 tablespoons olive oil
3–4 plum tomatoes, coarsely chopped
1/4 teaspoon salt
Several good grinds black pepper
3 cups chicken broth
1/2 teaspoon saffron threads
1/4 cup orzo
3 tablespoons finely snipped fresh dill
2 eggs

1. Scrub and debeard the mussels; discard any that are cracked or open.

2. In a large pot, combine the clam juice, 1 tablespoon of the lemon juice, and the garlic. Bring to the simmer, then add the mussels, cover, and cook over low heat for 5–10 minutes, until the mussels have opened.

3. Strain off the broth from the mussels and reserve (there should be about 1½ cups). Shell the mussels, discarding any that have not opened.

4. In the same pot, sauté the onion in the oil over moderate heat, stirring, until the onion wilts and begins to turn golden. Add the tomatoes and cook, stirring, for a few more minutes. Stir in the salt and the pepper.

5. Add the chicken broth, the reserved mussel broth, the saffron, and the orzo. Bring to the simmer, then cook, uncovered, over low heat for about 10 minutes, until the orzo is tender. Stir in the dill and the reserved mussels.

6. In a small bowl, whisk the eggs with the remaining 2 tablespoons of lemon juice. Slowly stir a little of the hot soup into the eggs, whisking as you add the liquid. Add some more of the hot soup, stirring constantly, until the egg mixture is quite warm. With the soup on very low heat, pour the eggs into the soup, whisking as you add them. Cook the soup, stirring, until it is very hot, but do not boil.

7. Serve the soup garnished with a sprig of dill, if desired.

Serves 4–6

New Orleans Bouillabaisse

In this heyday of creative "fusion" cuisine, when ethnic traditions and ingredients are tossed about with frequently reckless abandon, one hesitates to use the name of a classic dish for anything but the real thing. Still, this rich Creole fish soup is a legitimate offspring of the original, elaborating on the French model with Spanish, African, and local influences. Like its parent bouillabaisse, this one isn't quite sure whether it's a soup or a stew—but whatever it is, it's a meal.

1 medium onion, finely chopped
1 medium green pepper, seeded and finely chopped
1 rib celery, with leaves, finely chopped
2 tablespoons olive oil
4 cloves garlic, minced
2 tablespoons flour
2 cups bottled clam juice
½ cup dry white wine
2 large tomatoes, coarsely chopped
1 teaspoon saffron threads
2 teaspoons chopped fresh thyme, or 1 teaspoon dried
Plenty of freshly ground black pepper
8 ounces raw shrimp, peeled and deveined
8 ounces shucked oysters, with their liquor
4 ounces cooked crawfish meat, if available
4 ounces fresh crabmeat
½ teaspoon salt, or to taste
½ teaspoon liquid hot-pepper sauce, or to taste
Small handful flat-leaf parsley, finely chopped
Hot cooked rice, if desired (about ½ cup cooked per
    serving)

1. In a large heavy pot, sauté the onion, the green pepper, and the celery in the oil over moderate heat, stirring, until the vegetables are soft. Add the garlic and stir for a few minutes more.

2. Stir in the flour to make a roux, then cook, stirring, for 4–5 minutes, until the roux is nicely browned.

3. Whisk in the clam juice gradually until smooth, then add the wine, the tomatoes, the saffron, the thyme, and the black pepper. Bring to the simmer and cook, uncovered, over low heat for about 15–20 minutes.

4. Add the shrimp, the oysters with their liquor, and the crawfish, and cook just until the shrimp are pink and the oysters are curled.

5. Stir in the crabmeat, the salt, the hot-pepper sauce, and the parsley, and stir gently. Bring just to the simmer, then serve in bowls with hot cooked rice, if desired.

Serves 4–6

Fishiest of all fishy places was the Try Pots, which well deserved its name; for the pots there were always boiling chowders. Chowder for breakfast, and chowder for dinner, and chowder for supper, till you began to look for fish-bones coming through your clothes. . . . But when that smoking chowder came in, the mystery was delightfully explained. Oh, sweet friends! hearken to me. It was made of small juicy clams, scarcely bigger than hazel nuts, mixed with pounded ship biscuit, and salted pork cut up into little flakes; the whole enriched with butter, and plentifully seasoned with pepper and salt. Our appetites being sharpened by the frosty voyage . . . and the chowder being surpassingly excellent, we despatched it with great expedition. . . .

—Herman Melville,
Moby Dick

Down East Fish Chowder

The New England coast was the original home of many of America's most familiar and best-loved chowders—simple, hearty mixtures filled with fish and shellfish, thickened with potatoes, hard biscuit, or common crackers, and enriched with salt pork, butter, milk, and cream. The chowders of "Down East" Maine are traditionally made with halibut or lobster; you can use both for an exceptionally rich and delicious soup.

> 4 strips thick-sliced bacon, coarsely chopped, or 2 ounces
>   salt pork, diced
> 1 large onion, coarsely chopped
> 2 ribs celery, with leaves, finely sliced
> 1 large potato, peeled and diced
> 1/2 teaspoon salt
> Plenty of freshly ground black pepper
> Good dash cayenne pepper
> 1/4 teaspoon mace
> 1 cup water
> 3 cups milk or 2 cups milk and 1 cup light cream
> 3/4–1 pound boneless halibut or cod
> 1/2 cup lobster meat (meat from 1 small cooked lobster),
>   cut in small chunks (optional but good)
> 1–2 tablespoons unsalted butter
> Paprika, for garnish

1. In a heavy pot, fry the bacon or pork over moderate heat until it is crisp. Pour off and discard the fat, leaving enough to film the bottom of the pot generously.

2. Add the onion and the celery and cook over moderate heat, stirring, until the celery softens and the onion is just beginning to turn golden.

3. Stir in the potato, the 1/2 teaspoon of salt, the peppers, and the mace, and mix well. Add the water, bring to the simmer, then cook, uncovered, for about 15–20 minutes, until the potatoes are soft.

4. With a potato masher or heavy spoon, mash some of the potatoes coarsely. Don't mash them completely, because you want some potato pieces in the final soup.

5. Add the milk, then place the fish in the soup. Bring to the simmer and cook over low heat for about 10 minutes, or until the fish flakes easily when stirred.

6. Stir in the lobster and the butter and heat until very hot. Taste for salt and pepper; you will probably need to add some at this point.

7. Sprinkle individual servings with paprika.

Serves 4–6

Summer Salmon Chowder

Fresh salmon used to be a seasonal delicacy but is now being farm-raised and is available pretty much all the time. It has always seemed to me to go particularly well with the fresh produce of the American summer garden—corn, tomatoes, and the fresh tender leaves of young basil. If you are starting from scratch with your own stock made from salmon trimmings, proceed as per directions for Fish Stock (page 31), but add a half-dozen or so juniper berries, which give the soup a distinctive flavor.

6–8 scallions, finely chopped
1 carrot, sliced
2 ribs celery, with leaves, sliced
2 tablespoons butter or olive oil
3–4 plum tomatoes, coarsely chopped
1 medium new potato, diced
6 cups salmon or fish stock
½ pound boneless skinless fresh salmon, cut in small
    chunks
1 cup fresh corn kernels
Several good grinds black pepper
Good squeeze fresh lemon juice, or to taste
Salt to taste
Small handful fresh basil leaves, cut in thin strips

1. In a large pot, sauté the scallions, the carrot, and the celery in the butter or oil over moderate heat, stirring, for about 5–7 minutes, until the vegetables are wilted.
2. Stir in the tomatoes and the potato and cook for another few minutes.
3. Pour in the stock, bring up to the simmer, then add the salmon. Simmer for about 10 minutes, uncovered, then add the corn, the pepper, and the lemon juice. Simmer for a few minutes, then taste for salt, stir in the basil, and remove from the heat.

Serves 6–8

Thai Catfish, Corn, and Coconut Soup

From the Mississippi River to the Mekong Delta, people all over the world enjoy the sweet flesh of catfish, a plentiful species of fresh-water fish that is delicious batter-fried, sautéed, or stewed. In this Thai soup, with its typical flavors of coconut, chile, fish sauce, and corian-der, the succulent white fish teams up with canned creamed corn, a product used frequently by Asians to provide the sweet flavor of corn without use of dairy products (unlike homemade creamed corn, the commercial variety uses food starch rather than milk or cream to make the thick, creamy sauce).

2 medium shallots, finely chopped
4 cloves garlic, minced
2 small fresh hot chiles, seeded and minced, or
    1/4–1/2 teaspoon crushed dried hot peppers
2 tablespoons peanut oil
3/4 pound fresh boneless catfish, cut into 1-inch chunks
2 cups chicken stock
1 cup unsweetened coconut milk
2 cups (1 1-pound can) cream-style corn
1/2 teaspoon powdered lemon grass or 1 teaspoon finely
    chopped lemon grass
1 tablespoon fish sauce
1 tablespoon fresh lime juice
Good handful fresh coriander leaf, coarsely chopped

1. In a medium saucepan, sauté the shallots, the garlic, and the chiles in the oil over moderate heat, stirring, for 3–4 minutes, until the mixture is wilted and aromatic.
2. Add the fish chunks and turn them gently in the aromatics.
3. Add the stock, the coconut milk, the corn, the lemon grass, and the fish sauce. Bring to the simmer, then cook, uncovered, over low heat for about 30 minutes. Stir the mixture gently from time to time.
4. Just before serving, stir in the lime juice and the coriander leaf.

Serves 4–6

Veracruz Snapper Soup

From the eastern coast of Mexico, where red snapper—*huachinango*—and a rich variety of other seafoods are enjoyed, comes this light but full-flavored soup. As with many soups, its flavor develops if it stands a bit, so you may want to make it early in the day, or at least several hours before serving.

  1 medium onion, thinly sliced
  1–2 serrano chiles, seeded and minced
  1 medium carrot, thinly sliced
  1 small green bell or green frying pepper, seeded and
     cut into thin strips
  3 cloves garlic, minced
  2 tablespoons olive oil
  2 cups coarsely chopped plum tomatoes
  4 cups chicken stock or fish stock
  ½ cup zucchini, cut into matchstick strips
  1 tablespoon fresh lemon or lime juice
  ½ pound skinless red snapper fillets, cut into small chunks
     or strips
  ½ cup small shrimp, peeled and deveined, or large shrimp,
     coarsely chopped
  Small handful fresh cilantro, finely chopped
  Salt to taste

  1. In a medium saucepan, cook the onion, the chiles, the carrot, the pepper, and the garlic in the oil over moderate heat, stirring, until the onions wilt and just start to turn golden.
  2. Add the tomatoes and cook for another 5–7 minutes, stirring occasionally.
  3. Add the stock, the zucchini, and the lemon or lime juice, bring to the simmer, and cook, uncovered, over low heat for about 20 minutes.
  4. Add the fish and the shrimp and cook for another few minutes, just long enough to cook the fish. Stir in the chopped cilantro; taste for salt and lemon.

Serves 6

Creamy Bisque of Smoked Herring and Potato

In Northern Europe, herring is a way of life, eaten fresh, pickled, smoked, and sometimes even raw. It can turn up at any meal in salads, in sandwiches, or as a garnish for eggs and potatoes. Here it gives its special smoked flavor to a rich and unusual soup.

1 medium onion, coarsely chopped
2 medium carrots, sliced
1 medium parsnip, sliced
2 tablespoons butter
1 large potato, peeled and cut into chunks
Several good grinds black pepper
6 cups water
4–6 ounces smoked-herring fillets, cut into chunks
6 juniper berries
1/4 cup heavy cream
3–4 tablespoons finely snipped fresh chives

1. In a medium saucepan, sauté the onion, the carrots, and the parsnip in the butter over moderate heat, stirring, until the onion begins to turn a golden color.

2. Add the potato and the pepper and stir for a few minutes.

3. Add the water, the herring, and the juniper berries. Bring to the simmer, then cook, uncovered, over low heat for 30–40 minutes, until the vegetables are very soft.

4. Remove the soup from the heat and fish out the juniper berries (they should be floating on the top). With a slotted spoon, remove all the solids from the soup and place in a food processor. Add some of the cooking liquid and puree until smooth.

5. Return the puree to the pot, mix well, then bring to the simmer. If the soup seems too thick, you can add a bit more water. Stir in the cream and blend well. Garnish the soup with the snipped chives.

Serves 6–8

Chicken Stock

The richest sources of flavor for chicken stock are the bones, the fat, and the skin, rather than the flesh itself. Use necks and backs, which are sold inexpensively for soup, and wing tips, which you can cut off and freeze when preparing chicken wings. To my mind, the best flavor comes from chicken feet; these are almost always available in ethnic, particularly Chinese, groceries, if you can't find them in your own supermarket. Excellent stock can also be made from the remains of a roasted bird; this yields a stock with a somewhat less delicate, more "browned" flavor. Be sure to use as well any vegetables or stuffing that have cooked with the chicken, as well as all the pan juices. Both the roasted stock and the stock made from raw parts begin with a long, slow browning or "sweating" of the vegetables in oil or butter to produce the fullest flavor. Raw and cooked chicken are not customarily combined to make stock; use one or the other.

2 large onions, or 1 large onion and 1 large leek,
    coarsely chopped
3 carrots, sliced
3 ribs celery, with leaves, coarsely chopped
1 parsnip, sliced
2 tablespoons butter or vegetable oil
3–4 pounds chicken necks, backs, feet, wing tips, etc., or
    all the remains of a roasted chicken, including pan
    juices, etc.
4 quarts cold water
12 black peppercorns
Good handful coarsely chopped parsley
2 bay leaves
Couple of sprigs fresh thyme, or about ½ teaspoon dried
Salt to taste

1. In a large pot, cook the onions (or onion and leek), the carrots, the celery, and the parsnip in the butter or oil over moderate heat, stirring occasionally, for 20–30 minutes, until the vegetables are soft and beginning to turn a rich golden color.

2. Add the chicken, the water, and the peppercorns, the parsley, the bay leaves, and the thyme. Bring to the simmer, then cook, uncovered, over low to moderate heat for about 3 hours. Skim off and discard any scum that may rise to the top of the pot during cooking.

3. Strain the stock, pressing as much liquid as possible from the cooked ingredients. Measure the stock, then add salt, using about 1 teaspoon of salt per 1 quart of liquid.

4. Chill the stock, then skim off and discard the fat congealed at the top.

Makes about 2 quarts

Yugoslav Chicken and Red Pepper Soup

This chunky soup gets its beautiful ruddy color and rich flavor from three forms of red pepper—paprika, crushed dried hot chile, and fresh sweet red peppers. The capsicum peppers were introduced into Eastern Europe by the Turks after the opening of commerce with the Americas in the sixteenth century, and many varieties of pepper, both sweet and pungent, have become focal ingredients in Balkan cookery. For maximum flavor, select sweet, fully ripe, fleshy red peppers.

1 medium onion, coarsely chopped
2 cloves garlic, minced
1/4 teaspoon crushed dried hot peppers
2 medium sweet red peppers, seeded and diced
2 tablespoons olive oil
1 teaspoon paprika (preferably Hungarian sweet)
6–8 ounces boneless chicken (breast or thigh meat), cut
    into small chunks
Several good grinds black pepper
6 cups chicken stock (page 46)
1 medium potato, peeled and diced
1 cup small cauliflower florets
Salt to taste

1. In a medium saucepan, cook the onion, the garlic, the crushed hot peppers and the diced sweet peppers in the oil over moderate heat, stirring, until the onion wilts and begins to take on red color from the peppers.
2. Stir in the paprika, then add the chicken and brown it lightly in the mixture. Grind the black pepper over the chicken.
3. Add the stock, the potato, and the cauliflower. Bring to the simmer, then cook, uncovered, over low heat for about 1/2 hour. Taste for salt.

Serves 6–8

Thai "Monkey Ball" Chicken Soup

My children took great glee in intimidating their gastronomically less sophisticated friends with the picturesque name of this soup; the little guests were always relieved—and no doubt slightly disappointed—to learn that the "monkey balls" were nothing more exotic than little meatballs made from ground chicken, a kind of Asian "Chickarina." This is a very appealing soup—light, creamy, aromatic, with a full and complex flavor.

½ pound ground chicken
2 tablespoons fish sauce
¾ teaspoon powdered lemon grass or 2 teaspoons finely
    chopped lemon grass
2 ounces dried rice sticks (rice-flour noodles)
3 shallots, minced
1 small fresh hot green chile, seeded and minced, or ½ tea-
    spoon crushed dried hot peppers
1 carrot, cut into small julienne strips
1 tablespoon peanut oil
4 cups chicken stock (page 46)
5–6 ounces (1 small can) unsweetened coconut milk
½ teaspoon sugar
1 teaspoon minced fresh galangal root, or ¼ teaspoon
    galangal (laos) powder
1 cup finely shredded Napa cabbage
Small handful fresh basil leaves, coarsely chopped
Small handful fresh coriander leaf, coarsely chopped
1 tablespoon fresh lime juice
Asian chile sauce or paste, or liquid hot-pepper sauce,
    to add to taste

1. Combine the chicken with 1 tablespoon of the fish sauce and ¼ teaspoon of the dried lemon grass or 1 teaspoon of fresh. Mix well, then form into small balls, about the size of large cherries. If the mixture is too sticky to work with your hands, you can scrape rounded teaspoonfuls into the water. Poach the balls in boiling water for 3–4 minutes. Drain and set aside.

2. Soak the rice sticks in water to cover for ½ hour.

3. In a medium saucepan, sauté the shallots, the chile, and the carrot in the oil over moderate heat, stirring, until the shallots are wilted.

4. Add the stock, the coconut milk, the sugar, the remaining 1 tablespoon of the fish sauce, the remaining lemon grass, and the galangal, and bring to the simmer.

5. Drain the rice sticks, then add them along with the cabbage and the reserved chicken balls. Simmer the soup for about 5–10 minutes.

6. Stir in the basil, the coriander, and the lime juice. Add chile sauce or paste to taste.

Serves 4–6

Vietnamese Chicken Noodle Soup

And you thought your grandma's was the only chicken-noodle soup! This is one of the best—light and lemony, with a refreshing clean flavor, and chock-full of those wonderful rice-stick noodles that the Vietnamese have elevated to an art form.

6 ounces dried medium rice sticks
4 cups chicken stock (page 46)
1 cup water
1 medium onion, thinly sliced
1 tablespoon fish sauce
Several good grinds black pepper
Good pinch crushed dried hot peppers
1 tablespoon fresh lemon juice
1 teaspoon finely chopped fresh lemon grass or
    $1/4$ teaspoon powdered lemon grass
$1/2$ cup slivered cooked chicken
6 ounces fresh beansprouts
4 scallions, chopped, for garnish
Small handful fresh coriander leaf, chopped, for garnish
Lemon wedges, for garnish

1. Cover the rice sticks with tepid water and let stand for $1/2$ hour.

2. In a medium saucepan, combine the stock, 1 cup of water, the onion, the fish sauce, the black and hot peppers, the lemon juice, and the lemon grass. Bring to the simmer, then cook, uncovered, over low heat for about 15 minutes.

3. Drain the rice sticks, then add them, along with the chicken, to the soup. Simmer for another 10 minutes.

4. To serve: Place a small handful of beansprouts in each soup bowl. Ladle the hot soup, with plenty of noodles, over the sprouts, then garnish with chopped scallions and coriander leaf. Serve with lemon wedges.

Serves 4–6

Italian Escarole Soup

This soup is an old traditional Italian favorite, one of the simplest and still one of the best. It illustrates once again how a well-made stock with the addition of only a few select ingredients can be turned into a satisfying and delicious soup.

1 medium onion, finely chopped
2 tablespoons olive oil
3–4 cloves garlic, minced
Several good grinds black pepper
4 cups chicken stock (page 46)
1 head (about ½–¾ pound) fresh escarole, coarsely
    shredded or chopped
¼ cup small pasta (farfalline, ditalini, orzo, etc.)
Salt to taste
Freshly grated Parmesan cheese, for garnish

1. In a medium saucepan, sauté the onion in the oil over moderate heat, stirring, until the onion wilts and begins to turn translucent. Add the garlic and cook for another few minutes.

2. Add the pepper, the stock, and the escarole. Bring to the simmer, then cook, uncovered, over low heat for about 15 minutes.

3. Add the pasta and cook for another 5–10 minutes, or until the pasta is tender. Taste for salt and pepper.

4. Pass the grated Parmesan for diners to add as desired.

Serves 4

Sopa de Tortilla

(Mexican Chicken and Vegetable Soup)

This zesty soup, popular throughout Mexico, is called "tortilla soup" because it is served garnished with crisp strips of fried tortillas. Other vegetables such as diced zucchini, cut green beans, or chickpeas, can be added or substituted, if desired.

4–5 tablespoons vegetable oil
1 medium onion, coarsely chopped
2 serrano chiles, seeded and minced
1 small sweet red or green pepper, seeded and diced
2–3 plum tomatoes, coarsely chopped
1 small potato, diced
1 carrot, sliced
1 rib celery, sliced
6 cups chicken stock (page 46)
Kernels from 1 ear fresh corn (about ½ cup)
1 cup cooked chicken cut in small chunks
6 small corn tortillas, cut in thin strips (see Note)
1 tablespoon fresh lime juice
Good handful fresh cilantro, finely chopped
Salt to taste

1. In a medium saucepan, heat 2 tablespoons of the oil over moderate heat. Add the onion, the chiles, and the sweet pepper and sauté, stirring, until the onion begins to turn golden.

2. Stir in the tomatoes, the potato, the carrot, and the celery, and cook, stirring, for another few minutes.

3. Add the stock, bring to the simmer, then cook, uncovered, over low heat for about 20–30 minutes, until all the vegetables are tender.

4. Add the corn and the chicken and simmer a few minutes more.

5. In a large skillet, heat the remaining 2–3 tablespoons of oil over moderate to high heat. Add the tortilla strips and fry, turning

frequently, until the strips are nicely browned and crisp. Remove the strips from the pan and drain on paper towels.

6. Just before serving, add the lime juice and the cilantro to the soup. Taste for salt. Garnish each serving with a handful of the tortilla strips.

Serves 6–8

NOTE: If you're feeling lazy or want to save time, you can, of course, substitute coarsely crumbled tortilla chips for the fried tortilla strips.

Cock-a-Leekie with Vegetables and Barley

This traditional soup from Scotland was originally made with a tough old bird, cooked for hours to extract whatever virtue remained in the ancient bones and flesh. Here is an updated, quicker version, but still rich with the wonderful flavor of leeks and chunky with vegetables and barley.

2 large leeks, mostly white parts, coarsely chopped
1 large carrot, coarsely diced
1 rib celery, with leaves, coarsely chopped
2 tablespoons butter
6 cups chicken stock (page 46)
¼ cup barley
1 medium turnip, diced
1 cup coarsely chopped cabbage
1 cup coarsely chopped cooked chicken
Several good grinds black pepper
3 tablespoons chopped parsley
Salt to taste

1. In a medium pot, sauté the leeks, the carrot, and the celery in the butter over moderate heat, stirring occasionally, until the leeks become very soft.

2. Add the stock, the barley, the turnip, and the cabbage, and cook, uncovered, over low heat for about 45–60 minutes, until the barley is tender.

3. Add the chicken, the pepper, and the parsley, and heat to the simmer. Taste for salt and pepper, and add if necessary.

Serves 6

Sesame Chicken and Asparagus Soup

Like Chinese stir-fried food, this soup is very quickly made once the components have been prepared and assembled. It plays with interesting varieties of texture, as well as rich and complex flavors, with chewy mushrooms, crisp asparagus, and firm little nuggets of chicken in a leek-and-sesame-flavored chicken broth.

6–8 large Chinese dried black mushrooms
1 large leek, mostly white part, finely chopped
2 teaspoons grated gingerroot
1 tablespoon plus 2 teaspoons Asian sesame oil
6 cups chicken stock (page 46)
3 tablespoons rice wine
1/2 teaspoon sugar
Good dash white pepper
2 tablespoons cornstarch
1/2 pound medium asparagus, cut on the sharp diagonal
    into 3/4-inch pieces
4 ounces skinless, boneless chicken breast, cut in small
    (about 1/2-inch) pieces

1. Combine the mushrooms with just enough lukewarm water to cover. Let stand for 30–40 minutes. When the mushrooms are soft, drain them, reserving the liquid. Cut out and discard any hard stems, then chop the mushrooms coarsely.

2. In a medium saucepan, sauté the leek and the gingerroot in the 1 tablespoon of oil over low to moderate heat, stirring occasionally, until the leek wilts and the mixture becomes aromatic.

3. Add the stock, the rice wine, the sugar, the pepper, and the chopped mushrooms; bring to the simmer and cook for about 5 minutes.

4. In a small cup, combine the cornstarch with 2 tablespoons of the mushroom liquid. Mix into a smooth paste.

5. Bring the soup to the boil, then add the asparagus and the chicken. Stir briefly, then bring the mixture to the boil again.

6. When the liquid is at the boil, stir in the cornstarch paste, mixing constantly. Stir until the soup is clear and very slightly thickened. (The amount of cornstarch is just enough to provide a slight liaison, not a real thickening.)

7. Stir in the remaining 2 teaspoons of sesame oil.

Serves 6

Indonesian Coconut Vegetable Soup

This is a full-flavored but light soup, fragrant with aromatics and creamy with coconut milk. The fried onion flakes that are sprinkled on at the end are a pervasive garnish throughout Malaysia and Southeast Asia. They are available ready-made in Asian groceries and they keep well, tightly covered, on the pantry shelf. If you want to make your own, there are instructions at the end of the recipe.

2 shallots, minced

2 cloves garlic, minced

2 teaspoons minced gingerroot

1/4 teaspoon crushed dried hot peppers

2 tablespoons peanut oil

1 carrot, cut in small julienne strips

1 medium zucchini, cut in small julienne strips

1 1/2 cups finely sliced or shredded Napa cabbage

1 rib celery, finely sliced

4 cups chicken stock (page 46)

5–6 ounces (1 small can) unsweetened coconut milk

2 teaspoons finely chopped fresh lemon grass, or

   ½ teaspoon lemon-grass powder

½ teaspoon turmeric

Salt to taste

6 ounces (about) fresh beansprouts

Fried Red Onion or Shallot Flakes (recipe follows) or

   commercial fried onion flakes, for garnish

Lemon wedges, for garnish

1. In a medium saucepan, cook the shallots, the garlic, the ginger-root, and the hot peppers in the oil over moderate heat, stirring, for about 4–5 minutes, until the mixture becomes aromatic.

2. Stir in the carrot, the zucchini, the cabbage, and the celery and stir for a few minutes.

3. Add the stock, the coconut milk, the lemon grass, and the turmeric. Bring to the simmer, then cook, uncovered, over low heat for about 15–20 minutes, until the vegetables are just tender. Taste for salt.

4. Put a small handful of beansprouts into each soup bowl. Ladle the hot soup over the beansprouts, then garnish with the fried onion or shallot flakes and serve with lemon wedges.

Serves 4–6

Fried Red Onion or Shallot Flakes

An Indonesian friend taught me that cassava flour is the secret for the crispest fried onion flakes. Coarsely chop as many shallots or small red onions as desired, dredge them lightly with cassava flour, then fry until crisp in hot peanut oil. Drain on paper towels, then store in a tightly covered container.

Bulgarian Leek, Cabbage, and Potato Soup

The combination of leeks, cabbage, and potatoes is common throughout Europe in a variety of hearty soups that fill the belly and satisfy the taste buds. This thick peasant soup contains elements of Mediterranean, Middle Eastern, and Central European cooking, a combination characteristic of much of the food of the Balkans.

2 large leeks, mostly white parts, finely sliced (about 2 cups)
2 large cloves garlic, minced
2 tablespoons olive oil
2 medium potatoes, peeled and cut in small cubes
2–2½ cups coarsely chopped cabbage
2 cups canned crushed tomatoes
4 cups chicken stock (page 46)
Several good grinds black pepper
1 tablespoon fresh lemon juice
3 tablespoons finely snipped fresh dill
Salt to taste
Plain yogurt, for garnish, if desired

1. In a large pot, cook the leeks and the garlic in the oil over moderate heat, stirring occasionally, until the leeks wilt and just begin to turn golden.

2. Add the potatoes, the cabbage, the tomatoes, the stock, and the pepper. Mix well, then bring to the simmer and cook, uncovered, over low heat for about 40 minutes, until all the vegetables are very tender.

3. Stir in the lemon juice and the dill. Taste for salt. Serve the soup with a bowl of yogurt to pass, as garnish, if desired.

Serves 6

Egyptian Lentil and Chickpea Soup

Throughout North Africa and the Near and Middle East, a variety of pulses, peas, and beans have been cooked for thousands of years into hearty, filling soups—remember Esau's pot of red lentils? These soups frequently do not contain meat but are based on stocks made from meat bones, usually lamb or chicken, that give depth, body, and rich flavor. This simple Egyptian soup, which can serve as a meal with bread and salad, is delightfully seasoned with garlic, cumin, mint, and coriander.

1 medium onion, coarsely chopped
2 large cloves garlic, minced
2 tablespoons olive oil
1 cup lentils
6 cups chicken stock (page 46)
Plenty of freshly ground black pepper
1 cup cooked or canned chickpeas (if canned, drained
   and rinsed)
1 teaspoon ground cumin
1 tablespoon crushed dried mint
1 tablespoon fresh lemon juice
Small handful fresh coriander leaf, coarsely chopped
Salt to taste

1. In a medium saucepan, sauté the onion and the garlic in the oil over moderate heat, stirring, until the onion wilts and begins to turn golden.
2. Add the lentils, the stock, and the pepper, bring to the simmer, then cook, uncovered, over low to moderate heat for about 40 minutes, until the lentils are tender.
3. Add the chickpeas, the cumin, and the mint, mix well, and continue to cook for another 15 minutes.
4. Just before serving, stir in the lemon juice and the coriander. Taste for salt.

Serves 6–8

Curried Cream of Plantain Soup

The plantain was brought from Africa to the Caribbean, where it has become a staple ingredient in the exciting, eclectic cooking we call "creole." Unripe, the plantain functions as a basic starch, like potato; in its ripe state, it has a subtle banana flavor, not too sweet, that is very enticing in this rich and savory soup.

1 medium onion, coarsely chopped
2 tablespoons vegetable oil
2 large ripe plantains, peeled and sliced
2 cloves garlic, minced
1 tablespoon curry powder (preferably Jamaican or
    West Indian)
Several good grinds black pepper
1/4 teaspoon grated nutmeg
4 cups chicken stock (page 46)
1/3 cup light cream
Salt to taste
1/4 cup coarsely chopped or broken cashews, freshly toasted,
    for garnish

1. In a medium saucepan, sauté the onion in the oil over moderate heat, stirring, until the onion wilts and becomes translucent.

2. Add the plantains and cook, stirring, for another 5 minutes or so.

3. Add the garlic, the curry, the pepper, and the nutmeg and cook, stirring, for a few minutes.

4. Add the stock, bring to the simmer, then cook, uncovered, over low heat for 15–20 minutes.

5. Remove all the solids from the soup with a slotted spoon and place in a blender or food processor. Blend until smooth, using a little of the stock if necessary.

6. Return the puree to the pot and blend in thoroughly. Stir in the cream and heat to the simmer. Taste for salt.

7. Serve the soup garnished with a sprinkle of toasted cashews.

Serves 4–6

Provençal Soup of Pureed White Beans with Rosemary and Roasted Garlic

This is an easily made, smooth and creamy soup of French origin, in which chicken stock provides the essential foundation for the earthy and robust flavors of rosemary and roasted garlic.

1 medium onion, coarsely chopped
2 tablespoons olive oil
1 head roasted garlic
1 tablespoon fresh rosemary, or 1 teaspoon dried
3 cups cooked or canned white kidney beans, drained
3 cups chicken stock (page 46)
Several good grinds black pepper
Salt to taste
Chopped parsley and crisp croutons, for garnish

1. In a medium saucepan, sauté the onion in the olive oil, stirring, until the onion just turns golden.
2. In a food processor, combine the sautéed onion, the pulp squeezed from the head of roasted garlic, the rosemary, the beans, and a little of the stock. Puree the mixture until smooth.
3. Return the puree to the pot, add the remaining stock and the pepper, and bring to the simmer. Cook over low heat, uncovered, for about 10–15 minutes, stirring occasionally. Taste the soup for salt and pepper, and adjust seasoning if necessary.
4. Serve the soup very hot, garnished with a bit of chopped parsley and some croutons.

Serves 6

Chapter Three
Potluck

It's easy 'nough to titter w'en de stew
  is smokin' hot,
But hit's mighty ha'd to giggle w'en
  dey's nuffin' in de pot.

   Paul Laurence Dunbar
   (American poet)

The bubbling pot, brimming with savory stew, has always been the symbol of abundance, of comfort, of security, defining home with the fragrance of familiar, nourishing food.

Though our first liquid-cooked food may well have been some kind of soup, a quantity of water to which a variety of ingredients was added, it may also have been what we would call a stew, a mixture of foods cooked in liquid that serves as the main course or a filling meal-in-one. The distinction between the soup and the stew has always been somewhat blurred; America's most famous commercial soup maker advertises a soup "so chunky you can eat it with a fork." How we define a soup or a stew depends on such issues as the thickness or texture of the liquid, the amount and size of the solid substances, the dish we eat it in, and the utensils we use, and these criteria are by no means cast in stone.

Furthermore, just as all cultures bring their own unique perspectives to the definition of these different food categories, they also have their own criteria for the techniques of preparation and the appropriate characteristics of the finished dish. Are the foods to be cooked whole or in chunks, sliced, or chopped into small pieces? Is a rolling boil desirable or a barely discernible simmer? What should the food look like, taste like, smell like, feel like between our teeth? Nowhere have these issues been so simply and so eloquently addressed as they were by Ishi, the last surviving member of a tribe of Indians from central California, the Yahi, who existed into the twentieth century on a technological level comparable with that of Stone Age people. The anthropologist Theodora Kroeber recorded Ishi's fine distinctions between Yahi and American food practices:

> The white man's stove he found good for roasting and broiling as in his own earth oven or open-fire cooking, but he considered that the modern stove ruined boiled food. Said Ishi, "White man puts good food in pot full of boiling water. Leaves a long time. Food cooks too fast, too long. Meat spoiled. Vegetables spoiled. The right way is to cook like acorn mush. Put cold water in basket. Place hot rocks in water till it bubbles. Add acorn meal. It cooks *pukka-pukka*. Then it is done. Same way, make deer stew. Or rabbit stew. Cook *pukka-pukka*. Not too long. Meat firm, broth clear, vegetables good, not soft and coming apart."

What Ishi so neatly put into perspective is the issue of taste and the variety of standards that different cuisines bring to bear on the preparation of their food, as well as the selection of ingredients and the choice of seasonings. These differences are what make the foods of any culture unique and recognizable, and account for the marvelous diversity in the world's food. Still, there is a basic underlying similarity among the many varieties of pot-cooked food: the liquid functions not only as the cooking medium but as the agent of flavor exchange, the meat giving savor to the vegetables, the vegetables enhancing the flavor of the meat, the fat and the seasonings bathing everything in a flavorful liquid gravy or sauce.

Think of the meals-in-a-pot that are emblematic of so many cuisines: the French pot-au-feu, the Louisiana gumbo, the Hungarian goulash, Irish stew, and New England boiled dinner. Remember how fundamental is the tajin to Moroccan cooking, the cholent to Jewish cuisine, the mole to Mexico, the curry to India, the groundnut stew to West Africa. How much less interesting our tables would be without the savory red-cooked foods of China, the simmered nabemono (literally translated as "things in a pot") dishes of Japan, the rich meat-and-vegetable stews of the Middle East, the spicy chile, meat, and bean mixtures of our own Southwest.

However they may differ in terms of ingredients and seasonings, these simmered liquid-based meals seem to offer the same advantages to everyone—an economy of time, labor, and utensils, a variety of wholesome, nourishing foods cooked into flavorful ragouts that provide sustenance in an easy, homespun, nurturant form. Like the soups from which they probably derive, they shine as the beacon of home cooking and the domestic hearth, with heavy pots and blackened kettles bubbling their aromatic contents at the back of the stove or suspended over the hearth fire. They endure as the undisputed triumph of female cookery—unlike grilled, spitted, and fire-roasted food, which has traditionally been the province of the male, associated with the festive, the ritual, and a more public domain. (It is interesting that the simmering stewpot, symbol of benign and desirable female domesticity, has been transformed in times of cultural stress and paranoia into the bubbling cauldron of poisonous witch's brew.)

As Ishi celebrated his acorn meal and venison stew, cooking *pukka-pukka,* so do we all participate in a kind of cooking that is nearly as old as we are. The savory stew, the meal-in-a-pot, is simple food—but it is real food, with all the comfort, satisfaction, and pleasure that have always been so much a part of its appeal.

RECIPES

Afghani Lamb and Onion Stew
Braised Spiced Lamb Shanks (Middle Eastern)
East African Beef and Plantain Stew
Rendang (Sumatran Spiced Beef)
Beef Cholent (Jewish)
Braised Veal Shanks with Mixed Exotic Mushrooms (Italian)
Goulash of Veal, Sausage, and Vegetables (Hungarian)
Pot-Roasted Loin of Pork with Wine and Herbs (French)
Smothered Pork with Apples, Onions, and Sage (American)
Polish Sausage, Apple, and Sauerkraut Stew
Venison Stew with Dried Cranberries (American)
Red-Cooked Duck with Crispy Skin (Chinese)
Stifatho of Duck with Onions and Mushrooms (Greek)
Mediterranean Braised Olive Chicken
Korean Braised Chicken with Mushrooms and Cucumbers
Senegalese Chicken and Vegetable Curry
Creole Chicken and Shrimp in Coconut-Cashew Curry
Pollo Almendrado (Chicken with Garlic-Almond Sauce) (Mexican)
Ceylonese Chicken Korma
Kentucky Burgoo
Spicy Burmese Fish in a Pot
Southern-Style Catfish Stew (American)
Red-Cooked Salmon (Chinese)
Iraqi Barley, Lentil, and Vegetable Stew
Ethiopian Mixed Vegetable Stew
Beans and Greens with Red Chile (New Mexican)
Spiced Chickpeas and Potatoes (Pindi Chole) (Indian)
Spanish Pisto of Peppers, Tomatoes, and Squash

Afghani Lamb and Onion Stew

Central Asia is an ancient hearth of lamb cookery, whether grilled on skewers over an open fire or cooked in a pot into a savory stew. This dish features the onion-mint-coriander combination character-istic of the Afghani kitchen in a thickly sauced and richly flavorful stew to serve with rice or freshly baked nan.

3 large onions, coarsely chopped

2 tablespoons vegetable oil

2 pounds boneless lean lamb, cut in ½-inch pieces

½ teaspoon salt

¼ teaspoon freshly ground black pepper

¼ teaspoon crushed dried hot peppers

1 tablespoon ground coriander

4 large plum tomatoes, coarsely chopped

1 tablespoon crushed dried mint leaves

1 cup plain yogurt mixed with a small handful chopped
    fresh coriander leaf, for garnish

1. In a heavy pot or Dutch oven, cook the onions in the oil over moderate heat, stirring, for about 5–7 minutes, until the onions wilt and begin to turn golden.

2. Push the onions to the side of the pot and add the lamb chunks in small batches to brown. Do not overcrowd the pot. When all the lamb has been browned, sprinkle on the salt, the black pepper, the hot peppers, and the ground coriander, and mix well.

3. Add the chopped tomatoes, mix well, then bring to the sim-mer. Cover and cook over low heat for about 1–1½ hours, until the lamb is tender. Stir the stew from time to time while cooking.

4. When the meat is tender, uncover the pot and cook down the sauce until it is quite thick. Stir in the crushed mint and taste for salt.

5. Serve the stew with rice or nan; pass the yogurt sauce for diners to add as desired.

Serves 4–6

Braised Spiced Lamb Shanks

The shanks are among the least expensive cuts of lamb, yet when lovingly cooked can become the most glorious of braised meat dishes. The meat must be slowly cooked for a long time, until it comes away from the bone in tender, succulent chunks. This traditional Middle Eastern dish, with its savory spiced sauce, should be served with rice or couscous.

2 large onions, finely chopped
2 tablespoons olive oil
3–4 pounds lamb shanks, trimmed of excess fat
½ teaspoon salt
¼ teaspoon freshly ground black pepper
½ teaspoon ground cumin
½ teaspoon ground coriander
¼ teaspoon grated nutmeg
½ teaspoon cinnamon
1 teaspoon paprika
1 teaspoon grated lemon zest
1 cup tomato sauce
1 cup water
1–2 cups cooked or canned white beans or chickpeas
    (optional) (if canned, drained and rinsed)
Cooked rice or couscous

1. In a large, heavy pot or Dutch oven, sauté the onions in the oil over moderate heat, stirring, until the onions begin to turn golden.

2. Push the onions to the side, then brown the lamb shanks lightly, turning them to brown on all sides.

3. Sprinkle the lamb with the salt, the pepper, and the spices. Add the lemon zest, tomato sauce, and water, bring to the simmer, then cover and cook over low heat for 2–3 hours, or until the meat is very tender and coming off the bone. Turn the shanks in the sauce from time to time while cooking.

4. If the sauce seems too watery, uncover the pot and cook it down quickly until it is thick. A cup or two of white beans or chick peas can be added to the sauce for the last few minutes of cooking.

5. Serve the lamb shanks hot with rice or couscous.

Serves 4

East African Beef and Plantain Stew

Like the potato, the green or unripe plantain can be boiled and mashed to serve as a base for a savory sauce or stew; in this form it is known in Africa as "plantain foo foo." It can also be sliced thinly and fried into chips or, as in this recipe, cut into slices or chunks and cooked with meat and spices. Its texture is somewhat denser than that of potatoes, and its flavor, though bland, is a little nutty.

2 tablespoons peanut oil

1½–2 pounds boneless beef, cut into 1-inch chunks

½ teaspoon salt

Several good grinds black pepper

2 medium onions, coarsely chopped

2 carrots, sliced

2 medium sweet red and/or green peppers, seeded and
   coarsely chopped

1 tablespoon finely minced gingerroot

2–3 small fresh hot chile peppers, seeded and minced, or
   ½–1 teaspoon crushed dried hot peppers

4 large cloves garlic, minced

2 cups canned Italian-style tomatoes, with juice

2 green (unripe) plantains, cut in ¾–1-inch slices
   and peeled (see Note)

1 cup coarsely chopped greens (spinach, kale, collards,
   mustard greens, etc.)

(continued)

1. In a large, heavy pot or Dutch oven, heat the oil over moderately high heat. Add the beef cubes and brown, turning to brown on all sides.

2. While the meat is browning, add the salt and pepper, the onions, the carrots, the peppers, the gingerroot, and the chiles. Stir-fry the meat and vegetables until the beef is browned and the onions are beginning to brown.

3. Stir in the garlic, mix well, then add the tomatoes. Bring to the simmer, then cover and cook over low heat, stirring from time to time, for about 1 hour.

4. Add the sliced plantains and the chopped greens, mix well; cover and cook over low heat for about 2 hours, stirring from time to time. If the stew becomes too dry, you can add some water or tomato juice.

5. When the meat and the plantains are tender, taste for salt and chile. Serve the stew with hot sauce to pass.

Serves 4–6

NOTE: Plantains do not peel as easily as the bananas they so closely resemble; the skin is tough and adheres firmly to the flesh. For easiest peeling, cut the plantains into slices, then cut off the skin with a sharp knife.

Rendang
(Sumatran Spiced Beef)

This is a traditional dish from Indonesia which, like the goulash of Hungary and the gumbo of Louisiana, is prepared in as many different varieties as there are cooks. After the long, slow cooking, the meat is dark, tender, and richly coated with a thick spicy sauce. Serve the rendang with plain rice, a vegetable or salad, and a spicy relish.

1 large onion, coarsely chopped
6 cloves garlic, minced

1 tablespoon finely minced gingerroot

1 teaspoon crushed dried hot peppers

2 tablespoons peanut oil

2–2½ pounds boneless beef round, sliced ½ inch thick,
    then cut into pieces about 2 × 1 inches

1 teaspoon ground cumin

½ teaspoon ground coriander

2 teaspoons finely chopped fresh lemon grass, or
    1 teaspoon lemon-grass powder

2 teaspoons minced fresh galangal root, or ½ teaspoon
    galangal (laos) powder

1 teaspoon turmeric

½ cup water

⅔ cup unsweetened coconut milk

½ teaspoon salt

1. In a heavy pot or Dutch oven, cook the onion, the garlic, the gingerroot, and the hot peppers in the oil over moderate heat, stirring, until the onions wilt and the mixture becomes aromatic.

2. Add the beef in small batches and brown the pieces on all sides.

3. Add the cumin, the coriander, the lemon grass, the galangal, and the turmeric to the browned beef and mix well. Pour in the water, then bring to the simmer and cook, covered, over low heat for 2–2½ hours, until the beef is very tender.

4. Add the coconut milk and the salt, mix well, and continue to cook, uncovered, until the sauce is thick. Taste for salt.

Serves 4–6

Beef Cholent

Cholent is the traditional Jewish version of the meal-in-a-pot, a culinary enactment of the ancient tenet that no work be done on the sabbath. Since the Jewish housewife was forbidden to cook or even to light her stove between sundown on Friday and sundown on Saturday, she started her sabbath meal on Friday and kept it cooking over a very low flame or in a very slow oven until the family was ready to eat it on Saturday. Many ingredients were used in the cholent, but one of the most common mixtures was that of beef, root vegetables, fruit, and some beans or grains. The long, slow cooking creates a dish in which many of the vegetables eventually dissolve to form a rich, thick, deeply flavorful sauce. This cholent uses many traditional ingredients but substitutes fresh beans for dried ones.

2 tablespoons oil
2–2½ pounds boneless bottom-round beef roast
½ teaspoon salt
1 teaspoon paprika
¼ teaspoon freshly ground black pepper
2 large onions, coarsely chopped
2 large carrots, thickly sliced
1 parsnip, sliced
1 medium turnip, cut in small chunks
2 medium sweet potatoes, peeled and cut in small chunks
3 cloves garlic, minced
2 cups canned Italian-style plum tomatoes, with juice
1 cup pitted lemon-flavored prunes
2 cups fresh shelled cranberry beans or lima beans

1. In a large, heavy pot or Dutch oven, heat the oil over moderate heat. Sprinkle the beef on all sides with the salt, the paprika, and the pepper, then brown in the oil, turning to brown evenly on all sides.

2. While the meat is browning, add the onions, the carrots, and the parsnip and stir them to cook in the oil.

3. When the meat is thoroughly browned, add the turnip, the sweet potatoes, the garlic, the tomatoes, and the prunes. Bring to the simmer, then cover and cook over very low heat for 2–2½ hours. Turn the meat in the sauce from time to time.

4. Remove the meat from the pot and let stand for 10 minutes. At the same time, add the beans to the pot.

5. Carve the meat in even slices and return to the pot, poking the meat down into the sauce. Cover and cook again over very low heat for another 2 hours or so. By this time, the meat should be very tender and the sauce thick and velvety. Taste for salt.

Serves 6

Braised Veal Shanks with Mixed Exotic Mushrooms

The Italian kitchen has a special affinity for veal, prepared as savory roasts, tender sautéed scaloppine, and succulent stews. This recipe for slow-cooked veal shanks is similar to the classic osso buco, except that it adds a variety of exotic mushrooms that give a wonderful flavor and texture. The dish is traditionally served with a risotto, but it is also very good with a simple polenta or a buttered small pasta like orzo or seme di melone ("melon seeds").

1 medium onion, finely chopped
2 large carrots, diced
1 tablespoon butter
2 tablespoons olive oil
2 pounds meaty veal shanks (figure on 1 meaty shank, about ½ pound, per serving)
Flour for dredging
3 cloves garlic, minced
½ teaspoon salt
¼ teaspoon freshly ground black pepper
12–16 ounces mixed exotic mushrooms (oyster, shiitake, portobello, etc.), coarsely chopped
1 teaspoon chopped fresh rosemary
1 cup chicken stock
½ cup dry white wine or vermouth
3–4 tablespoons finely chopped flat-leaf parsley
1 teaspoon grated lemon zest

1. In a heavy pot or Dutch oven, sauté the onion and the carrots in the butter and 1 tablespoon of the oil over moderate heat, stirring, until the onion just begins to turn golden.
2. Dredge the veal shanks in flour, shaking off the excess. Add the remaining 1 tablespoon of oil to the pot, then push the vegetables to the side of the pot and put in the veal shanks to brown.

3. After turning the shanks to brown on the second side, add the garlic, the salt, and the pepper. Stir in the mushrooms and the rosemary.

4. Pour in the stock and the wine, bring to the simmer, then cover and cook over low heat for about 2 hours, or until the meat is very tender. Turn the shanks in the sauce once or twice while cooking.

5. When the meat is very tender, uncover the pot and cook the sauce down slightly. Stir in the parsley and lemon zest and cook for a few minutes more.

Serves 4

Goulash of Veal, Sausage, and Vegetables

The goulash is an ancient dish of meat—usually beef, lamb, or game—cooked in an iron pot over an open fire. It has evolved through the centuries, particularly with regard to the peppers, both sweet and hot, which were introduced into Hungary by the Turks after being discovered in the Americas by Columbus. There are now many kinds of goulash, containing a variety of meats and sausages, a good dose of fresh peppers, and, of course, the paprika that has become the hallmark of Hungarian cooking.

3–4 slices bacon, coarsely chopped

1 large onion, coarsely chopped

4 medium green bell or frying peppers, seeded and finely
    chopped

4 cloves garlic, minced

1 pound boneless veal, cut in 1-inch chunks

1 tablespoon Hungarian sweet (rose) paprika

½ teaspoon Hungarian hot paprika, or other crushed or
    ground hot pepper

½ teaspoon salt

Several good grinds black pepper

2 cups canned crushed tomatoes

½ teaspoon dried marjoram

2 cups coarsely chopped cabbage

2 cups coarsely chopped or sliced mushrooms

2 medium potatoes, peeled and cut in small chunks

1 pound smoked sausage (garlic, Polish, etc.), thickly sliced

1. In a large, heavy pot or Dutch oven, cook the bacon until it is crisp. Pour off and discard all but about 2 tablespoons of the fat.

2. Add the onion, green peppers, and garlic, and sauté, stirring, over moderate heat until the vegetables are wilted.

3. Push the vegetables to the side of the pot and add the veal cubes. Brown the veal lightly, turning the cubes to brown evenly.

Sprinkle the meat as it browns with the sweet and hot paprika, the salt, and the pepper.

4. Add the tomatoes, marjoram, cabbage, mushrooms, and potatoes. Mix well, then bring to the simmer, cover, and cook over low heat for about 1 hour, stirring occasionally, until the meat is tender.

5. Add the sliced sausage, mix well, then cover and cook for another 20–30 minutes. The goulash should be fairly thick, neither dry nor soupy. Serve with a tangy salad or pickled vegetables.

Serves 4–6

Pot-Roasted Loin of Pork with Wine and Herbs

From the country kitchens of France comes this aromatic and richly flavored pork, slow-cooked and succulent, with its complement of creamy white beans and tangy mustard. It is yet another example of the widespread and ancient alliance of pork and beans, which finds expression in such diverse dishes as the French cassoulet, the Brazilian feijoada, and our own Boston baked beans.

1 large onion, coarsely chopped
2 carrots, sliced
2 tablespoons olive oil
1½–2 pounds lean boneless loin of pork
4 cloves garlic, minced
½ teaspoon salt
¼ teaspoon freshly ground black pepper
1 cup dry white wine
¼ cup coarsely chopped sun-dried tomatoes
1½ tablespoons chopped fresh rosemary, or
    2 teaspoons dried
2 bay leaves
3 cups cooked or canned white beans, such as kidney, navy,
    marrow, etc. (if canned, rinse thoroughly in cold water,
    then drain)
1 heaping tablespoon Dijon mustard
Chopped parsley, for garnish

1. In a heavy pot or Dutch oven, sauté the onion and the carrots in the oil over moderate heat, stirring occasionally, for 7–10 minutes, until the onions are soft and becoming nicely browned.

2. Push the vegetables to the side of the pot and add the pork; brown the meat slowly on all sides. While the meat is browning, add the garlic to the pot and sprinkle the meat with the salt and the pepper.

3. When the meat is browned, add the wine, the tomatoes, the rosemary, and the bay leaves. Bring to the simmer, then cover and cook over low heat for 1½–2 hours, until the meat is very tender when pierced with a fork. Turn the pork in the liquid from time to time while cooking.

4. When the pork is tender, remove it to a carving board and let it rest for 5–10 minutes. Meanwhile, add the beans and the mustard to the pot and mix well.

5. Cut the pork into thick slices and return it to the pot. Cover and cook for another 10–15 minutes. Serve the pork and beans garnished with a bit of chopped parsley.

Serves 6

Smothered Pork with Apples, Onions, and Sage

The combination of pork and apples is old and tenacious; remember the classic suckling pig roasted with an apple in its mouth? This delicious dish is from the American South, where "smothered" foods—meats or vegetables coated with thick savory sauces—are a popular tradition. Don't rush the initial browning of the apples and onions; this step is crucial to the rich flavor of the finished sauce. The pork is excellent served with corn bread and a green vegetable or salad.

2 large onions, thinly sliced
2 Granny Smith or other tart crisp apples, peeled, cored,
  and thinly sliced
2 tablespoons peanut or vegetable oil
1½–2 pounds boneless loin of pork
½ teaspoon salt
Several good grinds black pepper
1 tablespoon chopped fresh sage, or 1 teaspoon
  crumbled dried
1 cup beef broth
Good squeeze lemon juice

1. In a heavy pot or Dutch oven, cook the onions and the apples in the oil over low to moderate heat, stirring occasionally, until they are very soft and a rich golden brown. This will take about 30–40 minutes

2. Push the apples and onions to the sides of the pot and brown the meat, turning it to brown evenly on all sides.

3. Sprinkle the meat with the salt and the pepper, then add the sage and the broth. Bring to the simmer, then cover and cook over low heat for about 1½ hours, turning the pork in the sauce once or twice, until the meat is fork-tender.

4. Remove the meat from the pot and place on a cutting board. Let it rest for 10 minutes. Meanwhile, cook the sauce down until it is quite thick. Stir in the lemon juice and taste for salt.

5. Cut the pork into thick slices, then return it to the sauce. Bring to the simmer and cook for a few minutes more. Serve the pork smothered with the sauce.

Serves 4–6

Polish Sausage, Apple, and Sauerkraut Stew

Hearty slow-cooked stews are hallmarks of Polish cookery; the national dish is the bigos, or hunter's stew, made from a variety of cooked meats, sausage, and game simmered with cabbage, sauerkraut, and fruit. Like so many popular ethnic dishes, the bigos can be found in dozens of varieties; this is a simplified version that uses kielbasa, the famous Polish smoked sausage. It makes a wonderful meal for a cold winter night.

1 large onion, cut in half and thinly sliced
2–3 carrots, sliced
1 tart crisp apple, peeled, cored, and thinly sliced
2 tablespoons vegetable oil
3 cloves garlic, minced
½ teaspoon salt
Several good grinds black pepper
½ teaspoon caraway seeds
½ cup dry red wine
3 tablespoons plum butter (if not available, substitute
    apple butter)
2 cups shredded cabbage
1½ pounds kielbasa (Polish smoked sausage), cut into
    1-inch chunks
2 cups sauerkraut, drained
1 tablespoon coarse-grained sharp mustard

(continued)

1. In a heavy pot or Dutch oven, sauté the onion, the carrots, and the apple in the oil over moderate heat, stirring occasionally, until the onion wilts and begins to brown. Stir in the garlic and cook for another few minutes.

2. Stir in the salt, the pepper, the caraway, the wine, and the plum butter. Mix well, then stir in the cabbage. Place the sausage chunks over the cabbage; place the sauerkraut over the sausage.

3. Bring to the simmer, then cover and cook over low heat for about ½ hour. Mix the stew gently but thoroughly. Cover and cook again for another ½ hour.

4. Taste for salt and sweetness; you may need a little more salt or plum butter. Stir in the mustard and mix well. Serve the stew with mashed or boiled potatoes.

Serves 4

Stewords

Our word "stew," used both as a noun and a verb, comes from the Old English *stuwe* and the Old French *étuvée*, meaning food slowly seethed in liquid. The word is related to the Spanish *estufado* and the Greek *stifatho;* the Creole *"étouffée"* is of the same derivation. French has replaced the old term with *ragout;* Italian uses both *stufato* and *ragù*. Many dishes that belong to the general category have descriptive names that refer to the primary solid ingredients: "chicken fricassee" and "chicken and dumplings" are stews, as are "lentil curry" and "corned beef and cabbage." The liquid part of the stew is also frequently designated, as in "coq au vin" or "meatballs in tomato sauce." "Goat water" is the name in Jamaica for a stew of goat meat and vegetables; in Persian, the term *abgusht* means "the water of the meat" and refers to the liquid in which meat is stewed with vegetables and seasonings.

There are two approaches to the basic process of stewing. The first is *braising*, in which aromatic vegetables and/or meats are sautéed or browned in fat or oil before the liquid is added. The second is *poaching*, in which there is no preliminary frying or browning; the ingredients are placed in the liquid, which is then brought to the simmer. Poaching produces a lighter, clearer liquid and is used more frequently with fish than with meat or poultry.

If *you're* stewing, you're obsessing about something; if you're in a stew, you're confused, worried, and all mixed up. If you're stewing in your own juices, you are suffering the consequences of your own ill-advised behavior, and if you're stewed . . . 'nuff said!

Venison Stew with Dried Cranberries

Venison—deer or elk meat—is probably one of mankind's most ancient red meats, and it remains a favorite of many. It is now being widely farm-raised, and coming more and more to resemble domesticated beef with its fat-marbled tenderness. Wild venison is very lean and usually requires a long, slow cooking to become tender—unless, like Ishi, you enjoy your meat firm to the tooth.

2 large onions, coarsely chopped
2 carrots, thickly sliced
1 parsnip, thickly sliced
2 tablespoons olive oil
2 pounds boneless venison, cut in 1-inch chunks
½ teaspoon salt
¼ teaspoon freshly ground black pepper
1½ tablespoons flour
1 cup dry red wine
2 tablespoons balsamic vinegar
⅓ cup dried cranberries
1 teaspoon dried thyme
2 bay leaves

1. In a heavy pot or Dutch oven, sauté the onions, the carrots, and the parsnip in the oil over moderate heat, stirring, until the onions wilt and begin to turn golden.

2. Push the vegetables to the side of the pot and add the venison chunks, in small batches so as not to crowd the pot, and brown on all sides, turning the meat to brown evenly.

3. When all the meat has been browned, add the salt and pepper, then sprinkle on the flour and cook, stirring, for 2–3 minutes.

4. Add the wine, the vinegar, the cranberries, the thyme, and the bay leaves, mix well, then bring to the simmer. Cover and cook over low heat for 2½–3 hours for wild venison, about 2 hours for farm-raised, stirring from time to time. If too much of the liquid cooks away, add some more wine or water.

5. When the meat is tender and the sauce thick, remove the bay leaves and taste for salt. Serve the stew with buttered noodles or potato pancakes.

Serves 4–6

Red-Cooked Duck with Crispy Skin

Most of us are familiar with Peking duck, that exquisite dish from northern China, whose crisp skin is achieved by long air-drying and the blowing of air between the flesh and the skin of the duck before roasting. The following dish is somewhat unusual, the duck poached in the spiced and soy-sauced liquid characteristic of red-cooking, then chilled, and the skin removed for separate roasting. It should be started the day before it is to be served, but it is well worth the time and the effort. The succulent meat and crisp skin are garnished with scallion slivers and hoisin sauce and wrapped in thin wheat or rice-flour pancakes.

1/4 cup soy sauce
1/4 cup rice wine
1 1/2 tablespoons sugar
4 slices fresh gingerroot, about 1/4 inch thick
6 scallions, sliced into 1-inch pieces
2 pieces star anise
1/2 teaspoon fennel seeds
1 cinnamon stick
6 whole cloves
2 cups water
1 4–5-pound duckling, or 4 whole duck breasts
6–8 scallions, slivered, for garnish
Hoisin sauce, for garnish
Sprigs of fresh coriander, for garnish
10–12 Peking doilies or thin wheat- or rice-flour wrappers

(continued)

1. In a medium-to-large heavy pot or Dutch oven, combine the soy sauce, rice wine, sugar, gingerroot, sliced scallions, spices, and water. Simmer, uncovered, for about 10 minutes.

2. Place the duckling, breast side down, or the duck breasts in the liquid. Bring to the simmer, then cover and cook, turning once, 2½ hours for the whole duckling, 1 hour for the duck breasts.

3. Let the duck cool in the broth, then remove. Pour the cooking liquid into a smaller container; cover and chill it overnight. Chill the duckling or the duck breasts overnight also.

4. With a small, sharp knife and your fingers, cut the skin and its underlying fat layer off the duck. Try to keep the skin in as large pieces as possible.

5. Place the pieces of skin on a rack over a pan. Bake in a 400° F. oven for 40–50 minutes, until the pieces of skin are dark brown and very crisp.

6. Remove the duck meat from the bones and cut into generous strips or chunks. Remove and discard the congealed fat on the top of the chilled cooking liquid.

7. In a skillet, gently heat the duck meat with a couple of table-spoons of the cooking liquid, just enough to moisten it. Do not cook the duck, just heat it until it is warm.

8. Serve the warmed duck meat and the crisp skin with slivered scallions, hoisin sauce, and fresh coriander. Wrap in Peking doilies or other wrappers and eat with the hands.

Serves 4

NOTE: The remaining cooking liquid should be stored, tightly covered, in the refrigerator. It can also be frozen. It becomes the "mother" sauce for other red-cooked foods, gaining greater flavor and depth with each use. Simply add water to bring its volume up to what is necessary for the next dish.

Stifatho of Duck with Onions and Mushrooms

The *stifatho* is the Greek rendition of the stew—meat or poultry and vegetables slowly cooked in savory liquids until tender and full of flavor. Except for the characteristic Greek ingredients of olive oil, cinnamon, and allspice, this dish bears an uncanny resemblance to the classic French *coq au vin*. It is a very rich preparation, ideal for a cold-weather meal.

2 tablespoons olive oil

12–16 small boiling onions, peeled

1–1½ cups small whole mushrooms

3–4 pounds duck parts (breast halves, legs, and thighs)

1 medium onion, coarsely chopped

2 carrots, sliced

½ cup full-bodied dry red wine

2 tablespoons tomato paste

2–3 bay leaves

1 teaspoon cinnamon

¼ teaspoon ground allspice

½ teaspoon salt

¼ teaspoon freshly ground black pepper

1 tablespoon red-wine vinegar

Rice, buttered orzo, or steamed new potatoes

1. In a heavy pot or Dutch oven, heat the oil over moderate heat. Add the whole onions and sauté, stirring, until they are nicely browned. Add the mushrooms and sauté, stirring, a few minutes longer. Remove the onions and mushrooms from the pot and set aside.

2. Add the duck parts in small batches so as not to crowd the pot, and brown slowly, turning the parts to brown evenly. When all the duck has been browned, remove it from the pot, then pour off and discard all the accumulated fat, leaving just enough to film the bottom of the pot.

3. Add the chopped onion and carrots and sauté, stirring, until the onion is soft and beginning to turn golden. Return the duck parts to the pot, and add the wine, the tomato paste, the seasonings, and the vinegar. Bring to the simmer, then cover and cook over low heat for 30–40 minutes.

4. Add the reserved onions and mushrooms, mix well, then cover and cook for another 30 minutes, until the duck is tender. Before serving, skim the fat off the top of the sauce.

5. Serve the duck with rice, buttered orzo, or steamed new potatoes. A tart green salad would go well with the dish.

Serves 4–6

Mediterranean Braised Olive Chicken

The most basic ingredients of the Mediterranean work to great advantage in this simple chicken dish, robust with garlic, olive oil, and cured olives, which give it a rich and intense olive flavor. It can be served with rice or couscous but is really best with chunks of crusty peasant bread.

1 medium onion, finely chopped
4–5 cloves garlic, minced
2 tablespoons rich, fruity olive oil
2–3 pounds chicken-breast halves, on the bone,
    skin removed
½ teaspoon salt
¼ teaspoon freshly ground black pepper
1 cup chopped tomatoes (fresh if they are ripe and
    flavorful, otherwise canned)
2 tablespoons fresh lemon juice
24 oil-cured unpitted black olives
Large handful finely chopped flat-leaf parsley
Additional chopped parsley, for garnish

1. In a heavy pot or skillet, sauté the onion and the garlic in the oil over moderate heat, stirring, until the onion wilts and just begins to turn golden.

2. Add the chicken pieces and turn briefly in the oil. Sprinkle the chicken with salt and pepper.

3. Add the tomatoes, lemon juice, olives, and parsley, mix well, then cover and cook over low heat for 40–50 minutes, until the chicken is very tender. If the sauce seems too liquid, uncover the pan and quickly cook it down until it is thickened. Garnish with additional parsley.

Serves 4–6

Korean Braised Chicken with Mushrooms and Cucumbers

The cooking of Korea shows clear influences from both Japan and China but retains its own unique hearty, full-flavored character, heavily dependent on garlic and sesame and spicy chile peppers. This dish of braised chicken and vegetables is a good example of how the simplest foods, lovingly cooked and seasoned, make feasts of our everyday meals.

1 large onion, coarsely chopped
½ teaspoon crushed dried hot peppers
2 tablespoons Asian sesame oil
4 cloves garlic, crushed
¼ cup soy sauce
1 teaspoon sugar
2–2½ pounds skinless chicken thighs, on the bone
2 cups coarsely sliced (about ½ inch) bok choy
2 cups thickly sliced fresh mushrooms, or small whole
    button mushrooms
2 medium cucumbers, peeled, seeded, and cut into strips
6 scallions, cut into 1-inch pieces
2 tablespoons toasted sesame seeds
Steamed or boiled rice

1. In a large, heavy skillet or pot, sauté the onion and the peppers in the oil over low to moderate heat, stirring, until the onion becomes soft and starts to turn golden. Add the garlic and sauté a few minutes more.

2. Add the soy sauce and the sugar, mix well, then place the chicken thighs in the pan. Cover and cook over low heat, turning the chicken occasionally, about 30 minutes.

3. Add the bok choy and the mushrooms, cover, and continue to cook for 15–20 minutes, until the chicken is very tender.

4. Mix in the cucumber strips and the scallions, cover, and cook for about 5 minutes.

5. Coarsely crush the toasted sesame seeds; garnish the chicken and vegetables with the seeds and serve with steamed or boiled rice.

Serves 4

Senegalese Chicken and Vegetable Curry

The cuisine of Senegal combines elements of West African, North African, and Indian cookery, all of which appear in this spicy chicken-and-vegetable curry. As in so many other areas to which Indian foods have been introduced, curry "powders" or blended spice mixtures are commonly used.

2–3 pounds chicken, cut in small serving pieces
    (thighs, drumsticks, breast quarters)
2 tablespoons peanut oil
Salt and pepper
2 medium onions, coarsely chopped
1 medium green pepper, seeded and chopped
1 carrot, sliced
1 small eggplant, peeled and diced
1 cup small cauliflower florets
1 medium potato, peeled and cut into small cubes
1 tablespoon Madras curry powder
1 teaspoon dried thyme
¼–½ teaspoon cayenne pepper
½ teaspoon salt
2 cups tomato sauce
⅓ cup raisins
1 tablespoon cider vinegar
Cooked rice or couscous

(continued)

1. In a heavy pot or deep skillet, brown the chicken pieces in the oil, turning the chicken to brown evenly. As the chicken browns, remove it from the pot; salt and pepper lightly.

2. In the oil remaining in the pot, sauté the onions and the green pepper over moderate heat, stirring, until the onion begins to turn golden.

3. Add the other vegetables, the curry powder, the thyme, the cayenne, and ½ teaspoon salt, mix well, and sauté, stirring, for a few minutes more.

4. Return the chicken to the pan and pour in the tomato sauce. Bring to the simmer, then cover and cook over low heat for about 1 hour, until the chicken and vegetables are very tender. Stir the mixture occasionally while cooking.

5. Add the raisins and the vinegar; taste the sauce for salt and hotness.

6. Serve the curry over hot cooked rice or couscous.

Serves 4–6

Creole Chicken and Shrimp in Coconut-Cashew Curry

Elements of Asian, African, Caribbean, and Brazilian cooking come together in this slowly simmered hot pot of chicken, shrimp, and vegetables, in a rich, spicy coconut-cashew sauce.

2–2½ pounds chicken, cut in serving-size pieces (thighs, wings, drumsticks, breast quarters)
2 tablespoons vegetable oil
1 medium onion, coarsely chopped
2 green peppers, seeded and cut into small chunks
2 carrots, thickly sliced or cut into small chunks
2 fresh hot green chiles, seeded and minced

1½ tablespoons curry powder, preferably a Jamaican or
   West Indian variety
1 medium sweet potato, peeled and cut into small chunks
2 medium tomatoes, coarsely chopped
4–5 ounces unsweetened coconut milk (1 small can)
½ teaspoon salt
Several good grinds black pepper
⅓ cup cashew butter
1 tablespoon fresh lime juice
1 pound shrimp, peeled and deveined
Hot cooked rice

1. In a large, heavy pot or Dutch oven, brown the chicken parts in the oil over moderate to high heat, turning the chicken parts to brown evenly. As the chicken browns, remove it from the pot and set aside. Pour off and discard all the oil, leaving just enough to film the bottom of the pot.

2. Add the onion, the green peppers, the carrots, and the chiles, and sauté over moderate heat, stirring, until the onion begins to wilt and turn golden. Stir in the curry powder and mix well.

3. Add the sweet potato, the tomatoes, and the coconut milk and mix well. Return the chicken to the pot and sprinkle with the salt and pepper. Bring to the simmer, then cover and cook over low heat for about 40–45 minutes, turning the chicken occasionally, until it is very tender.

4. Remove the chicken from the pot and set aside; cover and keep warm. To the mixture in the pot add the cashew butter and the lime juice and blend in thoroughly. Taste for salt and hotness; add more salt and cayenne to taste.

5. Add the shrimp to the sauce, then cover and cook for about 4–5 minutes, just until the shrimp turn pink and opaque.

6. Spoon the shrimp-and-vegetable mixture over and around the chicken on a large serving platter or bowl. Serve hot with rice.

Serves 4–6

Pollo Almendrado
(Chicken with Garlic-Almond Sauce)

This is a slow-cooked, savory chicken dish of Spanish origin that has been adopted and influenced by the cuisine of Mexico, particularly with the little serrano chiles, which give it a subtle bite. Long before the Spanish arrived, Mexican cooks thickened and flavored their sauces with a variety of nuts and seeds, and the Spanish almond fit right into that tradition.

2 tablespoons olive oil
2½–3½ pounds chicken, cut into serving pieces
   (thighs, drumsticks, breast halves)
1 large onion, finely chopped
4 cloves garlic, minced
2 serrano chiles, seeded and minced
½ teaspoon salt
Several good grinds black pepper
2 cups chicken stock
½ cup lightly toasted chopped almonds
2 cloves garlic, sliced
3–4 tablespoons chopped cilantro
Hot cooked rice

1. In a heavy pot or Dutch oven, heat the oil over moderate to high heat. Add the chicken pieces and brown, turning the pieces to brown on all sides.

2. While the chicken is browning, add the onion, the minced garlic, and the chiles, stirring them to cook in the oil.

3. When the chicken is all browned, sprinkle it with the salt and the pepper. Add the stock, bring to the simmer, then cover and cook over low heat for about 1 hour, until the chicken is tender. Turn the chicken in the sauce from time to time while cooking.

4. In a blender or food processor, combine the almonds, the sliced garlic, and about ½ cup of the liquid from the pot. Process the mixture into a coarse paste.

5. Stir the almond paste into the pot and continue to cook, uncovered, until the sauce has reduced and thickened a bit. Taste for salt. Stir in the cilantro at the last minute. Serve the chicken and sauce over hot cooked rice.

Serves 4–6

Ceylonese Chicken Korma

The korma is a slow-cooked braised dish of meat or poultry that originated in the north of India and traveled throughout the subcontinent,
taking on the distinctive spice and seasoning traditions of regional Indian cuisines. The korma of Ceylon (now called Sri Lanka), an island
nation on the southern tip of India, is highly aromatic, with a rich
browned-spice flavor. It is a good example of why Westerners are frequently apprehensive about Indian cookery: it seems to require so
many ingredients! But if you buy small amounts of the spices and keep
them tightly covered on a dark pantry shelf, you will give yourself the
opportunity for unparalleled flavor experiences.

1 tablespoon coriander seeds
2 teaspoons cumin seeds
1 teaspoon fennel seeds
1 teaspoon fenugreek seeds
6 cardamom pods
3 whole cloves
2 tablespoons dry flaked unsweetened coconut
2 tablespoons ground or very finely chopped cashew nuts
1/4 teaspoon lemon-grass powder or 1/2 teaspoon finely
    chopped lemon grass
1/4 teaspoon cinnamon
1/4–1/2 teaspoon cayenne pepper
1 teaspoon turmeric
2 1/2–3 pounds chicken thighs, on the bone, skin removed
1 medium onion, finely chopped
3 cloves garlic, minced
1 tablespoon finely minced gingerroot
2 tablespoons vegetable oil
1/2 teaspoon salt
1 medium tomato, coarsely chopped
1 cup plain yogurt
1 tablespoon fresh lime juice

3–4 small potatoes, cut into small cubes
Chopped fresh coriander, for garnish
Hot cooked rice

1. In a small frying pan, toast the coriander, cumin, fennel, and fenugreek seeds over moderate heat, stirring, until the seeds are nicely browned and aromatic. Be careful not to overbrown. Let the seeds cool, then grind them in a spice grinder together with the cardamom and the cloves. Add the coconut and grind it with the spices.

2. Combine the ground-spice mixture with the nuts, the lemon grass, the cinnamon, the cayenne, and the turmeric, and mix thoroughly.

3. Pour the spice mixture over the chicken thighs, turning the chicken so that all sides are coated with the spice. Let stand in the refrigerator 1–2 hours.

4. In a heavy pot or large, heavy skillet, sauté the onion, the garlic, and the gingerroot in the oil over moderate heat, stirring, until the vegetables are soft and aromatic.

5. Place the chicken with all the spice mixture in the pot. Add the salt, the tomato, the yogurt, and the lime juice. Cover and cook over low heat for about ½ hour.

6. Remove the cover and add the potatoes. Continue to cook over low heat, uncovered, stirring occasionally, for another hour or so, until the chicken is very tender and the sauce is thickened. Taste for salt and lime. Garnish the chicken with chopped coriander leaf and serve over hot cooked rice.

Serves 4–6

Kentucky Burgoo

The burgoo is Kentucky's equivalent of the French *marmite*, a large cast-iron pot designed to stand in or be suspended over the hearth fire. In pioneer times, the burgoo, which referred not only to the vessel but to the food that was cooked in it, was a communal event, with all the participants contributing ingredients to the long-cooked stew. A number of different meats—fresh, cured, poultry, game— showed up in the pot, as well as a variety of vegetables, all blending their flavors in a savory meal-in-one. This version has been scaled down to suit a family rather than a whole neighborhood, but it retains many of the ingredients and much of the feel of the original.

2 tablespoons vegetable oil (or lard, if you want to be more authentic)
2½–3½ pounds chicken, cut into large serving pieces (thighs, drumsticks, breast halves)
1 large onion, coarsely chopped
2 ribs celery, with leaves, coarsely sliced
½ teaspoon salt
¼ teaspoon freshly ground black pepper
2 large carrots, cut into small chunks
1 medium turnip, cut into small chunks
2 medium potatoes, cut into small chunks
2 whole small dried hot peppers
½ pound smoked ham, cut in small chunks
2 cups canned crushed tomatoes
2 tablespoons Worcestershire sauce
1 tablespoon cider vinegar
2 cups fresh or frozen baby lima beans
1 cup fresh or frozen corn kernels
Good handful chopped parsley

1. In a large, heavy pot or Dutch oven, heat the oil over moderate heat. Add the chicken pieces and brown on all sides. While the chicken is browning, add the onion, the celery, the salt, and the pepper.

2. When the chicken is browned, add all the remaining ingredients except the lima beans, the corn, and the parsley. Mix well, bring to the simmer, then cover and cook over low heat for about 2 hours. Stir the stew gently from time to time.

3. Add the lima beans and the corn and cook for another 20 minutes or so.

4. Taste the stew for salt. Stir in the chopped parsley and serve hot, with corn bread or biscuits.

Serves 4–6

Fried Onions

Think how often recipes begin with the directions to cook (fry, sauté) the onions (garlic, peppers) in the oil (butter, fat). All over the world, flavor in cooked food is frequently initiated by the cooking of aromatic vegetables in oil or fat. The ingredients and the technique vary from cuisine to cuisine, but the basic practice is widespread and pervasive. Some member of the allium family is almost always involved, most frequently onions, but not uncommonly the onion's close relatives shallots, scallions, and leeks. Another member of the same lily family, garlic, is a frequent addition, along with carrots, celery, and both sweet and hot peppers. The fat can be a vegetable oil (olive, sesame, peanut), whole or clarified butter, or an animal fat like lard, beef suet, bacon, or chicken fat. The technique can vary from a low-heat "sweating" or slow browning of the vegetables to a high-heat quick stir-fry, but the purpose of the process is the same: a browning or caramelization of the natural sugars in the vegetables, and a release into the oil or fat of certain aromatic and flavorful compounds that contribute immeasurably to the flavor of the finished dish.

So fundamental is this technique that its product has been given a name in many cuisines. In Spanish tradition the *sofrito* refers to onions slowly stewed in olive oil, with the frequent addition of sweet peppers and garlic. In French cooking the *mirepoix* is a mixture of finely chopped onions, carrots, and celery sautéed in butter. Caribbean cooks often begin their dishes with the *achiotina,* lard flavored with onion and garlic and colored orange-red with achiote. The Louisiana creole version has been dubbed "The Holy Trinity," that ubiquitous combination of onions, celery, and bell peppers sautéed in butter or oil, with the frequent addition of garlic. In Malaysia, *rempeh* is the name for a mixture of fried ground or pounded aromatics—

garlic, shallots, and chile—that initiates the seasoning of most food.

In Italy, onions and garlic are sautéed in olive oil; in Hungary, onions and paprika are fried in lard or bacon fat. Eastern European Jews substituted chicken or goose fat for the prohibited pork fat and developed their own unique flavor of onions caramelized in chicken fat for such characteristic dishes as chopped liver. In China and throughout Southeast Asia, almost all sauced or liquid-cooked food is flavored with the initial frying of onions or scallions or shallots, along with garlic, gingerroot, and hot chiles, in some kind of vegetable oil; in India, the same aromatics are fried in butter or vegetable ghee, peanut or mustard oil.

The cooking of aromatic vegetables in oil or fat is a preliminary step in the preparation of much cooked food, providing a savory base on which the final flavor will depend. That ultimate flavor is generally more complex, resulting from the food itself, the length and nature of the cooking process, and the addition of other seasoning ingredients. But much of that food, no matter the cuisine, begins with an onion, chopped and fried.

Spicy Burmese Fish in a Pot

Burmese curries—foods slowly cooked in highly seasoned liquids—are generally characterized by two distinct flavoring traditions, the soy, fish sauce, and lemon grass of Southeast Asia, and the dry curry spices and aromatics of Indian cuisine. This delicious and unusual fish curry is more the Southeast Asian type and should be done with a firm, meaty, and full-flavored fish. I find that bluefish works very well, but you can substitute other varieties if you wish. Burmese sauces are almost never thickened with cornstarch or flour and are best served over plain boiled or steamed rice.

1 large onion, finely chopped

1½ tablespoons finely minced gingerroot

4 large cloves garlic, minced

2–3 fresh hot chiles, seeded and minced, or

   ½–1 teaspoon crushed dried hot peppers

2 tablespoons vegetable oil

2 cups coarsely chopped fresh very ripe tomatoes

1 teaspoon lemon-grass powder, or 2 teaspoons finely

   chopped fresh lemon grass

2 tablespoons fish sauce

1½–2 pounds thick bluefish fillet, cut in large chunks

1 tablespoon fresh lemon juice

Small handful chopped fresh coriander leaf

Hot cooked rice

1. In a heavy pot, sauté the onion, gingerroot, garlic, and chiles in the oil over moderate heat, stirring, until the onions are soft and the mixture becomes aromatic.

2. Add the tomatoes, the lemon grass, and the fish sauce and mix well. Simmer the sauce, stirring occasionally, for about 5 minutes.

3. Place the fish chunks on the tomato mixture, cover, and cook over low heat for about 30 minutes, until the fish is very tender.

4. Sprinkle the lemon juice and the chopped coriander over the fish; serve the curry with individual bowls of hot cooked rice.

Serves 4–6

Southern-Style Catfish Stew

This is real Southern country cooking, a unique blend of the cuisines of African, Anglo, and Native American peoples, all of whom contributed their long-held traditions of bubbling pots of savory stew. Catfish has long been esteemed in the South, valued for its sweet, meaty flesh; it is now farm-raised and widely available, sometimes even in nuggets or chunks, which are perfect for this dish.

3–4 slices bacon, coarsely chopped

1 medium onion, coarsely chopped

1 medium green pepper, seeded and diced

2 ribs celery, with leaves, sliced

3 large cloves garlic, minced

1½ pounds boneless catfish, cut in large chunks

½ teaspoon salt

Several good grinds black pepper

1 medium sweet potato or white potato, peeled and diced

2 cups canned Italian-style tomatoes, with juice

½ teaspoon dried thyme

1 tablespoon Worcestershire sauce

½ teaspoon liquid hot-pepper sauce

3 cups coarsely chopped collard greens

1 cup fresh or frozen corn kernels

Good handful finely chopped flat-leaf parsley

1. In a heavy pot or Dutch oven, fry the bacon until it is crisp. Pour off and discard the fat, leaving enough to film the bottom of the pot generously.

2. Add the onion, green pepper, and celery and cook over moderate heat, stirring, until the onion begins to turn golden. Stir in the garlic and cook for a few minutes more.

3. Add the catfish chunks; sprinkle them with the salt and pepper. Add the potato, the tomatoes, the thyme, the Worcestershire, the pepper sauce, and the chopped greens. Mix well, bring to the simmer, then cover and cook over low heat for about 30 minutes.

4. Uncover the stew and cook for another 20–30 minutes, stirring occasionally. Stir in the corn and the parsley and cook for another few minutes.

5. Serve the stew hot, with biscuits or corn bread, and pass additional hot-pepper sauce at the table.

Serves 4

Red-Cooked Salmon

The Chinese practice of red-cooking, poaching foods in spiced, soy-flavored liquids, is commonly used with meat and poultry but not often with fish, which is thought to be too delicate in flavor and texture to stand up to the technique. I find that fresh salmon, however, with its rich, meaty, succulent flesh, does beautifully with red-cooking; its fine full flavor needs only some simple steamed greens and rice to complete the dish.

6 scallions, cut into 2-inch pieces
6 slices fresh gingerroot, about ⅛ inch thick
3 pieces star anise
¼ teaspoon five-spice powder
1 tablespoon sugar
¼ cup regular soy sauce
2 tablespoon black soy sauce
1 cup rice wine
1½–2 pounds skinless salmon fillets, cut 1 inch thick, or
    4–6 small salmon steaks, cut 1 inch thick
12–16 ounces fresh spinach or Chinese broccoli, cut into
    2-inch pieces
1 tablespoon cornstarch
1 tablespoon cold water
2–3 tablespoons chopped fresh coriander, for garnish
Steamed rice

1. In a heavy pot or Dutch oven, combine the scallions, ginger-root, star anise, five-spice powder, sugar, soy sauces, and rice wine. Bring to the simmer, then cook, uncovered, over low heat for 10 minutes. Let cool completely.

2. Place the salmon fillets or steaks in the cooled sauce, then refrigerate for about 1 hour, turning the fish once in the sauce.

3. At cooking time, bring the pot to the simmer, then cover and cook over low heat for about 15 minutes, carefully turning the fish once in the sauce. Remove from the heat.

4. Steam the spinach or the broccoli until just tender; drain thoroughly. Place the cooked greens on a rimmed serving platter or a shallow bowl. Carefully place the salmon fillets or steaks over the greens.

5. With a slotted spoon, remove the star anise and ginger slices from the cooking broth and discard. Mix the cornstarch and water into a smooth paste.

6. Bring the cooking liquid to a full boil, then mix in the cornstarch paste. Cook, stirring, until the sauce is smooth and slightly thickened. Pour the sauce over the salmon and the greens; garnish with a bit of chopped coriander. Serve with steamed rice.

Serves 4–6

Iraqi Barley, Lentil, and Vegetable Stew

Barley, lentils, and chickpeas have been eaten in the Middle East for at least ten thousand years, and they endure as familiar, nourishing, and inexpensive foods of the people. This hearty pot of grains, legumes, and vegetables, enriched with sesame paste—another traditional food—makes a tasty and filling vegetarian meal.

1 large onion, coarsely chopped
3 large cloves garlic, minced
1 tablespoon olive oil
1/2 cup barley
1/2 cup lentils
3 cups water
2 cups canned crushed tomatoes
2 medium sweet red or green peppers, seeded and coarsely chopped
1 pound Swiss chard, stems and leaves, coarsely chopped (about 4–5 cups chopped)
1 1/2 cups cooked or canned chickpeas, drained (1-pound can); if canned, rinse thoroughly in cold water and drain
2 teaspoons salt
1/4 teaspoon freshly ground black pepper
2 tablespoons fresh lemon juice, or more to taste
3 tablespoons sesame paste (tahini)
Chopped parsley, for garnish

1. In a large pot, sauté the onion and the garlic in the oil until the onion wilts and becomes translucent. Add the barley, the lentils, and the water. Bring to the simmer, then cover and cook over low heat for about 1/2 hour.

2. Add the tomatoes, the peppers, the chard, the chickpeas, 1 teaspoon of the salt, the pepper, and the lemon juice. Mix well, then cover and cook over low heat for another 1/2 hour.

3. Stir in the tahini and the remaining 1 teaspoon of salt. Mix thoroughly, then taste for salt and lemon. Garnish the vegetables with some chopped parsley.

Serves 6–8

Ethiopian Mixed Vegetable Stew

Ethiopians like meat as well as anyone; indeed, their warriors traditionally ate plenty of raw meat, spiced with hot chile, to strengthen
their bodies and fortify their spirits. For the ordinary daily diet, however, vegetables play a more important role, and though meat or
poultry is often added to the pot, simple vegetable mixtures are eaten
during Lent and as accompanying dishes in a meal. These stews are
frequently incendiary, with their lavish use of both fresh and dried
chile peppers, but you can adjust the pungency to suit your taste.

1 large onion, coarsely chopped
4 cloves garlic, minced
1 tablespoon finely minced gingerroot
2–3 small fresh hot chiles, seeded and minced
2 tablespoons vegetable or peanut oil
2 medium potatoes, cut into small chunks
    (about 2 cups chunks)
2 carrots, cut into small chunks
2 cups green beans, cut into 1-inch pieces
1 large green pepper, seeded and cut into small chunks
1 teaspoon salt
Several good grinds black pepper
¼–1 teaspoon cayenne or other ground hot red pepper
1 teaspoon cinnamon
1 teaspoon ground cardamom
¼ teaspoon grated nutmeg
¼ teaspoon ground cloves
3–4 fresh tomatoes, coarsely chopped, or 2 cups canned
    crushed tomatoes
8–10 ounces fresh spinach, coarsely chopped
Cooked rice, couscous, or injera (Ethiopian fermented
    flat millet bread)

  1. In a heavy pot, cook the onion, the garlic, the gingerroot, and
the fresh chiles in the oil over moderate heat, stirring occasionally,
until the onion wilts and the mixture becomes aromatic.

(continued)

2. Add the potatoes, the carrots, the green beans, the green pepper, the salt, the pepper, and all the seasonings. Mix thoroughly, then add the tomatoes.

3. Cover the pot and cook over low heat for about 45 minutes. Stir the mixture from time to time while it is cooking.

4. Stir in the spinach, cover again, and cook for another 30–40 minutes. If the vegetables become too dry during the cooking, add some water.

5. When the vegetables are finished, they should be very tender, and the sauce thick and aromatic. Taste for salt and chile. Serve the stew with rice, couscous, or injera.

Serves 4–6

Beans and Greens with Red Chile

This simple pot of beans is traditionally served in New Mexico during the Lenten season, when many people observe a temporary abstinence from meat and meat products. It makes an earthy and satisfying vegetarian meal, particularly with the greens, called "quelites," which are frequently the first wild greens of the springtime. The epazote, a common herb traditionally used in Mexican bean cookery, and known in North America as pigweed or goosefoot, imparts an exceptional and unique herbal flavor to the beans.

2 cups dried pinto beans
8 cups cold water
1 large onion, coarsely chopped
2 large New Mexican dried red chiles, or 2 large dried
    Anaheim chiles, seeded and torn into small pieces
2 teaspoons dried epazote
2 cups (tightly packed) coarsely chopped greens—spinach,
    chard leaves, etc.
1 teaspoon salt
Warm corn tortillas

1. Soak the beans in cold water overnight. Drain the beans, then place in a large pot and cover with 8 cups of fresh cold water.
2. Add the onion, the chiles, and the epazote, bring to the simmer, then cook, uncovered, over low to moderate heat for about 2 hours, or until the beans are very tender and have a soft creamy texture. (You can add some water if too much cooks away.)
3. Add the chopped greens and the salt and cook for another 15–20 minutes. Taste for salt and chile. Serve the beans hot with fresh warm corn tortillas.

Serves 6–8

Spiced Chickpeas and Potatoes
(Pindi Chole)

Forced by geography, economics, and ritual belief into a heavy reliance on plant foods, the cuisine of India has developed what is certainly some of the world's most complex and sophisticated vegetarian cookery. A wealth of aromatic herbs and spices has from ancient times provided a range of flavor and variety that brings humble vegetables to new heights of gastronomic richness. This pot of potatoes and chickpeas in a spiced tomato sauce can serve as the main course of a vegetarian meal, or as one part of an Indian meal.

1 tablespoon cumin seeds
2 tablespoons vegetable oil
1 large onion, finely chopped
1 tablespoon minced gingerroot
4 cloves garlic, minced
1/4–1/2 teaspoon crushed dried hot peppers
1/2 teaspoon cinnamon
1/2 teaspoon ground coriander
Several good grinds black pepper
2 medium potatoes, peeled and cut into small cubes
    (about 3 cups cubes)
1 cup canned crushed tomatoes
2 cups cooked or canned chickpeas (if canned, drained and
    rinsed)
2 tablespoons fresh lime juice
1/4 teaspoon salt
2–3 tablespoons chopped fresh coriander leaf, for garnish
Cooked rice or chapatis (traditional Indian flat
    wheat breads)

1. In a small skillet, toast the cumin seeds over moderate heat, stirring, until they begin to brown and become aromatic. Remove from the heat and let cool, then grind in a spice grinder.

2. In a medium to large pot, heat the oil over moderate heat. Add the onion, the gingerroot, the garlic, and the hot peppers, and cook, stirring, until the onion wilts and the mixture becomes aromatic.

3. Add the cinnamon, the coriander, the black pepper, and 1½ teaspoons of the ground cumin. Sauté for a few minutes, then add the potatoes and stir them into the spice mixture.

4. Add the tomatoes, bring to the simmer, then cover and cook over low heat for about 20 minutes, or until the potatoes are tender.

5. Add the chickpeas, the lime juice, and the salt, and mix well; cook, stirring, for another 5 minutes or so. Taste for salt, then stir in the remaining ½ teaspoon of ground cumin.

6. Garnish the mixture with the chopped coriander and serve hot with cooked rice or chapatis.

Serves 4–6

Spanish Pisto of Peppers, Tomatoes, and Squash

Cousin to the French ratatouille, the pisto is a simple mixture of fresh vegetables slowly simmered in their own juices with olive oil. The dish has many variations: some use eggplant instead of squash, and others include ham or bacon. The pisto is one of those wonderfully versatile preparations, delicious warm or at room temperature, as a main course, as a vegetable accompaniment to other foods, or as part of a spread of tapas.

1 very large onion, cut in quarters and thinly sliced
   (about 2–2½ cups)
¼ cup olive oil
2 cups coarsely chopped fresh tomatoes
2 large sweet red peppers, seeded and coarsely chopped
2–3 small yellow summer squash, cut in small chunks
   (about 2 cups)
2–3 small zucchini, cut in small chunks (about 2 cups)
4–5 cloves garlic, minced
½ teaspoon salt, plus more to taste
Plenty of freshly ground black pepper

1. In a heavy pot, cook the onion in the oil over moderate heat, stirring occasionally, for about 10–15 minutes, until the onion is wilted and beginning to turn golden.

2. Add all the remaining vegetables and the garlic, mix well, then cook, uncovered, over moderate heat, stirring from time to time, for about 1 hour, until the vegetables are very soft and the liquid has cooked away. Stir in the salt and pepper, mix well, then taste and adjust the seasoning if necessary.

Makes about 4 cups

Chapter Four

Garnished Grains

Pease porridge hot,
Pease porridge cold,
Pease porridge in the pot
Nine days old!

Along with the animal foods—the flesh, the bones, the fat—
that found their way into pots of simmering liquid everywhere was
an even larger assortment of plant foods—roots and tubers, fruits
and nuts, leafy greens, legumes, and grains. These many vegetable
foods not only added a rich variety of flavors, textures, and colors,
but were a crucial source of nourishment, providing for many if not
most people throughout history the actual bulk of the diet.

Foremost among the plant foods that have sustained humans
from the very earliest times are the cereal grains, the seeds of wild
grasses that originated in a number of different habitats throughout
the world. These seeds are nutritionally useful to humans because, as

the propagative agents of plants, they contain many essential nutrients: some protein, dietary fat in the form of vegetable oil, many vitamins and minerals, and a great deal of carbohydrate. Though none of the common cereal grains is, by itself, a complete and satisfactory source of nourishment, each can, with supplements or garnishes of other complementary foods, provide a full and balanced diet.

The cereal grains that feed most of the world's people today originated as wild plants that were domesticated starting about ten thousand years ago: wheat and barley in the Near and Middle East, rice in Southeast Asia, millet in Africa, maize in the Americas, rye and oats in Central Europe. But long before these grains were deliberately cultivated and bred for higher yield and for drought and disease resistance, they were gathered as wild seeds by our prehistoric ancestors and used for many of the same kinds of dishes we enjoy today—pilafs, porridges, and an impressive variety of bread and pasta products. Some of the grains, like wheat and rice, have traveled successfully and been enthusiastically accepted all over the world, whereas others, like millet and oats, have remained more geographically and culturally limited. Whatever the grain, however, and whatever the traditions that shape its use, it endures as the substantive underpinning of the human diet, the bread, the staff of life. And although the cereal grains provide basic plant nourishment for most people, a number of starchy fruits and vegetables serve the same function in some areas of the world.

But the staff of life, essential for the very survival of so many people, can be by itself undeniably monotonous; an unremitting diet of plain rice, boiled potatoes, cornmeal mush, or millet porridge proves boring and ultimately unpalatable. The human animal requires more than mere nourishment; variety and excitement are crucial to the eating experience. And so, wherever in the world people have relied on cereal grains and starchy plant foods, they have developed traditions for garnishing those foods with an enormous range of ingredients, from a simple sprinkle of seasonings to a more complex assortment of meats, vegetables, spices, fats, and oils. This practice reflects the universal human desire for novelty and variety, the inclination to dress up bland, starchy foods, to make them more interesting, more exciting, more palatable, to improve their appearance, their flavor, their texture, and their nutritional value.

The Chinese cook who stir-fries his noodles with gingerroot, scallions, and soy sauce is performing the same operation as the Italian who tosses his linguine with olive oil, garlic, and basil, or the Hungarian who mixes his noodles with butter and paprika and poppy seed. The Thai housewife who cooks her rice with chile peppers and fish sauce and coconut milk is doing the same thing as the Polish grandma who simmers her barley with a savory mixture of onions and butter and mushrooms. The grains can be whole, partially refined, or ground into flour or meal; the garnish can be simple or elaborate, cooked in or added on, and can consist of an almost limitless number of ingredients—but the practice is remarkably similar and pervasive across cultures.

The cereal grains, along with other plant foods—such as yams, potatoes, and cassava—have been from the most ancient times the bedrock of the human diet, and for good reason. With our growing contemporary appreciation of their value, as we turn away from the meat-heavy meals to which we have become accustomed, we can look with renewed interest at traditional cuisines to see how imaginative cooks throughout history have elaborated these simple foods into a myriad of splendid dishes.

RECIPES

Vegetable Pilau (Indian)

Saffron Garlic Rice with Clams (Spanish)

Green Chile Rice with Crab (Mexican)

Jollof Rice with Shrimp (West African)

Creamy Asparagus Risotto (Italian)

Turkish Mussel Pilaf

Gingery Chicken Congee (Chinese)

Fried Wild Rice with Vegetables and Duck (American)

Barley Pilaf with Fresh and Dried Mushrooms (Eastern European)

Carrot and Barley Kugel (Eastern European Jewish)

Tomato Bulgur and Toasted Noodle Pilaf (Middle Eastern)

Buttery Three-Grain Pilaf (American)

Mashed Potatoes with Leeks and Garlic Chives (American)

Papitas con Chorizo y Queso (Diced Potatoes with Chorizo and
    Cheese) (Southwest)

Spiced Yam and Peanut Casserole (African)

Herbed Polenta with Seared Portobello Mushrooms (Italian)

Sopa Seca de Tortilla (Tortilla Casserole with Chiles and Cheese)
    (Mexican)

Spiced Vegetable Couscous (North African)

Toasted Orzo Pilaf (Mediterranean)

Philippine Pan-Fried Noodles

Spicy Peanut-Sesame Noodles (Chinese)

Spaghetti with Anchovy and Garlic Cream (Italian)

Vegetable Pilau

India is an ancient hearth of rice cookery, with an enormous variety of dishes that range from the simplest boiled rice to the most extravagantly garnished festive preparations. The success of this delicious vegetable pilau rests on two critical ingredients: basmati rice, with its large firm grains and unique nutty flavor, and panch phora, a five-seed mixture consisting of cumin, black cumin, mustard, fennel, and fenugreek, frequently used to aromatize rice and vegetable dishes.

1 medium onion, finely chopped
1 carrot, diced
2 tablespoons butter or butter ghee
1 tablespoon panch phora (five-seed mixture)
1 teaspoon turmeric
1 cup basmati rice
Several good grinds black pepper
2 cups chicken stock or vegetable stock
1/2 cup very small cauliflower florets
1/2 cup fresh or frozen peas

1. In a medium saucepan, sauté the onion and the carrot in the butter or ghee over moderate heat, stirring. Add the panch phora and continue to cook, stirring, until the seeds begin to pop and the onion turns golden.
2. Add the turmeric, the rice, and the pepper and stir until the rice is evenly coated with the spiced butter.
3. Add the stock, bring to the simmer, then cover and cook over low heat for 10 minutes.
4. Add the cauliflower and the peas, cover, and cook for another 10 minutes or so, until all the liquid has been absorbed.

Serves 4–5 as a side dish

Saffron Garlic Rice with Clams

Rice came to Spain from the Arab world many centuries ago; it gracefully joined hands with the indigenous olive oil, garlic, and seafood that are so fundamental to much Spanish regional cuisine. The alliance was further enriched in the sixteenth century with the introduction of tomatoes and peppers from the New World. Though the paella is probably Spain's most famous dish, it is only one of a large variety of such preparations based on richly flavored and garnished rice.

1 large onion, finely chopped
2 tablespoons olive oil
4–5 cloves garlic, minced
1½ cups long-grain rice
¼ teaspoon freshly ground black pepper
3 cups chicken stock
½ teaspoon saffron threads
1 cup fresh or frozen peas
24 littleneck clams
1–2 roasted sweet red peppers, cut in strips, for garnish
3–4 tablespoons finely chopped parsley, for garnish

1. In a large, shallow top-of-range casserole or paella pan, sauté the onion in the oil over moderate heat, stirring occasionally, until the onion turns a deep golden color.

2. Add the garlic, the rice, and the black pepper and cook, stirring, for another few minutes.

3. Add the stock and the saffron, bring to the simmer, then cover and cook over low heat for about 10 minutes.

4. Stir in the peas, then place the clams on top of the rice, pushing them slightly down into the rice. Cover and cook until the clams open and all the liquid has been absorbed by the rice, about 10–15 minutes.

5. Garnish the dish with roasted pepper strips and chopped parsley.

Serves 4–6 as a main dish

Green Chile Rice with Crab

Rice was unknown in Mexico before the arrival of the Spanish early in the sixteenth century, but it was enthusiastically adopted as an attractive addition to the indigenous grains and starchy vegetables. Fresh coriander (cilantro) was also an import from the Mediterranean, one that has become fundamental to the flavor of post–Columbian Mexican food.

6 scallions, finely chopped
3 cloves garlic, minced
1 rib celery, finely chopped
1 large green pepper, seeded and finely chopped
1–2 serrano chiles, seeded and minced
2 tablespoons olive oil
1 cup long-grain rice
2 cups chicken stock
1 teaspoon epazote (optional but good)
½ teaspoon dried oregano
1 cup (8 ounces) fresh lump crabmeat
1 tablespoon fresh lime juice
Good handful fresh cilantro, finely chopped

1. In a medium saucepan, sauté the scallions, garlic, celery, green pepper, and chiles in the oil over moderate heat, stirring, until the vegetables are soft.

2. Add the rice and stir it into the sautéed vegetables.

3. Add the stock, the epazote, and the oregano, mix well, then bring to the simmer. Cover and cook over low heat for about 20 minutes.

4. Just before the rice is done, when most of the liquid has been absorbed, add the crabmeat, the lime juice, and the cilantro. Mix gently but thoroughly.

5. Cover and cook for about 5 minutes more.

Serves 4 as a main dish

Jollof Rice with Shrimp

In much of West Africa, rice is a valued staple grain; jollof rice is a seasoned and garnished dish that can include vegetables, meat, chicken, fish, or shellfish. The African jollof combined with another famous garnished-rice preparation, the Spanish paella, to create the extravagant and exciting rice dishes of creole Louisiana, including jambalaya and dirty rice.

1 pound peeled and deveined raw shrimp
6 cloves garlic, minced
½ teaspoon paprika
½ teaspoon cayenne pepper
½ teaspoon ground cumin
1 medium onion, coarsely chopped
1 tablespoon minced gingerroot
1 small fresh hot chile pepper, seeded and minced
2 tablespoons peanut oil
1 cup long-grain rice
3–4 fresh plum tomatoes, coarsely chopped
2 cups chicken stock (page 46)
1 teaspoon dried thyme
2–3 cups coarsely chopped any fresh greens (chard, kale, mustard, etc.)

1. In a small bowl, combine the shrimp with 2 of the minced garlic cloves, the paprika, the cayenne, and the cumin. Mix well, cover, then let stand in the refrigerator for 1 hour.

2. In a medium to large saucepan, sauté the onion, the gingerroot, the fresh chile, and the remaining garlic in the oil over moderate heat, stirring, until the onion wilts and the mixture becomes aromatic.

3. Add the rice and stir it into the onion mixture for a few minutes.

4. Add the tomatoes, the stock, the thyme, and the chopped greens. Mix well, bring to the simmer, then cook, covered, over low heat for about 10 minutes.

5. Place the marinated shrimp on top of the rice mixture. Cover and continue to cook, about 10–15 minutes, until the rice is tender and all the liquid has been absorbed. Stir the shrimp into the rice mixture and serve.

Serves 4 as a main dish

Creamy Asparagus Risotto

Though Italian cuisine is perhaps better known for its grain dishes based on wheat, in the form of bread and pasta, it has developed a distinctive rice cookery as well. The risotto, a flavored and garnished rice preparation, uses a plump, short-grained, starchy rice, primarily the Arborio variety, that produces a thick, rich, and creamy texture. Risottos can be enriched with all kinds of vegetables, bits of meat, sausage, or shellfish, seasonings, and cheese, and, left over, make good fillings for stuffed peppers or omelets.

1 pound medium asparagus
1 tablespoon butter
1 tablespoon olive oil
1 medium onion, minced
1 carrot, diced
1 cup Arborio rice
3½ cups chicken stock (page 46)
1 teaspoon chopped fresh rosemary, or ½ teaspoon dried
1 teaspoon chopped fresh sage, or ½ teaspoon dried
Several good grinds black pepper
¼ cup light cream (optional but good)
2 tablespoons freshly grated Parmesan cheese
Chopped parsley, for garnish

(continued)

1. Trim off the tough ends, then cut the asparagus into ½-inch pieces. Cook the asparagus in boiling water for 1–2 minutes, until just tender but still crisp. Drain and set aside.

2. In a medium saucepan, heat the butter and the oil over moderate heat. Add the onion and the carrot and sauté, stirring, for 4–5 minutes, until the onion wilts and begins to turn golden.

3. Add the rice and stir it for a few minutes into the onion mixture.

4. Keeping the heat moderate, add about 1 cup of the stock, bring to the simmer, and cook, stirring, until all the liquid has been absorbed. As soon as the rice becomes dry, add another cup of stock, along with the rosemary, sage, and pepper. Continue cooking, stirring, until once again all the liquid becomes absorbed.

5. Continue to cook the rice, adding the stock in half cupfuls, until all the stock has been used and all the liquid has been absorbed. This will take about 30 minutes in total. Taste the rice to make sure it is fully cooked; it should be creamy but not soupy and should have some texture but no crunch or hardness. If it does not seem soft or creamy enough, you can add a bit more stock.

6. Stir in the reserved cooked asparagus and the cream and cook until the risotto is hot. Stir in the cheese and mix well. Garnish the risotto with a bit of chopped parsley.

Serves 4–6 as a side dish

Turkish Mussel Pilaf

Mussels are a popular food in Turkish cuisine, served fried, steamed, marinated, or stuffed. In this recipe, along with pine nuts and currants, they garnish a rich tomatoey rice pilaf that can be eaten either hot or cold.

1 medium onion, finely chopped
2 tablespoons olive oil
1 cup long-grain rice
2 cups chicken stock
½ cup tomato sauce
Several good grinds black pepper
⅓ cup currants
1 tablespoon fresh lemon juice
2–2½ pounds fresh mussels, steamed and shelled
2 tablespoons pine nuts
3 tablespoons finely chopped parsley
Salt to taste

1. In a medium saucepan or top-of-range casserole, sauté the onion in the olive oil over moderate heat, stirring, until the onion wilts and begins to turn golden.

2. Stir in the rice and cook, stirring, for a couple of minutes, until the rice absorbs the oil and begins to turn golden.

3. Add the stock, the tomato sauce, the pepper, the currants, and the lemon juice. Mix well, then bring to the simmer and cover. Cook over low heat for about 20 minutes, until the rice is tender and all the liquid has been absorbed.

4. Stir in the mussels, the pine nuts, and the parsley. Cover and let stand for 5–10 minutes. Taste for salt.

Serves 4 as a main dish

Gingery Chicken Congee

All cuisines that use cereal grains and starchy plant foods make porridges, puddings, and gruels, thick, nourishing, slow-cooked mixtures that are frequently eaten for breakfast or given as special food to invalids, the very young, and the elderly. They are the world's comfort foods—soft, bland, easy to eat. Congee is the Chinese version, a kind of savory rice pudding, eaten throughout Asia as a comforting, familiar, restorative dish—and a lot more tasty, I think, than farina or cream of wheat!

1 cup medium- or short-grain rice
2 cups water
6 cups chicken stock
4–5 slices fresh gingerroot, about ¼ inch thick
1½ cups cooked diced chicken
6–8 scallions, finely chopped
1 tablespoon soy sauce
1 tablespoon Asian sesame oil
Chopped roasted peanuts, chopped fresh coriander leaves,
    minced fresh hot chile peppers, for garnish

1. In a heavy pot, cook the rice in the water for 15–20 minutes, until all the liquid has been absorbed.
2. Add the stock and the ginger slices to the rice, mix well, then cover and cook over low heat, stirring occasionally, until the rice is very soft and all the liquid has been absorbed.
3. Combine the chicken, the scallions, the soy sauce, and the sesame oil. Mix well, then stir the mixture into the rice.
4. Serve the congee hot in small bowls, with chopped peanuts, coriander, and chile for garnish. Remove the ginger slices before serving.

Serves 6 as a main dish

Fried Wild Rice with Vegetables and Duck

Wild rice is not a rice at all, but the seed of a wild grass native to Minnesota and Canada and now cultivated in California. It is not widely known outside its ancestral North American home, but it is very good seasoned and garnished in the style of Asian fried-rice dishes, adding an attractive nutty flavor and chewy texture.

2¼ cups water
½ teaspoon salt
1 cup wild rice
1 cup fresh or frozen corn kernels
3 tablespoons soy sauce
2 tablespoons Chinese oyster sauce
½ teaspoon sugar
3 tablespoons peanut oil
6–8 scallions, finely chopped (about ½ cup chopped)
1 tablespoon finely minced gingerroot
1 medium sweet red pepper, seeded and diced
½ cup coarsely chopped mushrooms
½ cup sugar snap peas
1 cup diced cooked duck meat

1. Early in the day or the day before, combine the water and salt in a medium saucepan and bring to the simmer. Stir in the wild rice, then cover and cook over low heat for about 45 minutes, until all the liquid is absorbed and the rice is just tender but still slightly crunchy. Let the rice cool thoroughly, at least several hours or overnight.

2. Blanch the corn kernels in boiling water for 1 minute. Drain and set aside.

3. Combine the soy sauce, oyster sauce, and sugar. Mix well and set aside.

4. Heat a wok or frying pan over high heat; add the oil and swirl it around. Add the scallions and gingerroot and stir-fry for a few minutes.

5. Add the cooled rice and stir-fry for a few minutes. Add the pep-

per, the mushrooms, the snap peas, and the corn and stir-fry for another few minutes.

6. Stir the duck into the mixture and fry for a few minutes.

7. Add the reserved sauce and mix in until everything is well blended and hot. Taste for salt.

Serves 4 as a main dish

Barley Pilaf with Fresh and Dried Mushrooms

In Central and Eastern Europe, barley and mushrooms have had a long and intimate relationship, particularly in the form of rich, hearty soups. But barley, one of the most nutritious of the cereal grains, works very well as a pilaf, its pleasant nutty flavor and firm chewy texture complemented by the meaty flavor of fresh portobello mushrooms and the intense aromatic earthiness of dried porcini. You can serve this as a side dish, but for me it's the main course!

1 ounce dried porcini mushrooms
2 tablespoons butter
2 tablespoons olive oil
8 ounces fresh portobello mushrooms, coarsely chopped
Salt and freshly ground pepper
1 medium onion, finely chopped
2 carrots, diced
1 cup barley
3 cups chicken stock (page 46)

1. Place the porcinis in a small bowl and pour in just enough lukewarm water to cover. Let stand for ½–1 hour.

2. In a medium skillet, heat 1 tablespoon of the butter and 1 tablespoon of the oil over moderate heat. Add the chopped portobellos and sauté, stirring, until the mushrooms are nicely browned. Salt and pepper lightly, then remove from the heat and set aside.

3. In a medium saucepan, heat the remaining butter and oil over moderate heat. Add the onion and the carrots and sauté, stirring, for 4–5 minutes, until the onion is beginning to turn golden.

4. Stir the barley into the onions, then add the stock. Bring to the simmer, and cook, covered, over low heat for about 40–45 minutes, until the barley is tender and all the liquid has been absorbed.

5. Drain the porcinis, reserving the liquid. Strain the liquid through cheesecloth, and add it to the barley along with the porcinis and the reserved portobellos. Mix well, then cover and cook for another few minutes. Taste for salt and pepper; adjust seasoning if necessary.

Serves 4–6 as a side dish

Carrot and Barley Kugel

From Eastern European Jewish cuisine comes the kugel, a baked dish of starches, vegetables, or grains that can be prepared either savory or sweet. Noodles and potatoes are frequent components of the kugel; this one is made from barley and root vegetables, enriched with chicken fat. If you don't want to use chicken fat, which does add a delicious and traditional flavor, you can go with all olive oil. Serve the kugel as a savory accompaniment to meat or poultry.

3 cups chicken stock
1 cup barley
2 tablespoons olive oil
1 tablespoon rendered chicken fat
1 large onion, shredded
1 medium parsnip, shredded
2 large carrots, shredded
1 teaspoon salt
1/4 teaspoon freshly ground black pepper
2 eggs

(continued)

1. In a medium saucepan, combine the stock and the barley. Bring to the simmer, then cover and cook over low heat for about 45 minutes, until the barley is tender and all the liquid has been absorbed.

2. In a skillet, heat the oil and the chicken fat over moderate heat. Add the onion, the parsnip, and the carrots and sauté, stirring occasionally, for about 10–15 minutes, until the vegetables are soft and the onions are becoming richly golden. Stir in the salt and the pepper.

3. Stir the vegetable mixture into the cooked barley and mix well. Preheat the oven to 350° F.

4. Whisk the eggs thoroughly, then mix them into the barley. Spread the mixture evenly in an oiled shallow casserole or baking dish, about 9 by 12 inches. Drizzle a little olive oil over the top of the kugel.

5. Bake the kugel for 40–45 minutes.

Serves 6 as a side dish

Tomato Bulgur and Toasted Noodle Pilaf

Bulgur, cracked parboiled wheat, is yet another form of the valuable grain that was native to the Near and Middle East and was first cultivated there at least ten thousand years ago. Though wheat found its most successful expression ground into flour for bread and pasta, it is still popular as a grain cooked into pilafs or salads. This one is nice with roast or grilled chicken or used as a stuffing for peppers or cabbage leaves.

1 cup fine egg noodles
1 medium onion, finely chopped
2 tablespoons olive oil
1 cup bulgur, medium- or coarse-grain
2 cups chicken or vegetable stock
1 cup tomato sauce
1 tablespoon fresh lemon juice
Several good grinds black pepper
2 tablespoons finely snipped fresh dill

1. Spread the noodles evenly on a baking sheet; toast in a 350° F. oven for 7–10 minutes, until lightly browned. Remove from the oven and set aside.

2. In a medium saucepan, sauté the onion in the oil over moderate heat, stirring, until the onion wilts and just starts to turn golden.

3. Stir the bulgur into the onion mixture, then add the stock, the tomato sauce, the lemon juice, and the pepper. Bring to the simmer, cover, and cook over low heat for 10 minutes.

4. Mix the toasted noodles into the bulgur, cover, and continue to cook for another 5–10 minutes, until the noodles are soft and all the liquid has been absorbed.

5. Remove from the heat, stir in the dill, then cover and let stand for 5–10 minutes. Fluff up the pilaf with a fork before serving.

Serves 4–6 as a side dish

Buttery Three-Grain Pilaf

Grains from three very different areas of the world—rice from Asia, barley from the Middle East, wild rice from North America—are combined in a simple but delicious pilaf that can serve as a main course or as an accompaniment to meat or poultry. If you want to make the dish completely vegetarian, you can substitute a well-flavored vegetable stock for the chicken stock.

1 medium onion, finely chopped
3 tablespoons butter
¼ cup barley
¼ cup wild rice
Several good grinds black pepper
3 cups chicken stock or vegetable stock
1 cup long-grain rice
⅓ cup golden raisins
⅓ cup coarsely chopped cashews

1. In a heavy pot, sauté the onion in 2 tablespoons of the butter over moderate heat, stirring, until the onion just begins to turn golden. Add the barley, the wild rice, the pepper, and the stock, bring to the simmer, then cover and cook over low heat for about 40 minutes.

2. Stir in the white rice and the raisins, cover, and cook for another 15–20 minutes, or until all the grains are tender and the liquid has been completely absorbed.

3. In a small skillet, sauté the cashews in the remaining 1 tablespoon of butter until just lightly browned. Mix the sautéed nuts into the pilaf.

Serves 4–6 as a main dish, 6–8 as a side dish

Roots and Tubers

Though a great many of the world's people are nourished with the cereal grains, many others depend for basic sustenance on a number of plant carbohydrates—roots and tubers like potatoes, sweet potatoes, yams, cassava, and taro, and starchy fruits such as plantain and breadfruit. These foods, which generally contain almost no fat and much less protein than the grains, are nonetheless valuable, because they contain rich supplies of carbohydrates and provide a basic source of nourishment in geographic areas where the cereal grains cannot so easily be cultivated. These starchy fruits and vegetables are treated much the same way as grains—pounded, grated, and dried into flour to make various breadlike products, or cooked and mashed into thick porridges and pastes. Like the cereal grains, they function as the basic staple food, bland and filling, garnished with spices and sauces and enriched with fats and oils and bits of meat and vegetables. The cuisines of Northern Europe, with their rich repertoire of filling potatoes flavored with onions or leeks and enriched with butter or bacon fat or sour cream, are parallel to the foo foo tradition of Africa, a variety of yam, cassava, and potato mashes eaten with spicy peppers and savory peanut sauces. Despite clear differences in seasoning and style, these widely disparate cultures reveal an underlying similarity in the choice and preparation of their basic foods, starchy plant foods garnished with other, more enlivening ingredients.

Mashed Potatoes with Leeks and Garlic Chives

Wherever the potato was accepted as a basic food, it turned up in some form of mash or puree, enlivened with a variety of herbs and seasonings and frequently enriched with fat and, in the Western world, dairy products. Here in America, mashed potatoes are comfort food, simply prepared with butter, milk, and salt. This is a somewhat more elaborate version of that tradition, with two members of the onion family that add wonderful flavor. Garlic chives are somewhat larger than ordinary chives, with a pronounced garlic flavor. They are usually available in Asian markets.

4 medium potatoes, peeled and cut into quarters
2 tablespoons butter
1 large leek, mostly white part, finely chopped
½ cup milk
½ cup finely snipped garlic chives
½ teaspoon salt
Plenty of freshly ground black pepper
1–2 tablespoons additional butter (optional)

1. Cook the potatoes in boiling water until tender. Drain and set aside.

2. In the same pot, heat the 2 tablespoons of butter over moderate heat. Add the leek and cook, stirring, for 5–7 minutes, until it is soft.

3. Add the milk and the chives to the leek and heat until the milk is hot. Add the drained potatoes and mash them into the milk. Stir in the salt and pepper and mix well. Taste for salt; you may need to add more to taste. Stir in the additional butter, if desired.

Serves 4 as a side dish

Papitas con Chorizo y Queso
(Diced Potatoes with Chorizo and Cheese)

For potato lovers everywhere, here is a dish from the Southwest, an area that, with its traditional and evolving blend of Mexican, Anglo, and native traditions, has given America some of its liveliest and most flavorful food. In this preparation, diced pan-fried potatoes are spiced with chile, flavored with chorizo and tomato, and enriched with a topping of melted cheese.

1 large onion, coarsely chopped

1–2 fresh hot chiles, seeded and minced

4 medium potatoes, waxy-fleshed type, diced

3 tablespoons olive oil

½ cup tomato sauce

6 ounces cured chorizo, thinly sliced or diced

1 teaspoon dried oregano

½ teaspoon salt

1 cup shredded jack, pepper jack, or mild Cheddar

1. In a large, heavy skillet, cook the onion, the chiles, and the potatoes in the oil over moderate heat, turning occasionally with a spatula, until the potatoes are lightly browned and just tender.

2. Add the tomato sauce, chorizo, oregano, and salt, mix well, and cook, stirring occasionally, until the potatoes are soft and all the liquid has been absorbed. Add a bit more tomato sauce or water if the mixture dries out before the potatoes are fully cooked.

3. Sprinkle the cheese over the potatoes and cover the pan until the cheese melts, or run the pan under the broiler just long enough to melt the cheese.

Serves 4 as a side dish

Spiced Yam and Peanut Casserole

The yam is native to both Africa and Southeast Asia and is thought to be the oldest cultivated food plant in sub-Saharan Africa, where it has served as a staple since prehistoric times. In its simplest preparation, the yam is roasted in hot ashes or boiled and mashed into foo foo, the generic carbohydrate base that serves as the underpinning of much African cuisine. In this recipe, mashed yams are enriched with tomatoes, peppers, peanuts, and spices. The dish goes very well with ham and other meats and makes a delicious accompaniment to the Thanksgiving turkey; it can also serve as a main course for a vegetarian meal.

3 medium to large yams (about 1½ pounds total)
1 medium onion, coarsely chopped
1 medium green pepper, seeded and diced
½ teaspoon crushed dried hot peppers
2 tablespoons peanut oil
1 cup canned crushed tomatoes
½ teaspoon salt
1 teaspoon curry powder
½ cup finely chopped roasted salted peanuts

1. Bake the yams in a preheated 400° F. oven for about 45–55 minutes, or until they are fork-tender. Remove from the oven and let cool.
2. In a medium skillet, sauté the onion, the green pepper, and the hot peppers in the oil over moderate heat, stirring, until the onion wilts and begins to turn golden.
3. Add the tomatoes, the salt, and the curry powder, mix well, and cook over low heat, uncovered, stirring occasionally, for about 15–20 minutes, until the mixture is thick and most of the liquid has cooked away.
4. Peel the cooked yams, then mash them in a bowl. Add the tomato mixture and the chopped peanuts and mix well.
5. Spoon the yams into a lightly oiled shallow casserole. Cover lightly and bake in a preheated 375° F. oven for 20–25 minutes, just enough to heat through.

Serves 4–6 as a side dish, 3–4 as a main course

Herbed Polenta with Seared Portobello Mushrooms

The ancient grain of the Americas, maize, ground into a meal or flour, made its way to Europe, where it was accepted by many of the rural poor, who could not afford more expensive foods. Like the cornmeal mush of colonial Americans, polenta was for many Italians a cheap and filling dish; only in recent years has it become a trendy item on restaurant menus. In this recipe, it is cooked in herbed chicken stock and garnished with meaty portobello mushrooms and melted cheese.

1 medium onion, finely chopped
2 tablespoons olive oil
3½ cups chicken stock (page 46)
1 tablespoon chopped fresh sage, or 1 teaspoon dried
1 tablespoon chopped fresh rosemary, or 1 teaspoon dried
Several good grinds black pepper
1 cup stoneground coarse cornmeal
2 tablespoons finely chopped flat-leaf parsley
6–8 ounces portobello mushrooms, sliced ½ inch thick
Additional olive oil
Salt to taste
1 cup shredded fontina or mozzarella

1. In a heavy saucepan, sauté the onion in the 2 tablespoons of olive oil until the onion becomes translucent.

2. Add the stock, the sage, the rosemary, and the pepper, and bring to the boil.

3. Keeping the liquid at a boil, add the cornmeal in a slow, steady stream with one hand, while whisking or stirring briskly with the other. When all the cornmeal has been added, lower the heat and continue to cook, stirring occasionally, for about 15 minutes. Stir in the parsley.

4. Spread the polenta in a lightly buttered 9-inch baking dish or shallow 1-quart casserole.

5. Brush the mushroom slices generously on both sides with olive oil. Heat a heavy skillet (cast iron is best) over moderate to high heat.

(continued)

6. When the pan is very hot, add the mushroom slices and sear for a few minutes on each side. Salt and pepper the mushrooms lightly, then place them in a layer over the polenta.

7. Sprinkle the cheese evenly over the mushrooms. If the polenta is still warm, run the casserole under the broiler for a few minutes, until the cheese is melted and bubbly. If the polenta has cooled, bake it in a 400° F. oven for about 20 minutes, until the cheese is melted and bubbly.

Serves 4 as a main dish

Sopa Seca de Tortilla
(Tortilla Casserole with Chiles and Cheese)

Mexican cuisine includes an interesting category of food called *sopa seca,* or "dry soup"—grains or grain products, like pasta and bread, cooked in a savory liquid or sauce until the liquid is absorbed. It is, in other words, a garnished grain dish. In this recipe, stale tortillas are the grain, cooked in a rich chile sauce and enriched with cream and cheese. It makes a marvelous meatless main course.

10 corn tortillas (9-ounce package)
1 tablespoon vegetable oil
1 medium onion, coarsely chopped
1 medium sweet red or green pepper, seeded and coarsely
    chopped
2 tablespoons olive oil
4 cloves garlic, minced
2 cups canned crushed tomatoes
1 whole chipotle pepper (smoked jalapeño)
1 tablespoon ground ancho chile, or 1 whole ancho chile,
    seeded and chopped
½ teaspoon salt

½ teaspoon dried oregano
½ teaspoon ground cumin
1 cup chicken broth (or vegetable broth)
1½ cups shredded jack cheese
1 cup light cream

1. Cut the tortillas into ½-inch strips. Spoon 1 tablespoon of vegetable oil onto a large baking sheet; toss the strips lightly in the oil. Spread the strips evenly over the tray.

2. Bake the strips in a 400° F. oven for about 20 minutes, until they are lightly browned and crisp. (The time may vary slightly; if the tortillas are stale, the baking time will be a little less; if they are fresh, the time will be a little more.) Remove the browned strips from the oven and set aside.

3. In a medium saucepan, cook the onions and the sweet pepper in the oil over moderate heat, stirring, until the onion begins to brown. Stir in the garlic and cook for a few minutes more.

4. Add the tomatoes, the chiles, the salt, and the seasonings. Cook, uncovered, over low to moderate heat for about 10 minutes.

5. Add the broth, mix well, then bring to the simmer and cook, uncovered, for about 30 minutes, stirring occasionally. Remove and discard the chipotle. Preheat the oven to 350° F.

6. Lightly grease a 2–2½-quart casserole. Spoon in just enough sauce to cover the bottom of the casserole lightly. Arrange the tortilla strips over the sauce. Spoon the remaining sauce over the strips.

7. Sprinkle the cheese evenly over the top, then carefully pour the cream all over the casserole.

8. Bake, uncovered, for about 30 minutes, until the casserole is bubbly.

Serves 4 as a main dish

Spiced Vegetable Couscous

Popular throughout North Africa and the Near East, couscous looks like a grain and eats like a grain, but is actually a kind of pasta made from finely milled semolina-wheat flour. Steamed in water or stock, it serves as a simple base for all sorts of spiced meat, poultry, and vegetable stews, but it can be dressed up and used as a main course or savory side dish.

1 medium onion, finely chopped
1 medium sweet red pepper, seeded and diced
1 medium green pepper, seeded and diced
1 carrot, thinly sliced or diced
2 tablespoons olive oil
½ teaspoon ground coriander
½ teaspoon ground cumin
½ teaspoon ground ginger
½ teaspoon turmeric
1 cup cooked or canned chickpeas (if canned, thoroughly
    drained and rinsed)
1 cup small cauliflower florets
2 cups chicken stock or vegetable stock
2 tablespoons fresh lemon juice
Several good grinds black pepper
1½ cups couscous
¼ cup currants

1. In a medium saucepan, sauté the onion, the red and green peppers, and the carrot in the oil over moderate heat, stirring, until the onion begins to turn golden.
2. Stir in the coriander, cumin, ginger, and turmeric, then add the chickpeas and the cauliflower and mix well.
3. Add the stock, the lemon juice, and the black pepper and bring to the simmer; cook for 2–3 minutes.
4. Bring the liquid to the boil, then stir in the couscous and the

currants, mix well, cover, and remove from the heat. Let the couscous stand for 5 minutes, then fluff it up with a fork before serving.

Serves 4–6 as a side dish

Toasted Orzo Pilaf

Although it looks like a grain, orzo, like couscous, is a pasta made
from wheat flour, shaped and cut to provide a grain- or seedlike appearance and texture. The toasting of noodles and other pasta products is a common practice of the Sephardim, those Jews who settled
throughout the Mediterranean and North Africa; the toasting gives a
rich brown color and a subtle nutty flavor.

1 cup orzo
1 medium onion, finely chopped
2 tablespoons olive oil
2 cups chicken stock
½ teaspoon cinnamon
Several good grinds black pepper

1. Spread the orzo on a baking tray and place in a 375° F. oven
for 7–10 minutes, turning occasionally, until the pasta is a deep
golden brown. Remove from the oven and let cool.
2. In a medium saucepan, sauté the onion in the olive oil over
low to moderate heat, stirring occasionally, until the onion becomes
a rich golden brown.
3. Stir the orzo into the onion and mix well.
4. Add the stock, the cinnamon, and the pepper, bring to the
simmer, then cover and cook over low heat for 15–20 minutes, until
the orzo is just tender and all the liquid has been absorbed. Remove
from the heat and let stand, covered, for 5–10 minutes.

Serves 4 as a side dish

Flour and Water

We must acknowledge with awe and admiration the accomplishments of our ancient ancestors, who, long before history recorded their doings, fashioned some of our most basic and best-loved foods from nothing but flour and water. The cereal grains were, as they still are, consumed whole in pilafs and porridges, but they were from the earliest times ground or pounded into flours and meals that, mixed with water, formed products that stuck to the ribs and gave pleasure to the palate. Long before the discovery of leavened bread and the addition of such enriching ingredients as eggs, fats, and dairy products, there were the flatbreads, simple baked loaves and cakes made from ground grains and water. The wheat-flour pita of the Middle East and the chapatis of India, the millet-flour injera of Ethiopia, the rice-flour papers and skins of Asia, the corn tortilla of Mexico, and the corn pone of North America—all are ancient flatbreads that have their origin in the universal practice of milling grains on stone grinders and baking the cakes in the hot ashes or on flat stone griddles. The simple mixtures of flour and water, if boiled in water instead of grilled or baked, produced such worldwide favorites as dumplings and noodles; many examples from the contemporary pasta repertoire are nothing more than flour mixed with water into a dough that is stretched and shaped and cut into a multitude of shapes and forms, to be cooked fresh or dried for longer storage. We will never know the name of the culinary genius who first thought to grind up some seeds or grains and mix them with water, but we salute her—the inventor of bread, the mother of spaghetti, the goddess of dim sum.

Philippine Pan-Fried Noodles

Philippine cooking combines elements from all parts of Asia, as well as a number of Spanish influences that entered the cuisine in colonial times. Extremely popular is a variety of noodle dishes, similar to other Southeast Asian dishes of cooked noodles pan-fried in oil and garnished with a tasty assortment of meats and vegetables. Note the use of both soy sauce and fish sauce, and the characteristic addition of annatto (achiote), a tiny seed that gives an intense red or orange color to food.

1 pound fresh Chinese egg noodles
4 tablespoons vegetable oil
1 medium onion, cut in half and finely sliced
4 large cloves garlic, finely chopped
1 teaspoon ground annatto (achiote) (if not available,
     you can substitute paprika)
2 cups finely shredded Napa or savoy cabbage
1 cup finely sliced celery
3 ounces Chinese sausage, cut on the diagonal into thin slices
½ pound cooked shrimp, peeled and deveined
½ cup diced cooked chicken
2 tablespoons soy sauce
2 tablespoons fish sauce
Several good grinds black pepper
Lemon wedges and tomato quarters, for garnish

1. Cook the noddles in boiling salted water for 1–2 minutes, until they are just tender but still quite firm. Drain, rinse in cold water, then drain again. Toss the noodles with 1 tablespoon of the oil and set aside.

2. In a large skillet or wok, heat the remaining oil over moderate heat. Add the onion and the garlic and cook, stirring, until the onion wilts and the mixture becomes aromatic.

3. Add the annatto, the cabbage, the celery, and the sausage. Cook, stirring, until the cabbage is just wilted, about 5–7 minutes.

4. Add the reserved noodles and mix well. Cook, stirring gently,

until the noodles are heated through. Stir in the shrimp and the chicken.

5. Add the soy sauce, fish sauce, and pepper and cook, mixing gently, until everything is very hot. Turn the noodles out onto a serving platter and serve garnished with lemon wedges and tomato quarters.

Serves 4–6 as a main dish

Spicy Peanut-Sesame Noodles

These savory noodles are common fare throughout China, eaten with as much gusto as is spaghetti with tomato sauce in Naples or New Jersey. Chinese sesame paste differs from its Middle Eastern counterpart, tahini, in that the seeds are darkly roasted before they are ground into paste or pressed for their oil, resulting in the characteristic dark color and rich nutty flavor. This dish is usually eaten at room temperature and is quite spicy; a platterful makes a wonderful addition to the buffet table.

1 pound fresh Chinese noodles

2 tablespoons Asian sesame oil

6 scallions, finely chopped

1 tablespoon minced gingerroot

4 large cloves garlic, minced

1 tablespoon peanut oil

¼ cup soy sauce

¼ cup rice wine

¼ cup peanut butter or Chinese sesame paste

1 tablespoon sugar

1 teaspoon Chinese chile paste with garlic

1 teaspoon crushed dried hot peppers

2 cups fresh beansprouts

2–3 tablespoons chopped peanuts, for garnish
4–6 chopped scallions, for garnish
Good handful chopped fresh coriander leaf, for garnish

1. Cook the noodles in boiling salted water for 2–3 minutes, until just tender but still firm. Rinse with cold water, then drain well. Toss the noodles lightly but thoroughly with the sesame oil and set aside.

2. In a small saucepan, sauté the scallions, the gingerroot, and the garlic in the peanut oil over moderate heat, stirring, for a few minutes, until the mixture becomes soft and aromatic.

3. Add the soy sauce, rice wine, peanut butter or sesame paste, sugar, chile paste, and hot peppers. Mix well, then cook for a couple of minutes, stirring, until the mixture is smooth and well blended.

4. Pour the sauce over the noodles and toss until all the noodles are evenly coated with the sauce. Add the beansprouts and toss with the noodles.

5. Spread the noodles on a serving platter and garnish with the chopped peanuts, the scallions, and the coriander.

Serves 4 as a main dish; more if served with other foods

Spaghetti with Anchovy and Garlic Cream

The myth still persists that Marco Polo brought back noodles to Italy from China in the thirteenth century, though the evidence is clear that pasta was produced in Italy long before that historic voyage. Since people all over the world seem ultimately to do the same kinds of things with their food, it is not unreasonable to assume that two such disparate cultures as China and Italy should have developed independently the same kinds of products, given an appropriate grain and an appropriate technology for milling it into flour. It is not hard to believe that both the Chinese and the Italians have, in addition to the common human culinary imperative, some extra genetic endowment that makes them exquisitely tuned to the pleasures of the palate—a noodle gene, perhaps? Here, at any rate, is an extravagantly garnished pasta that Marco Polo himself might have enjoyed. Because the dish is so rich, it is best served in small portions as a separate pasta course.

1 2-ounce can anchovies packed in olive oil
6 cloves garlic, minced
2 cups heavy cream
1/8 teaspoon freshly ground black pepper
1/2 cup finely chopped flat-leaf parsley
1 pound spaghetti or linguine, cooked (hot)
1/3 cup finely chopped freshly toasted walnuts

1. Carefully pour the oil from the anchovies into a heavy skillet.
2. Add the garlic and sauté, stirring, just until the garlic wilts.
3. Add the anchovies and mash them into the garlic.
4. Add the cream and simmer, stirring occasionally, over low heat, for about 5–7 minutes.
5. Stir the parsley into the sauce. Pour the sauce over hot cooked pasta and garnish with the chopped nuts.

Serves 4–6

Chapter Five
Little Bits of Meat

Though a variety of plant foods—primarily the cereal grains, the legumes, and a number of starchy roots and tubers—have always had a central role in the human diet, they have not for the most part supplanted or erased our taste for meat and animal foods, which seem to give us an extraordinary measure of nutritional, sensory, and aesthetic gratification. Vegetable foods are almost always cheaper and easier to come by, however, so most ordinary people throughout history have had to refashion their preferences to cope with lower-meat, higher-plant diets.

An obvious and widespread response to the problem is to make the most of whatever meat is available, to maximize the unique and distinctive characteristics of this desired and desirable food in order to provide variety and excitement without undue cost. Bits of meat in relatively small quantities are skillfully designed as embellishing additives to the monotonous vegetable base on which so many of us depend for basic nourishment, literally "beefing up" starchy, bland carbohydrate foods with satisfying meaty flavor and texture.

There are many strategies for stretching bits of meat into pleasing and inexpensive meals, as thrifty cooks from ancient times to the present can affirm. One of the most popular is to grind or mince the meat or cut it into very small pieces, mix it with a variety of other ingredients, and then cook the mixture in savory sauces that are spooned as an enhancing garnish over rice or noodles or potatoes, or used as stuffings for dough and vegetable containers. This category includes such familiar dishes as spaghetti with meat sauce, or chicken à la king served over rice or noodles, or chili con carne spooned into folded tortillas. In all these dishes, the meat sauce is of crucial importance in giving the food its character, its savor, its vitality; yet the meat remains in general a relatively small proportion of the finished preparation. And of course the sauces and seasonings that accompany the bits of meat are critical in providing color, flavor, and good coating or enrobing qualities, demanding from the cook some degree of virtuosity. A good hunk of prime steak doesn't need much, after all, by way of seasoning additives or extravagant technique, to provide gratification, but little bits and scraps of meat may require more care and creativity.

Another common tactic for stretching the meat involves combining bits of meat, either raw or cooked, with a grain or starch, then cooking the two together as a single cohesive mass. This practice results in such familiar products as corned-beef hash or fish cakes or chicken croquettes, dishes in which the meat may play a minor role in terms of quantity but is perceived and experienced as the crucial ingredient. In India, finely minced lamb is mixed with ground lentils, highly spiced, and then fried to make tasty little croquettes called shami kabobs; in Jamaica, bits of salt cod are mixed with a thick flour batter and fried into the savory fritters known as "stamp-and-go." The Pennsylvania Dutch combine bits and shreds of meat rescued from all parts of the butchered pig with highly seasoned cornmeal mush to make scrapple, a name exquisitely evocative of its composition. All these loaves, fritters, croquettes, and hashes share the same basic strategy of stretching the meat by combining the bits with vegetable substances in a dry rather than liquid medium.

Throughout the world and from ancient times, frugal cooks have devised all sorts of clever techniques to make us feel that we have eaten fully and well, by making the most of small amounts of meat to provide savor and excitement to boring vegetable diets. In so doing they have, perhaps unwittingly, developed a healthier and more environmentally sound way to eat. A little meat goes a long way, in terms both of its nutritional and its gustatory impact. Artfully prepared in small amounts and used as an enriching garnish, little bits of meat may well serve us better than the main-course slabs and chunks to which we have become accustomed. And traditional cuisines, wise perhaps from necessity rather than true preference, can show us a trick or two.

R E C I P E S

Central Asian Spiced Meat and Lentil Sauce
Chinese Five-Spice Beef Sauce
Thai Green Curry Sauce with Pork
Vietnamese Beef, Eggplant, and Basil Sauce
Armenian Meat Sauce
Piccadillo (Latin American)
Keema Curry (Indian)
Scandinavian-Style Veal and Mushroom Sauce
Sicilian Sausage Sauce with Fennel and Peppers
Thai Duck in Fragrant Curry Sauce
Smoky Chicken and White Bean Chili (Mexican)
Cantonese Crab and Leek Sauce
Malaysian Spicy Shrimp Sauce
Nigerian Smoked Fish and Peanut Sauce
Mexican Carnitas and Chinese Meat Shreds
Cypriot Spiced Sausage Roll
Fresh Chorizo (Mexican)
Costa Rican Chicken-Tortilla Nuggets
Spiced Chicken-Falafel Croquettes (Israeli)

Central Asian Spiced Meat and Lentil Sauce

Set strategically on the ancient trade routes connecting Asia, India, and the Middle East, the highlands of Central Asia have a long-established and unique cuisine that blends indigenous foods with exotic ingredients from many lands. Ground-meat sauces containing herbs and spices and a variety of grains, legumes, and vegetables are popular served over rice or noodles, frequently garnished with the yogurt that is a staple food of the area.

1 cup lentils
1 pound lean ground beef or lamb
1 large onion, coarsely chopped
2 tablespoons vegetable or olive oil
1 teaspoon salt
Several good grinds black pepper
1/2 teaspoon cayenne pepper
1 teaspoon ground cumin
1 teaspoon cinnamon
1 1/2 cups tomato sauce or canned crushed tomatoes
1/2 cup water
1/2 cup finely chopped parsley
1/2 cup finely snipped dill
1/2 cup finely chopped fresh coriander leaf
Cooked rice or noodles
Plain yogurt for garnish, if desired

1. Cook the lentils in boiling water for about 1/2 hour. Drain.
2. In a heavy skillet, brown the ground meat over high heat, crumbling the meat as it browns. When all the pink color has disappeared, remove the meat from the pan with a slotted spoon and set aside. Pour off and discard the fat from the pan.
3. In the same pan, sauté the onion in the oil over moderate heat, stirring, until the onion wilts and just begins to turn golden.
4. Add the reserved meat and the lentils, then stir in the salt, the peppers, the cumin, and the cinnamon, and mix well.

5. Add the tomato sauce, the water, the parsley, and the dill. Mix well, then bring to the simmer and cook, uncovered, over low heat for about 30 minutes, until the sauce is thick.

6. Stir in the chopped coriander and taste for salt. Serve the meat sauce over rice or noodles; if you wish, pass yogurt to add as desired.

Serves 4–6

Chinese Five-Spice Beef Sauce

Chinese five-spice powder is a traditional and widely used seasoning blend, containing cinnamon, cloves, fennel, star anise, and either Szechuan brown pepper or chile pepper; ginger or dried orange peel is sometimes added. The mixture imparts a forthright sweet, spicy, and aromatic flavor to sauces and cooking liquids, like this easy and delicious ground-beef-and-vegetable sauce to serve over rice or noodles.

1 pound lean ground beef
6–8 scallions, mostly white parts, chopped (reserve green
 tops for garnish)
1 tablespoon finely minced gingerroot
2 tablespoons peanut or vegetable oil
2 tablespoons soy sauce
1/4 cup rice wine
2 tablespoons hoisin sauce
1 teaspoon five-spice powder
1/2 teaspoon Chinese chile paste with garlic
1 teaspoon sugar
1/2 cup water
2 cups finely chopped bok choy or Napa cabbage
1/2 cup fresh or frozen peas
Salt to taste
1 tablespoon Asian sesame oil
Reserved green scallion tops, chopped, for garnish
Small handful fresh coriander leaf, chopped, for garnish

1. In a large skillet, brown the ground beef over high heat, breaking up the clumps. When the meat is thoroughly browned, remove from the pan with a slotted spoon and set aside. Pour off and discard any fat in the pan.

2. In the same skillet, sauté the scallions and the gingerroot in the oil over moderate heat, stirring, until the mixture becomes aromatic.

3. Return the browned meat to the pan, along with the soy sauce, rice wine, hoisin, five-spice powder, chile paste, sugar, water, and cabbage. Mix well, bring to the simmer, then cook uncovered over low heat for about 30 minutes, stirring occasionally, until the mixture is fairly thick.

4. Stir in the peas and cook for a few minutes more. Taste for salt and hotness; adjust seasoning if necessary.

5. Stir in the sesame oil, then top the sauce with the chopped green scallions and coriander. Serve hot over noodles or rice.

Serves 4

Thai Green Curry Sauce with Pork

Thai cooking, like so much Asian cuisine, is complex and appealing, manipulating a wide variety of ingredients and seasonings with skill and imagination. Meat products are used sparingly but to great effect, and a small amount—properly cut, cooked, sauced, and seasoned—can become an adventure in the mouth. In this dish, ground pork can be used, but the texture will be much better if the meat is finely cut or slivered.

    2 tablespoons peanut oil
    3–4 shallots, minced
    3 cloves garlic, minced
    1–2 fresh hot green chile peppers, seeded and minced
    1 pound lean boneless pork, cut in pea-sized bits or slivered
        (easiest to do if meat is partially frozen)
    5–6 ounces unsweetened coconut milk (1 small can)
    1 tablespoon fish sauce
    1 tablespoon fresh lime juice
    2 teaspoons finely chopped fresh lemon grass or
        1/2 teaspoon powdered lemon grass
    2 teaspoons minced galangal or 1/2 teaspoon galangal (laos)
        powder
    1/2 teaspoon Asian bottled shrimp or crab paste
    1 carrot, thinly sliced on the diagonal
    1 cup sugar snap peas
    1 cup fresh beansprouts
    1/3 cup finely chopped fresh basil
    1/3 cup finely chopped fresh coriander leaf
    Salt to taste

1. In a skillet or wok, heat the oil over moderate heat. Add the shallots, the garlic, and the chiles and fry, stirring, until the shallots wilt and the mixture becomes aromatic.

2. Add the pork to the pan, turn the heat up, and stir-fry the meat to brown it lightly.

3. Turn the heat down to low and add the coconut milk, the fish sauce, the lime juice, the lemon grass, the galangal, and the shrimp paste. Mix well, then cook, uncovered, stirring occasionally, for about 10 minutes.

4. Add the carrots and the snap peas and cook for another few minutes, until the vegetables are just tender but still crisp.

5. Stir in the beansprouts, the basil, and the coriander and mix well. Heat just to the simmer. Taste for salt; add as needed. Serve the sauce with plain steamed rice or noodles.

Serves 4

Vietnamese Beef, Eggplant, and Basil Sauce

In many ways, this sauce bears a remarkable resemblance to the sugo di carne of Italy and the yakne of Lebanon, both ground meat and vegetables in rich tomato sauces. This one, however, is wholly Asian in flavor, complex and spicy. It is best to use the small, skinny Asian eggplants, which have a sweeter flavor and more velvety texture, but if you can't get them you can substitute the common eggplant, peeled and diced. Serve the sauce over cooked rice noodles and garnish with fresh mint.

1 pound lean ground beef

2 tablespoons vegetable oil

3 small to medium Asian eggplants, diced
   (about 2 cups diced)

1/2 cup chopped scallions

1–2 small fresh hot chile peppers, seeded and minced, or
   1/2–1 teaspoon crushed dried hot peppers

2 carrots, thinly sliced on the diagonal

1/3 cup chili sauce (the American tomato variety)

1 cup water

1 tablespoon soy sauce

1 tablespoon fish sauce

2 pieces star anise

1/2 teaspoon cinnamon

1/2 cup chopped fresh basil leaves

1. In a large skillet, brown the beef over high heat, breaking up the meat coarsely as it browns. When all the pink color has disappeared, remove the meat from the pan with a slotted spoon and reserve. Pour off and discard any fat in the pan.

2. Add the oil to the pan and heat over high heat. Add the diced eggplant, the scallions, the hot peppers, and the carrots, and cook, stirring, for 3–4 minutes, until the eggplant is lightly browned.

3. Turn the heat down; add the reserved beef, the chili sauce, the water, the soy and fish sauces, the star anise, and the cinnamon. Mix well, then cook, uncovered, over low heat for 20–30 minutes, stirring occasionally, until the mixture is soft and thick.

4. Stir in the chopped basil and mix well. Taste the sauce for hotness, and add some more chile if desired. Remove the pieces of star anise before serving.

5. Garnish the sauce with some fresh mint and serve over hot cooked rice noodles.

Serves 4

Armenian Meat Sauce

Stews and sauces of ground or chopped meat are a common feature of Middle Eastern and Central Asian cuisines—inexpensive, flavorful mixtures served over rice or bulgur or noodles or used as stuffings for vegetables, pasta, and breads. This Armenian version is delicious served in any of the traditional ways and is especially good as the meat spread for Lahmajun (page 285).

1 pound lean ground lamb
1 large onion, finely chopped
1 large green pepper, seeded and finely chopped
2 tablespoons olive oil
3 cloves garlic, crushed
2 cups canned crushed tomatoes (a good chunky variety)
½ teaspoon salt
Several good grinds black pepper
½ teaspoon paprika
Good dash cayenne pepper
1 cup finely chopped flat-leaf parsley

1. In a large skillet, brown the lamb over high heat, breaking up the meat as it cooks. When all the pink color has disappeared, remove the meat from the pan with a slotted spoon; pour off and discard all the fat from the pan.

2. In the same skillet, sauté the onion and green pepper in the oil over moderate heat, stirring, until the vegetables are wilted and the onions are just beginning to brown. Stir in the garlic and cook another few minutes.

3. Return the meat to the pan and add all the remaining ingredients. Mix well, then cook, uncovered, over low heat, stirring occasionally, for about ½ hour, until the mixture is thick and most of the liquid has cooked away. Taste for salt.

4. Serve the sauce over rice or bulgur, or use for Lahmajun.

Serves 4

Piccadillo

Piccadillo is the Latin American version of the meat sauce, showing in its many different varieties the fascinating mix of ingredients from Spain, Mexico, and the Caribbean. Cubans eat their piccadillo with rice and black beans; Mexicans and Costa Ricans use it as a filling for tacos. It turns up frequently as a filling for empanadas, those tasty little turnovers that are popular throughout South America and the Caribbean. This piccadillo has some surprising ingredients that play wonderful games in the mouth—salty olives, tart raisins, sweet pineapple, and the delightful spike of serrano chiles.

1 pound lean ground beef

1 medium onion, coarsely chopped

1 medium green pepper, seeded and diced

2 serrano chiles, seeded and minced

2 tablespoons olive oil

3 cloves garlic, minced

1 teaspoon salt

1 teaspoon cinnamon

½ teaspoon ground cumin

¼ teaspoon ground allspice
12–15 pimento-stuffed green olives, coarsely chopped
½ cup dark raisins
1 cup finely chopped fresh pineapple, with juice
1 cup tomato sauce
⅓ cup chopped almonds

1. In a skillet, brown the ground beef over moderate to high heat, crumbling the meat as it browns. When all the pink color has disappeared, remove the meat from the pan with a slotted spoon and set aside. Pour off and discard all the fat in the pan.

2. In the same pan, sauté the onion, the green pepper, and the chiles in the oil over moderate heat, stirring, until the onion just begins to turn golden. Stir in the garlic and cook a few minutes more.

3. Return the meat to the pan, along with all the remaining ingredients except the almonds. Mix well, then bring to the simmer and cook, uncovered, over low heat for 20–30 minutes, stirring occasionally, until the mixture is quite thick.

4. Stir in the almonds, mix well, and cook for a few more minutes. Taste for salt and chile. Serve the piccadillo with hot cooked rice, as a filling for tacos, or as a stuffing for green peppers or empanadas.

Serves 4

Keema Curry

In the Indian kitchen, "keema" means ground or minced meat, and "curry" refers to a spiced sauce. Keema curry is thus the Indian equivalent of the Latin American piccadillo, the Italian meat sauce, and the American chili. It is customarily eaten with rice or chapatis, but, like so many other ground-meat sauces, it can be used as a stuffing for cabbage leaves or peppers, or as a filling for samosas.

1 pound lean ground beef
1 medium onion, finely chopped
1 tablespoon finely minced gingerroot
1 tablespoon vegetable oil
2 teaspoons ground coriander
1 teaspoon ground cumin
1 teaspoon cinnamon
1/2 teaspoon ground fenugreek
1/2 teaspoon turmeric
1/2 teaspoon crushed dried hot peppers
1 teaspoon salt
Several good grinds black pepper
2–3 medium tomatoes, coarsely chopped, or 1 cup canned
    crushed tomatoes
3/4 cup unsweetened coconut milk
1 medium potato, peeled and diced
2 carrots, diced
1/2 cup fresh or frozen peas
1 tablespoon fresh lime juice
Small handful fresh coriander leaf, chopped, for garnish
    (optional)

1. In a heavy skillet, brown the ground beef over high heat, breaking up the meat as it browns. When all the pink color has disappeared, remove the meat from the pan with a slotted spoon and reserve. Pour off and discard all the fat from the pan.

2. In the same pan, sauté the onion and the gingerroot in the oil over moderate heat, stirring, until the onion wilts. Stir in the spices, the dried peppers, the salt, and the pepper, and cook for a few minutes.

3. Return the beef to the pan, then add the tomatoes, the coconut milk, the potato, and the carrots. Mix well; bring to the simmer and cook, uncovered, over low heat, stirring occasionally, for about ½ hour, until the vegetables are tender and the mixture is thick.

4. Stir in the peas and the lime juice and cook for another few minutes. Taste for salt and chile. Garnish the keema with chopped coriander, if desired, and serve with hot cooked rice or chapatis.

Serves 4

Scandinavian-Style Veal and Mushroom Sauce

Allspice, dill, and sour cream flavor this chunky sauce of ground veal and mushrooms, which should be served with boiled or mashed potatoes or buttered noodles. Its rich flavor is enhanced by the contrasting tartness of pickled beets or a sweet-and-sour cucumber salad.

1 pound ground veal
1 medium onion, finely chopped
1 tablespoon butter
2 cups coarsely chopped mushrooms
½ teaspoon salt
Several good grinds black pepper
1 teaspoon paprika
1 teaspoon ground allspice
1 cup beef broth or veal stock
Several good dashes liquid hot-pepper sauce
3–4 tablespoons finely snipped fresh dill
½ cup sour cream
Sprigs of fresh dill, for garnish

(continued)

1. In a medium skillet, brown the veal over moderate to high heat, breaking up the meat as it browns. When all the pink color has disappeared, remove the meat from the pan with a slotted spoon and set aside. Pour off and discard any fat in the pan.

2. Cook the onion in the butter over moderate heat, stirring, until the onion just turns translucent.

3. Add the mushrooms, the reserved meat, and the salt, pepper, paprika, and allspice. Mix well and cook, stirring, for a couple of minutes.

4. Add the broth and the hot-pepper sauce, then bring to the simmer and cook, uncovered, over low heat for about 30 minutes, stirring occasionally, until the mixture is thick and most of the liquid has cooked away.

5. Stir in the finely snipped dill and the sour cream and mix well. Bring to the simmer and cook for a few minutes. Taste for salt; you may need to add some more at this point.

6. Serve hot, with potatoes or noodles, and garnished with some sprigs of dill.

Serves 4

Sicilian Sausage Sauce with Fennel and Peppers

The kitchens of southern Italy gave America the foods that have become as entrenched and well loved as fried chicken and apple pie—spaghetti with tomato sauce, eggplant parmigiana, and, of course, pizza. From that same tradition comes another robust sauce for pasta, rich with garlic, olive oil, and tomatoes and perfumed with the unique aroma and flavor of fresh fennel.

1 pound bulk fennel-flavored Italian sweet sausage

1 medium onion, coarsely chopped

1 small bulb fresh fennel, thinly sliced (reserve some of the feathery green leaves for garnish)

2 tablespoons olive oil
3 cloves garlic, minced
1 medium green pepper, seeded and cut into small strips
4 cups canned tomato sauce or crushed tomatoes
½ teaspoon salt
Several good grinds black pepper
½ teaspoon dried oregano
Freshly grated Parmesan or Asiago cheese, for garnish

1. In a large skillet, brown the sausage meat over moderate to high heat, crumbling the meat coarsely as it cooks. When all the pink color has disappeared, remove the meat from the pan with a slotted spoon; pour off and discard the fat from the pan.

2. In the same skillet, sauté the onion and the fennel in the oil over moderate heat, stirring, until the onion begins to turn golden. Add the garlic and the green pepper and sauté a few minutes more.

3. Add the tomatoes, salt, pepper, and oregano. Bring to the simmer, then cook, uncovered, over low heat, stirring occasionally, for about 15 minutes.

4. Add the reserved sausage meat, mix well, then continue to cook for another 10–15 minutes. Stir in the chopped feathery leaves of the fennel.

5. Serve the sauce over hot cooked pasta. Pass the grated cheese to add to taste.

Serves 4

Thai Duck in Fragrant Curry Sauce

A complex mix of flavors—sweet, pungent, citrusy, aromatic—characterizes this curry of duck in creamy coconut milk. It is a very rich dish, even though it contains little fat.

1–2 small fresh hot red chiles, seeded
2 shallots, coarsely chopped
Juice of 1 lime
2 teaspoons shrimp paste
2 teaspoons chopped fresh lemon grass, or ½ teaspoon
    lemon-grass powder
2 teaspoons chopped fresh galangal, or ½ teaspoon
    galangal (laos) powder
1 clove garlic
1⅓ cups unsweetened coconut milk
1 tablespoon fish sauce
¼ teaspoon sugar
3 tablespoons finely chopped fresh young basil leaves
2 cups boneless, skinless cooked duck meat cut into bite-sized
    pieces (about the yield from half of a 5-pound duckling)
Hot cooked rice

1. In a food processor, combine the chiles, the shallots, the lime juice, the shrimp paste, the lemon grass, the galangal, and the garlic. Process the mixture into a paste.
2. In a medium saucepan, combine the paste with the coconut milk, the fish sauce, and the sugar. Bring to the simmer, then cook, stirring, over low heat, for 5–10 minutes. Taste for chile and lime. Stir in the basil and the duck and bring to the simmer. Serve with hot cooked rice.

Serves 4

Smoky Chicken and White Bean Chili

The operative ingredient in chili is chile, and this one contains two of the best, the ancho, which is the dried form of the poblano pepper, and the chipotle, which is a smoked jalapeño. They both have a unique seasoning capacity as well as pungency, and show how a rich, mouth-filling flavor can make a little meat go a long way.

2 ancho chiles
2 chipotle chiles
1 medium onion, finely chopped
2 tablespoons vegetable oil
1 pound boneless skinless chicken, cut into pea-sized pieces
    (easiest to do if chicken is partially frozen)
3 large cloves garlic, minced
1/2 teaspoon salt
2 cups canned crushed tomatoes
1/2 teaspoon dried oregano
1 teaspoon ground cumin
2 cups cooked or canned small white beans—white kidney,
    pea, navy, etc. (if canned, rinse thoroughly in cold water
    and drain)
Fresh corn tortillas or large corn chips, finely chopped
    onion, sour cream, guacamole, for garnish

1. Remove the stem end from each ancho; scrape or shake out the seeds and discard. Tear the anchos into coarse pieces. Cover the anchos and the whole chipotles with about 1/2 cup warm water and let stand for about 30 minutes.

2. In a heavy skillet or saucepan, cook the onion in the oil over moderate heat, stirring, until the onion wilts.

3. Add the chicken and brown quickly, turning the pieces to brown evenly. While the chicken is browning, stir in the garlic and the salt.

4. Add the tomatoes, the chiles with their liquid, the oregano, and the cumin. Mix well and bring to the simmer, then cook over low heat, uncovered, for about 30 minutes, stirring occasionally.

5. Stir in the beans and simmer for another 10–15 minutes. Remove the whole chipotles before serving. Serve the chili with fresh tortillas or corn chips, and with finely chopped onion, sour cream, and guacamole to garnish.

Serves 4

Cantonese Crab and Leek Sauce

Southern China is one of the great gastronomic centers of Asia, with a rich tradition of seafood cookery. In this simple preparation, the delicate flavor of fresh crab combines with stir-fried leeks for a savory sauce to serve with steamed rice.

2 tablespoons rice wine
2 teaspoons soy sauce
1 teaspoon sugar
Good dash white pepper
1 tablespoon plus 1 teaspoon cornstarch
2 tablespoons peanut oil
2 cups finely chopped leeks (mostly white parts)
1 tablespoon finely minced gingerroot
8 ounces fresh lump crabmeat
1 cup chicken broth
3–4 tablespoons finely chopped scallions, for garnish

1. In a small bowl or cup, combine the rice wine, the soy sauce, the sugar, the pepper, and the cornstarch. Mix thoroughly, blending out all the lumps of cornstarch, and set aside.

2. Heat a wok or skillet over high heat. When it is very hot, swirl in the oil, then add the leeks and the gingerroot and stir-fry for about 2 minutes.

3. Add the crabmeat and mix into the leeks, stirring gently so as not to break up the crabmeat. Pour in the chicken broth and bring to the boil.

4. Mix the reserved sauce mixture again, then add it to the boiling broth mixture. Stir gently until the sauce is thickened and clear. Garnish the sauce with chopped scallions and serve with steamed rice, if desired.

Serves 2–3; more if other foods are served

Malaysian Spicy Shrimp Sauce

Yet another illustration of the Asian genius for getting as much mileage as possible from bits of meat and seafood. The real impact of this sauce comes from the marvelous mix of flavors, but the small amount of shrimp adds satisfying texture and substance.

2 ounces bean-thread vermicelli
2 tablespoons peanut or vegetable oil
2 shallots, minced
1 tablespoon finely minced gingerroot
3 cloves garlic, minced
1 small fresh hot chile pepper, seeded and minced
1 large ripe tomato, coarsely chopped
1 tablespoon regular soy sauce
2 tablespoons black soy sauce
1 teaspoon sugar
½ cup chicken stock
½ cup fresh or frozen peas
½ pound raw shrimp, peeled, deveined, and
    coarsely chopped
2 scallions, chopped, for garnish

(continued)

1. Cover the bean threads with warm water and let stand for 10–15 minutes. Drain the noodles and chop coarsely.

2. In a medium skillet or wok, heat the oil over moderate heat. Add the shallots, the gingerroot, the garlic, and the chile and sauté, stirring, until the vegetables soften and become aromatic.

3. Add the tomato, the soy sauces, the sugar, and the stock and bring to the simmer. Add the chopped bean threads and cook, stirring occasionally, over low heat until the noodles are tender and almost all the liquid has been absorbed, about 15–20 minutes.

4. Stir in the peas and the shrimp and cook just until the shrimp turn pink. Garnish with chopped scallions and serve over hot cooked rice.

Serves 4

Nigerian Smoked Fish and Peanut Sauce

In much of sub-Saharan Africa, smoking and drying are pervasive preservative techniques, and delicacies like smoked monkey and smoked elephant, as well as a variety of smoked dried fresh and salt-water fish, add rich flavor and substance to stews and sauces. Almost any kind of smoked fish will serve; I have done this with bluefish, mackerel, and whitefish, and all are very good. Though the combination of ingredients may seem exotic, the sauce is attractive and very tasty and makes a satisfying meal served over rice, couscous, or cornmeal foo foo.

1 medium onion, coarsely chopped
2 medium sweet red and/or green peppers, seeded and
  diced
3 cloves garlic, minced
2 tablespoons peanut oil
1/4 teaspoon ground hot red pepper (mombassa,
  cayenne, etc.)

1 28-ounce can Italian-style tomatoes, coarsely chopped,
   with juice
6 ounces boneless smoked fish, coarsely flaked
5–6 ounces coarsely chopped spinach
¼ teaspoon salt
3 tablespoons peanut butter
1 cup cooked or frozen black-eyed peas

1. In a heavy skillet or pot, sauté the onion, the sweet peppers, and the garlic in the oil over low to moderate heat, stirring occasionally, until the mixture is soft and becoming aromatic.

2. Stir in the hot pepper, then add the tomatoes, the fish, the spinach, and the salt. Mix gently, and cook, uncovered, over low heat for about 30 minutes, stirring from time to time.

3. Stir in the peanut butter and blend in until smooth. Add the black-eyed peas, mix well, then cook over low heat for about 10 minutes. Taste for salt and hot pepper. Serve the sauce over rice, couscous, or cornmeal foo foo.

Serves 4–6

Mexican Carnitas and Chinese Meat Shreds

Many cultures, including our own, make their meat sauces and garnishes from chopped or ground meat, but others have different techniques for achieving the same goal. The cuisines of Mexico and China, so far apart and so different in many ways, use the same process to make a savory meat garnish: chunks or slices of pork are simmered in a flavored broth until the meat becomes very tender and the fat is rendered out; when all the liquid has cooked away, the meat is shredded and cooked in its own fat, producing brown shreds of meat that are both crispy and soft, and very tasty. The technique requires a cut of pork that has a fair amount of fat in it, like shoulder or butt; if the meat is too lean, there will not be enough fat to render out, and the meat will not fry properly. Tightly covered, the cooked meat will keep well in the refrigerator for a week or so.

Mexican Carnitas

Carnitas—the name in Spanish means "little bits of meat"—are used as a filling for tacos, or as a garnish for bean and egg dishes.

1½ pounds boneless pork butt or shoulder, cut in
    large chunks or slices
1 onion, stuck with 4–6 whole cloves
3–4 cloves garlic, coarsely smashed
1 small whole dried chile pepper
1 teaspoon salt
2–3 cups water

1. Place the meat and all the other ingredients in a large, heavy skillet or pot. Bring to the simmer, then cover and cook over low to moderate heat for about 1 hour, until the meat is starting to become tender.
2. Uncover the pan and continue to cook, stirring occasionally,

over moderate heat, until the meat is very tender and almost all the liquid has cooked away. If the mixture becomes too dry before the meat is very tender, simply add some more water.

3. With a knife and fork, cut the meat into shreds. Continue to cook, stirring occasionally, until the meat is lightly browned. If there doesn't seem to be enough fat rendered out, you can add a table-spoon or two of oil. Fry the meat until it is nicely browned and crispy.

4. Remove and discard the whole spices and vegetables before serving.

Makes about 3 cups

Chinese Meat Shreds

The technique for Chinese Meat Shreds is exactly the same as that for Mexican Carnitas. The deliciously seasoned crispy shreds of pork are used as a garnish for rice and noodle dishes or as a component of fillings for dumplings and buns.

1½ pounds boneless pork butt or shoulder, cut in
    large chunks or slices
4–5 slices gingerroot
¼ cup soy sauce
¼ cup rice wine
1 tablespoon sugar
2 cups water
2–3 pieces star anise or ½ teaspoon five-spice powder

1. In a heavy skillet or pot, combine the meat and all the other in-gredients. Follow the instructions for the Mexican Carnitas (page 168).

Makes about 3 cups

Sausage

One of the oldest ways that people have used bits of meat is in the form of sausage. The word derives from the Latin *salsus,* meaning "salted," and is thus related to our words for both "salad" and "sauce"; it refers to the age-old practice of preserving meat by salting. Sausage-making was originally an exercise in frugality, for it uses the bits and scraps from a butchered animal, spiced and salted, then packed into the intestinal casings of the same animal. Thus prepared, the sausages can be consumed fresh or they can be cured—smoked and/or dried—for longer storage. Whether fresh or cured, sausage is almost always highly seasoned, with a wide variety of ingredients that frequently includes garlic, pepper, and chile. Hungarians lace their sausages with paprika; Italians love the flavor of garlic and fennel; Cypriots favor ground coriander; and the Chinese cure their sausages with soy sauce, wine, and sugar. Many native Americans traditionally made pemmican, cakes of minced buffalo and other game meats, flavored with cloudberries or juniper berries and preserved in melted buffalo fat. The texture of sausages has an enormous range, from the finely ground smooth liver sausages of Germany to the chunkier French andouille and the coarsely grained Spanish chorizo. Many of our familiar lunch meats—like bologna, salami, and pepperoni—are in fact sausages, and their names frequently denote their places of origin. Our beloved hot dog is also known as a frankfurter, or sausage from Frankfurt, or as a wiener, sausage from Vienna. Sausage is an extremely versatile food, functioning both as a meat and as a seasoning ingredient, adding meatiness, fat, and rich flavor to the foods it is cooked with. From its humble beginnings as a salted preserved product for lean times, it has become a food of great diversity, pleasing our palates as well as our pocketbooks.

Cypriot Spiced Sausage Roll

This highly seasoned roll, made of both beef and lamb, is baked in the oven like a meat loaf. Serve it thinly sliced in pockets of pita bread, with a lemony chopped-vegetable salad or a garlic-tahini sauce. It can also be sliced, cold, for sandwiches, or used as a sausage accompaniment for brunch or breakfast eggs.

1 medium onion, coarsely chopped
4 large cloves garlic
1 tablespoon fresh lemon juice
1 egg, lightly beaten
1½ teaspoons salt
¼ teaspoon freshly ground black pepper
Good pinch crushed dried hot peppers
1 teaspoon dried oregano
1 teaspoon ground cumin
1 teaspoon ground coriander
½ teaspoon allspice
⅓ cup bread crumbs
1 pound lean ground beef
½ pound lean ground lamb
½ cup tomato sauce (optional)

1. In a food processor, combine the onion, the garlic, and the lemon juice and process into a smooth puree.

2. In a large bowl, combine the onion puree, the egg, and all the seasonings, and mix well. Preheat the oven to 375° F.

3. Add the bread crumbs and the ground meats to the seasoning mixture. Mix thoroughly with a heavy spoon or your hands.

4. Form the mixture into a long sausage-shaped roll; place the roll in a lightly greased baking dish. Spoon the tomato sauce evenly over the top and sides, if desired.

5. Bake the roll for about 1 hour. Let stand for 5–10 minutes, then carefully pour off and discard the fat. Slice the roll thinly to serve.

Serves 4–6 as a main course; more for sandwiches or breakfast dishes

Fresh Chorizo

Chorizo, like other pork products, came to Mexican cuisine from Spain, where it is more commonly prepared as a cured sausage. In Mexico, the fresh sausage is popular as a filling for tacos or as an addition or garnish for a variety of egg, bean, and cheese dishes. Many excellent sausages are available ready-made, but fresh chorizo is not always easy to find, and it is an extremely useful and delicious ingredient in many Mexican and Southwestern dishes.

2 ancho chiles
2 tablespoons red wine vinegar
4 large cloves garlic
1 teaspoon salt
1 teaspoon ground coriander
½ teaspoon ground cumin
½ teaspoon dried oregano
1 teaspoon ground achiote
1 teaspoon paprika
½ teaspoon ground or crushed dried hot red peppers
1 pound coarsely ground pork, not too lean

1. Break open the chiles and discard the seeds; pinch off the stem ends and discard. Tear the chiles into small pieces and mix with the vinegar. Let stand for at least ½ hour.

2. In a food processor, combine the chiles, the vinegar, and the garlic. Blend into a paste. Combine the ancho paste with all the remaining seasoning ingredients and mix well.

3. Add the seasonings to the pork and mix very thoroughly. Cover the sausage closely with plastic wrap and place in the refrigerator for 24–48 hours. Cook as you would any bulk sausage, or form into small patties. The sausage can be frozen for longer storage.

Makes 1 pound fresh sausage

Costa Rican Chicken-Tortilla Nuggets

Masa harina is the lime-treated ground corn that is used throughout Mexico and Central America as the traditional flour for tortillas and the basis of the stuffing for tamales. In this recipe, it acts as a meat extender, while at the same time contributing its own distinctive flavor. These savory little nuggets make a terrific appetizer or hors d'oeuvre, served with a chile-laced dipping sauce.

1 medium onion, chopped

4 cloves garlic

2 fresh hot green chiles (serranos are particularly good),
    seeded and chopped

2 medium green frying peppers, seeded and chopped

2 tablespoons fresh lime juice

½ cup fresh cilantro

1 egg

1 pound ground chicken (turkey, beef, or pork can also
    be used)

¾ cup masa harina

1½ teaspoons salt

1 teaspoon liquid hot-pepper sauce

½ teaspoon dried oregano

3–4 tablespoons vegetable oil

1. In a food processor, combine the onion, the garlic, the chiles, the frying peppers, the lime juice, and the cilantro. Process into a paste.

2. In a large bowl, beat the egg lightly, then stir in the puree. Add the chicken, masa harina, salt, pepper sauce, and oregano. Mix very thoroughly, then cover and refrigerate for 1–2 hours.

3. Pinch off a piece about the size of a small walnut. Roll the piece into a ball, then flatten slightly to make a small croquette. Repeat with the rest of the mixture.

4. Fry the croquettes in the oil over moderate heat, turning once,

to brown nicely on both sides. Serve them warm or at room temperature with a spicy salsa or guacamole. They are particularly good with
the green chile–tomatillo sauce on page 271.

Makes 40–50 small nuggets

Spiced Chicken-Falafel Croquettes

Falafel are a popular Israeli snack, savory little fried croquettes made
from spiced ground chickpeas and fava beans. Falafel mix can be
used much like flavored bread crumbs or cornmeal, added to ground
meat as a binder and extender while contributing its own unique flavor. In this recipe, it combines with ground chicken and additional
herbs and spices to make delicious highly seasoned little bites that
are great as appetizers or cocktail nibbles.

Good handful flat-leaf parsley
Good handful fresh coriander leaf
1 medium onion, coarsely chopped
2 tablespoons fresh lemon juice
1 tablespoon olive oil
1 pound ground chicken
$\frac{1}{2}$ cup falafel mix
1 teaspoon salt
1 teaspoon ground cumin
1 teaspoon ground coriander
1 teaspoon paprika
$\frac{1}{4}$ teaspoon cayenne pepper
$\frac{1}{8}$ teaspoon freshly ground black pepper
Flour for dredging
Vegetable oil for frying
Coarsely chopped fresh mint, for garnish

1. In a food processor, combine the parsley, the coriander, the onion, the lemon juice, and the oil. Process into a puree.

2. Combine the puree with the chicken, the falafel mix, and all the seasonings. Mix very thoroughly, then cover and refrigerate for 1–2 hours.

3. Form the mixture by heaping tablespoons into small oval croquettes. Roll or dredge them lightly in flour, then fry in oil over moderate heat, turning to brown evenly.

4. Serve the croquettes warm or at room temperature, garnished with chopped fresh mint. They are very good with Sweet and Spicy Onion-Tomato Jam (page 259) or Mango Ketchup (page 265).

Makes about 24 small croquettes. Serves 4–6 as a main dish, more as an appetizer or hors d'oeuvre.

Chapter Six

Broken Eggs

The eighteenth-century revolutionary Robespierre declared, "You can't make an omelet without breaking some eggs." That pronouncement, surely more political than culinary in its rhetoric, provided an analogy to which his countrymen could certainly resonate: The French, perhaps more than most other people, are connoisseurs of the egg and masters of its preparation. From the humblest farmhouse table to the most sophisticated of three-star restaurants, the egg takes center stage as the crucial ingredient of the peasant omelet, the dessert soufflé, and a raft of voluptuous sauces.

But the French, though perhaps more adroit than most in the art of eggery, are by no means the only people to appreciate and exploit eggs as a wholesome, satisfying, and versatile food. Indeed, wherever they are available, eggs seem to be highly valued, and for very good reason. As the protective growing medium for animal embryos, they contain rich supplies of protein and fat, essential nutrients for proper growth and nourishment. Like seeds and nuts, the propagative agents of plants, animal eggs are a concentrated source of nutrition in a very compact form.

Our earliest ancestors almost certainly understood how valuable eggs are and gathered them in the same way they gathered other wild foods. Well before humans became organized hunters, and surely long before they domesticated a variety of animals for flesh and derivative foods like dairy products and eggs, they scavenged for their food. By watching the nesting behavior of birds, by observing how sea turtles laid their eggs in tidal flats, they would have had access to a rich source of nourishment that could be obtained with relative ease. The Bushmen of the Kalahari Desert still search out ostrich eggs, which have six times the volume of ordinary hens' eggs, and whose emptied shells make valuable storage and drinking containers.

Eggs can be prepared in a number of ways—boiled in their shells, poached in liquid, fried in a pan, baked in the oven. Some cultures, such as those of Northern Europe, pickle their eggs in brightly colored beet juice; others, like the Moroccans, stew hard-cooked eggs in slowly simmered spicy sauces. The Chinese marinate their eggs in soy sauce, or smoke them over tea leaves, or ferment them under straw into pungent, cheesy products known as "thousand-year-old eggs." And some of us occasionally consume eggs *au naturel*, not ordinarily as a gustatory treat but as a last-ditch effort to subdue the painful aftereffects of a night on the town. Indeed, the injunction "Go suck an egg!" is a clear index of our particular cultural response to uncooked eggs.

Though the ordinary domesticated hen's egg has emerged as the most esteemed and widely used egg throughout the world, other animals' eggs are enjoyed, frequently as rare and costly delicacies. The eggs, or roe, of some kinds of fish are painstakingly harvested and salted to produce, depending on the variety and the grade, one of the world's most expensive and luxurious of foods, caviar, or the less pricey but very delicious Greek tarama.

All these exotic practices notwithstanding, there is one way with eggs that is common to a great variety of cuisines: whisked or beaten eggs are mixed or spread with a wide assortment of other ingredients, then fried in a pan or baked in the oven. We may call them omelets or frittatas or tortas or scrambled eggs, but whatever their name, they turn up as remarkably similar dishes in kitchens throughout the world.

The advantages of these beaten egg dishes are clear. First of all, they are relatively inexpensive, a nutritionally equivalent but less costly alternative to meat. And from the point of view of the thrifty cook, these egg dishes inspire a creative use of leftovers, all sorts of odds and ends that add extra dimensions of flavor and texture. Finally, because eggs are both relatively bland and cohesive when cooked, an almost unlimited variety of ingredients and seasonings can be incorporated into them, providing an impressive range of interesting and varied dishes that are quickly and easily prepared.

Jews fry crumbled matzo with their eggs, while the people of Yemen use pieces of flat wholemeal bread and season the eggs with a spicy fenugreek paste. Swedes love anchovies with their eggs; Poles fancy mushrooms of every variety; Mexicans favor their beloved chiles to scramble with their eggs, or to season the sauces that cover them. Chinese egg foo young features a savory assortment of meat and vegetable tidbits; the city of Denver has given its name to the all-American version of the same dish. And the Italians of South Philadelphia construct an omelet in which the eggs are nearly smothered in an avalanche of sausage, meatballs, peppers, cheese, and spicy tomato sauce.

Eggs are good food, nourishing and delicious, to be eaten, like other animal foods, in moderation. Traditional cuisines show us how they can serve as versatile and satisfying meals, from the simplest omelet to the most extravagant creations garnished with sour cream and—yes—caviar!

RECIPES

Curried Vegetable Bake (Asian)
Bulgarian Farmer's Omelet with Mushrooms, Peppers, and Cheese
Portuguese Bean and Garlic Omelet
Scrambled Eggs with Chorizo and Pepper Strips (Mexican)
Korean Crab and Vegetable Pancake
Pipérade (French)
Persian Green Vegetable Cake
Spanish Potato and Onion Torta
Mushroom and Artichoke Frittata (Italian)
Lebanese Eggs with Squash and Tomato
Omelet Soufflé with Sour Cream and Caviar (French)

Curried Vegetable Bake

Throughout Asia, mixtures of beaten eggs and other ingredients are scrambled, baked, or fried into savory pancakes and omelets that add variety to meals and make thrifty use of leftovers. Generally they are served in small portions as garnishes or complements to other foods, but like so many egg dishes, they can also serve as brunch or light supper dishes. This recipe is really just a general guide; other cooked vegetables—such as cauliflower, zucchini, corn, and peas—can be substituted or added, and of course bits of cooked ham, chicken, and shellfish can be used, if desired.

    2 tablespoons peanut oil
    1 medium onion, coarsely chopped
    1–2 small fresh hot chile peppers, seeded and minced
    1 medium sweet red or green pepper, seeded and diced
    1 carrot, sliced
    1 medium potato, peeled and thinly sliced
    1 cup cooked string beans, cut in 1-inch pieces
    1 cup finely chopped cabbage
    ½ teaspoon salt
    Several good grinds black pepper
    2 teaspoons curry powder (preferably an Asian variety)
    1 tablespoon fresh lime juice
    1 cup fresh beansprouts
    4 eggs
    ½ teaspoon sugar
    2 teaspoons soy sauce

1. In a large skillet, heat the oil over moderate heat. Add the onion, chiles, sweet peppers, carrot, and potato. Cook, stirring, until the onion is turning brown and the potato is just tender.

2. Add the string beans, cabbage, salt, pepper, and curry powder, mix well, and continue cooking, stirring, until the cabbage is wilted.

3. Add the lime juice and the beansprouts, mix thoroughly, then remove from the heat. Preheat the oven to 350° F.

4. In a large bowl, beat the eggs thoroughly with the sugar and the soy sauce. Spoon the vegetable mixture into the eggs and mix well.

5. Spread the mixture in a buttered 9-inch baking pan or shallow casserole. Smooth to make it fairly even. Bake the omelet for about 30 minutes, until it is firm and just very lightly browned. Cut into small squares or wedges and serve warm or at room temperature.

Serves 3 as a light meal, more if used as garnish or appetizer

Bulgarian Farmer's Omelet with Mushrooms, Peppers, and Cheese

Henry James once observed that "an egg which has succeeded in being fresh has done all that can be reasonably expected of it." Exactly so: anything else has to do with the skill and ingenuity of the cook. Eggs can be used in the simplest and most complex of dishes. This recipe is one of the easiest—a simple peasant omelet spread with a richly flavored mixture of peppers and mushrooms. Wild mushrooms would have been the original choice, but almost any fresh mushroom will do; I find that portobellos, with their meaty texture and flavor, work very well.

1 medium onion, coarsely chopped
1 large green pepper, seeded and diced
1 small fresh hot green chili, seeded and minced, or
    ¼ teaspoon crushed dried hot peppers
2 cups coarsely chopped mushrooms
3 tablespoons olive oil
1 teaspoon salt
Freshly ground black pepper
6 eggs
1½ tablespoons butter
3–4 ounces softened cream cheese, cut into small pieces
Paprika
Sour cream or plain yogurt, for garnish, if desired

(continued)

1. In a skillet, cook the onion, the green and hot peppers, and the mushrooms in the oil over moderate heat, stirring occasionally, for 15–20 minutes, until the vegetables are very soft and all the liquid has cooked away. Stir in ½ teaspoon of the salt and several grinds of black pepper, mix well, and set aside.

2. Whisk the eggs thoroughly, then stir in the remaining ½ teaspoon of salt and several grinds of black pepper.

3. Heat the butter in a heavy 8- or 9-inch skillet over moderate heat. Swirl the butter so that it coats the bottom and a little of the sides of the pan.

4. Pour the eggs into the skillet, then sprinkle the pieces of cream cheese over them. Cook, without stirring, over moderate heat until the bottom begins to brown. With a spatula, lift up the sides of the omelet so that some of the egg mixture runs underneath.

5. When the top of the omelet is almost set but still creamy, spoon the reserved mushroom mixture over the eggs. Continue cooking for a few minutes more.

6. Sprinkle the omelet lightly with paprika. Cut into wedges, then serve with some sour cream or yogurt, if desired.

Serves 4

Portuguese Bean and Garlic Omelet

Cooked in a heavy skillet until the top is just set and the bottom browned and crusty, this hearty omelet is full of zesty flavor. Serve it with some good bread and a juicy tomato salad.

1 large onion, coarsely chopped
3 tablespoons olive oil
5 large cloves garlic, minced
½ cup diced good-quality cured ham
2 cups cooked or canned white kidney beans (if canned,
    rinse thoroughly in cold water and drain)
1 teaspoon salt
¼ teaspoon freshly ground black pepper
⅓ cup coarsely chopped flat-leaf parsley or
    fresh coriander leaf
6 eggs
Additional chopped parsley, for garnish

1. In a heavy 8- or 9-inch skillet (cast iron is great), cook the onion in the oil over moderate heat, stirring occasionally, for 5–7 minutes, until the onion is soft and beginning to brown.

2. Add the garlic and the ham and cook, stirring, for another few minutes.

3. Add the beans, ½ teaspoon of the salt, half of the pepper, and the parsley or coriander. Mix well and cook for a few minutes.

4. Whisk the eggs thoroughly with the remaining salt and pepper. Pour the eggs over the beans, then cover the pan and cook over moderate heat for about 5–7 minutes, or until the top is just set. Garnish with additional chopped parsley or coriander, and cut in wedges to serve.

Serves 4

Scrambled Eggs with Chorizo and Pepper Strips

The rich and varied cuisines of Mexico have many wonderful egg dishes, the most familiar of which is *huevos rancheros,* fried eggs served on a fresh corn tortilla and smothered with a spicy tomato-chile sauce. Here is another that can be served for breakfast, brunch, or a light supper, with fresh salsa and a side of stewed or refried beans. Unlike the cured variety, fresh chorizo is not always available, but you can easily make a batch yourself and store it in the freezer to use when needed (see recipe on page 172).

1 medium onion, thinly sliced
1 large green pepper, seeded and cut into strips
1 large sweet red pepper, seeded and cut into strips
3 tablespoons olive oil
½ cup cooked, crumbled fresh chorizo (about half the
    recipe on page 172)
6 eggs
½ teaspoon salt
Good dash cayenne pepper
Warm flour tortillas

1. In a heavy 8- or 9-inch skillet, cook the onion and the red and green peppers in the oil over moderate heat, stirring, until the onion is just beginning to turn golden and the peppers are wilted.

2. Add the crumbled chorizo and cook, stirring, another few minutes.

3. Thoroughly whisk the eggs with the salt and the cayenne. Pour the eggs over the vegetables and sausage and cook, stirring, over low heat until the eggs are set but still creamy.

4. Spoon the eggs over warm flour tortillas; serve with salsa and beans and additional warm tortillas.

Serves 4

Korean Crab and Vegetable Pancake

Savory egg cakes, filled with an assortment of tasty meat, seafood, and vegetable tidbits, are common throughout Asia. They are extremely versatile dishes that are used as snacks, as appetizers, or as garnishes for rice and noodle dishes.

4–5 scallions, chopped
1 carrot, finely sliced or diced
3 tablespoons Asian sesame oil
1 cup finely shredded or chopped Napa cabbage
½ cup fresh or frozen peas
3 extra-large eggs
1 tablespoon soy sauce
⅛ teaspoon salt
Good dash hot-pepper sauce
4 ounces fresh crabmeat
½ cup fresh beansprouts

1. In a heavy 8- or 9-inch skillet, sauté the scallions and the carrot in 1½ tablespoons of the oil over moderate heat. When the carrot is just tender, add the cabbage, and sauté, stirring, until the cabbage is just limp. Add the peas, mix well, and remove from the heat.

2. Whisk the eggs thoroughly with the soy sauce, salt, and hot-pepper sauce. Stir in the crabmeat and the beansprouts, then all of the vegetables from the pan.

3. Heat the remaining 1½ tablespoons of oil in the skillet over moderate to high heat. Pour in the egg mixture, even it out, then cook without stirring until the bottom is set. Cover the skillet and continue to cook until the top is set, about 7–10 minutes.

4. Remove from the heat and let stand for 5 minutes before cutting the pancake from the pan. Cut in small wedges or squares to serve as a snack, an appetizer, or a garnish.

Makes 1 9-inch pancake

Pipérade

The pipérade is a classic egg dish from the Basque country of France and Spain (in Spanish it is known as the "piparrada"). Its success depends on the sweet peppers and luscious tomatoes of the region; don't bother with this recipe unless you have high-quality, flavorful, fully ripe vegetables. Some purists insist that the pipérade be prepared in a double boiler, so that the slowly cooked eggs will be very creamy, but much the same effect can be achieved if you use a heavy pan, keep the heat low, and stir the mixture constantly. The pipérade is thought by some to be the ancestor of America's own "Spanish" omelet.

2 large onions, finely chopped
3 large or 6 small sweet red and/or green peppers, seeded
    and finely chopped
1/4 cup olive oil
3–4 fully ripe medium tomatoes, coarsely chopped
1 teaspoon salt
1/4 teaspoon freshly ground black pepper
6 eggs
Bit of chopped parsley, for garnish
Crusty bread and thin slices of good cured ham, if desired

1. In a heavy 8- or 9-inch skillet, cook the onions and the peppers in the oil over low to moderate heat, stirring occasionally, for 15–20 minutes, until the onions are nicely browned and the mixture is soft.

2. Add the tomatoes and continue to cook, stirring occasionally, until the mixture is thick and soft and most of the liquid has cooked away. Stir in 1/2 teaspoon of the salt and half of the pepper and mix well.

3. Whisk the eggs thoroughly, then stir in the remaining salt and pepper. Pour the eggs over the vegetables in the pan and cook over low heat, stirring, until the eggs are just set but still creamy.

4. Garnish the pipérade with a sprinkle of chopped parsley, then serve with crusty bread and thin slices of ham, if desired.

Serves 4

Persian Green Vegetable Cake

This one's for you, Dr. Seuss—the greenest eggs you've ever seen! It's a delicious and unusual dish, a baked egg cake chock-full of fresh green herbs and vegetables and served with yogurt as a sauce. It makes a fine brunch dish or vegetable accompaniment for other foods.

8 eggs
2 cups finely chopped fresh spinach
½ cup finely chopped flat-leaf parsley
½ cup finely chopped scallions
½ cup finely snipped fresh dill
½ cup finely chopped fresh coriander leaf
1 teaspoon salt
¼ teaspoon freshly ground black pepper
2–3 tablespoons butter, melted
Plain yogurt, as garnish

1. In a large bowl, whisk the eggs until they are light and frothy.
2. Add the chopped vegetables and herbs, salt, and pepper, and mix well. Preheat the oven to 350° F.
3. Butter a 9-inch gratin dish, shallow casserole, or cake pan. Pour the egg mixture into the dish and smooth into an even layer.
4. Drizzle the melted butter over the eggs.
5. Bake for about 25–30 minutes, until the cake is set and just lightly browned. Let stand for 5 minutes before cutting into wedges or squares. Serve warm or at room temperature, with yogurt to pass as a sauce.

Serves 4 as a main course, 6–8 as a side dish

Spanish Potato and Onion Torta

Omelets and egg cakes, called "tortas" or "tortillas," made with a variety of vegetables, cured ham, or sausage, are very popular in Spain. This is one of my favorites, with its savory fried potatoes and *sofrito* of onions—lots of them—slowly browned in olive oil. The best kind of pan is a heavy cast-iron 8- or 9-inch skillet that can go directly from the stove to the oven, but if you don't own one you can bake the torta in a greased shallow casserole.

4 cups finely chopped onions
4 tablespoons olive oil
2 medium potatoes, thinly sliced
1 teaspoon salt
¼ teaspoon freshly ground black pepper
6 eggs
Chopped parsley, for garnish

1. In a heavy skillet, cook the onions in 2 tablespoons of the oil over low to moderate heat, stirring occasionally, until the onions are richly browned and very soft. This will take about 30–40 minutes. When the onions are done, remove them from the pan and set aside.

2. Add the remaining 2 tablespoons of oil to the pan, then add the potatoes and fry over moderate heat, turning occasionally with a spatula, until the potatoes are tender and lightly browned, about 15–20 minutes. Preheat the oven to 400° F.

3. Stir the reserved onions into the potatoes, add ½ teaspoon of the salt and half of the pepper, and mix well. Remove from the heat.

4. Whisk the eggs thoroughly with the remaining salt and pepper. Pour the eggs over the potatoes and onions.

5. Bake for 12–15 minutes, until the eggs are set. If you want a slightly crisp top, you can run the torta under the broiler for a couple of seconds.

6. Garnish the torta with chopped parsley and cut in wedges to serve.

Serves 4–6

Mushroom and Artichoke Frittata

Who was the first to discover that gastronomic treasure, the secret hidden heart of the artichoke? Italy has long appreciated the bizarre but delicious vegetable and is responsible for introducing it to the French, who knew a good thing when they tasted it. This frittata is wholly Italian, however—a rich concoction of eggs baked with mushrooms, artichokes, fresh basil, and mozzarella.

1 medium onion, finely chopped
3 tablespoons olive oil
1 cup sliced mushrooms
4–5 freshly cooked artichoke bottoms, sliced
1 teaspoon salt
Freshly ground black pepper
Small handful coarsely chopped fresh basil
Small handful coarsely chopped flat-leaf parsley
6 eggs
⅛ teaspoon grated nutmeg
2 tablespoons freshly grated Parmesan cheese
1–1½ cups shredded mozzarella, about 6 ounces

1. In a medium skillet, sauté the onion in the olive oil over moderate heat, stirring, until the onion wilts and begins to turn golden.

2. Add the mushrooms and sauté, stirring, until they are just lightly browned.

3. Stir in the sliced artichokes, ½ teaspoon of the salt, and a couple of good grinds of pepper. Mix well and cook, stirring, for a few minutes. Stir in the basil and the parsley and remove from the heat.

4. Preheat the oven to 400° F. In a bowl, whisk the eggs thoroughly, then add the remaining salt, several good grinds of pepper, the nutmeg, and the Parmesan, and mix well.

5. Butter or oil a shallow casserole or baking dish. Spoon the mushroom-artichoke mixture into the casserole, pour the eggs over the vegetables, then sprinkle the mozzarella evenly over the top.

6. Bake the frittata for about 10 minutes, until the cheese is melted and the eggs are just set. Serve hot with good bread and a green salad.

Serves 4

Humpty Dumpty sat on a wall,
Humpty Dumpty had a great fall;
All the king's horses and all the king's men
Couldn't put Humpty together again.

If there are two truths on which we can depend, the first is that eggs, once broken, cannot be mended. The second is that there are two parts to the egg, the yellow or yolk, and the white or albumen ("yolk" comes from an Old English word for "yellow," and "albumen" from the Latin word for "white"). It is these two parts, with their separate and complex biochemistry, that give eggs their very special culinary properties. The yolk is made up mostly of water and fat with some additional protein; it is the fat that functions as an enriching, binding, and emulsifying agent, combining with liquids to form smooth, unctuous thickeners, coatings, and sauces. The egg yolk accounts for the thick creaminess of mayonnaise and contributes to the rich, smooth texture of high-quality ice cream. The albumen is composed mostly of water and proteins, the structure of which permits the incorporation of air to form a foam; the beaten egg-white foam can be cooked to form products like meringues or folded into other ingredients to provide puffiness and lightness for cakes and soufflés. When exposed to heat, the proteins in the egg coagulate—clump together and harden—a useful characteristic when you want scrambled eggs but not so appealing when you are making a custard sauce and let the heat get too high. For there is yet another truth that all cooks know only too well: an egg, once scrambled, cannot be unscrambled!

Lebanese Eggs with Squash and Tomato

The savory vegetable stews of the Middle East are versatile dishes that can be cooked with meat, served over rice, or used as tasty stuffings and sauces for vegetables and noodles. They are frequently combined with eggs to make hearty main-course entrées; in this one, a typical Lebanese vegetable mixture, scented with cinnamon, gives substance and rich flavor to a slowly cooked omelet. It is important to use a heavy skillet (cast iron is best), so that the eggs cook slowly and evenly.

1 medium zucchini, diced
1 medium yellow summer squash, diced
1 cup coarsely chopped fresh tomatoes
3 tablespoons olive oil
1 cup coarsely chopped scallions
1 teaspoon salt
Several good grinds black pepper
1 teaspoon cinnamon
6 eggs
3–4 tablespoons shredded Kefalotyri cheese or Cheddar

1. In a heavy 8- or 9-inch skillet, cook the zucchini, the squash, and the tomatoes in 2 tablespoons of the oil over moderate heat, stirring occasionally, for about 10 minutes, or until the vegetables are tender and most of the liquid has cooked away.

2. Add the scallions, ½ teaspoon of the salt, several grinds of pepper, and the cinnamon, mix well, and cook, stirring, for another few minutes, until the scallions are wilted. Add the remaining 1 tablespoon of oil to the pan.

3. Whisk the eggs thoroughly with the remaining ½ teaspoon of salt and several grinds of pepper. Pour the eggs over the vegetables, then sprinkle them with the cheese. Cover the pan and cook over low to moderate heat for about 10–12 minutes, until the eggs are completely set and the cheese is melted. Cut in wedges to serve.

Serves 4

NOTE: The omelet is very good left over as a stuffing for pita pockets, garnished with a spoonful of yogurt, if desired.

Omelet Soufflé with Sour Cream and Caviar

The omelet soufflé is, exactly as its name suggests, a pan-fried egg dish aerated and puffed with beaten egg whites. It can be flavored and garnished in any number of ways, but served with sour cream and as much of as many varieties of caviar as you can afford, it makes a delicious and festive brunch presentation.

4 extra-large eggs, separated
¼ cup milk or light cream
½ teaspoon salt
Several good grinds black pepper
2–3 tablespoons finely snipped chives
⅔ cup shredded Swiss cheese (Gruyère, Emmenthaler, etc.), about 3–4 ounces
1 tablespoon unsalted butter
Sour cream, caviar, and additional snipped chives, for garnish

1. Preheat the oven to 325° F. Whisk the egg yolks thoroughly, then mix in the milk, the salt, the pepper, the chives, and the cheese.

2. Beat the egg whites until they are stiff but not dry, just until they hold a firm peak. Fold the beaten whites into the omelet mixture.

3. Heat a heavy 8- or 9-inch ovenproof skillet or omelet pan over moderate heat. Add the butter and as it melts swirl it around to cover the bottom and part of the sides of the skillet.

4. Pour the egg mixture into the pan and cook for a couple of minutes, until the bottom is beginning to brown and the omelet starts to puff.

5. Carefully transfer the pan into the preheated oven and bake for 7–10 minutes, until the omelet is puffed and lightly browned. Serve immediately, cut into wedges and garnished with sour cream, caviar, and a sprinkle of snipped chives.

Serves 4

Chapter Seven

Vegetable Refreshment

The current American passion for salad belies the fact that for most of our short history we have not been a nation of salad lovers. Indeed, until only very recently the mainstream looked upon salad as "rabbit" food, "sissy" food, and, most damning of all, "ladies' " food! Our hardworking forebears, solid farmers and pioneers with a largely Northern European background, subsisted on flour, cornmeal, potatoes, and cured pork, regarding fresh and raw fruits and vegetables as effete and citified, appropriate for the French, perhaps, but not for real men. All that has changed, of course, and with astonishing rapidity; urbanization, ever-growing sophistication about food, and above all an overwhelming concern with improved health and nutrition have permitted the acceptance of the salad bar into the deepest recesses of the entrenched heartland. Even the cheeseburger, palpable icon of all we hold most dear, now sports a slice of tomato and a frill of (supposedly) fresh lettuce.

This long-overdue appreciation of fresh vegetables, raw greens, and salads of every kind is, like so much else about us, anomalous, for there is good evidence that such food has been highly valued in the human experience from earliest times. The word "salad" comes from the Latin *sal*, "salt," apparently because of the ancient practice of eating raw or cooked greens with salt. The tradition is far older than the Romans, however; the ancient Greeks esteemed wild greens, and to this day, in rural areas of the Aegean, a variety of wild plants, such as rocket, dandelion, nettle, and cress, are gathered by the women and eaten boiled and salted. Indeed, the tender young greens that first appear in the early spring are picked and eaten by rural people all over the world as a welcome relief from the stale stores of winter food, the fresh vegetable goodness providing a lift that is both nutritional and gustatory.

Though salt is certainly a basic and universal seasoning for salad—as it is, of course, for all savory food—it is not by itself enough to define the salad as it has evolved through our history. Rather more critical to salads as we understand them today is an acidic dressing of some kind, most commonly provided by vinegar, citrus juices, and sour fruits like tamarind. Cuisines that have a strong tradition of dairying frequently ferment or culture their milk into mildly acidic products like yogurt and sour cream that are also used as dressings for salad. And a tribe of California Indians, the Maidu, who cultivated no crops, were reported to gather the leaves of wild lettuce, which they placed near the nests of ants; the ants scurried all over the leaves, leaving behind a sour secretion (probably formic acid); the Maidu then consumed the lettuce, quite literally, with relish.

So, while salt is fundamental, acid of some kind also seems to be crucial. Two thousand years ago, the Roman writer Apicius offered this recipe:

> Dress lettuces with vinegar, and a little liquamen [salty fish sauce], to make them more easily digestible, to prevent flatulence, and so that the lettuces cannot harm your system.

It is entirely possible that acid helps us to process raw and fibrous plant foods, since as a species we do not possess the grinding molars, the multiple stomachs, and other digestive mechanisms of herbivorous animals. It is also likely that, because from ancient times salt and vinegar were the most widely known preservative agents, used to prevent spoilage in foods, their beneficial effects were thought to extend to the preparation of raw vegetables and greens, always a notorious source of bacterial contamination.

All these practical considerations aside, there is no question that the use of acid also has a significant gastronomic function. Vegetables and greens are frequently bland, with sometimes bitter, peppery, pungent, and even sweet flavors that are enhanced by the tartness of vinegar or lemon juice or the smooth mild sourness of yogurt. The oil, which joined the salt and the acid in relatively recent times, functions more critically as a coating agent, ensuring that every leaf and vegetable part is evenly enrobed with flavor. And because we are so enamored of fat in all its forms, the oil component of the salad dressing has had an ever-growing importance.

Just as the sauces and seasonings for salads have become more complex and elaborate, so too have salads themselves grown into baroque compositions that include not just the simple greens and vegetables that once defined them, but all manner of meats and seafoods, grains and legumes, pasta, cheese, and eggs. (The French classify salads in two basic categories: "simple" salads of lettuce or other greens; and "composed" salads, which are constructed of two or more ingredients.)

So when is a salad not a salad? When it is a soup? Ah, but what about gazpacho, often described as a liquid salad? When it is stewed in a pot? But then there's ratatouille! When it's served hot? Well, what about warm spinach salad and German hot potato salad? The criteria are constantly expanding, and it is for us as cooks and eaters to determine what "salad" means. Whatever it is, almost every cuisine produces it, and has done so consistently from the very earliest times. Perhaps the best understanding and appreciation were expressed two hundred years ago by the gastronome Brillat-Savarin. "Salad," he said, "freshens without enfeebling and fortifies without irritating . . . and makes us younger."

RECIPES

Fattoush (Lebanese)
Spinach and Mushroom Salad with Pine Nuts (Italian)
Sesame-Ginger Spinach Salad (Japanese)
Spanish Chicory Salad with Orange and Red Onion
Hungarian Wilted Pepper Salad
Roasted Pepper Salad with Yogurt, Garlic, and Walnuts (Balkan)
Mixed Vegetable Antipasto Salad (Italian)
Russian Mixed Vegetable Salad
Asparagus Salad with Oyster Sauce (Chinese)
Greek Salad of Beets and Beet Greens
Sesame Beansprout Salad (Korean)
Japanese Eggplant and Double Ginger Salad
Moroccan Eggplant Salad
Spicy Szechuan Eggplant Salad (Chinese)
Burmese Spiced Green Bean Salad
Middle Eastern Tomato and Cucumber Salad
My Grandma's Unburnt Cucumber Salad (Brooklyn)
Tomato and Red Onion Salad with Avocado Vinaigrette (American)
Mediterranean Layered Salad
Really Red Slaw (American)
Beefsteak Tomatoes with Anchovy, Lemon, and Basil (Mediterranean)
Turkish White Bean Salad
Spiced Lentil and Golden Orzo Salad (Middle Eastern)
Multicolored Potato and Pepper Salad with Sun-Dried Tomatoes and
    Basil (Italian-American)
Portuguese-Style Redskin Potato Salad with Tomatoes and Garlic
Salad of Shrimp and Sugar Snap Peas with Ginger Peanut Vinaigrette
    (Nouvelle Indonesian)
Spanish Squid and Rice Salad
Salade Niçoise (French)
Vietnamese-Style Jicama, Beansprout, and Chicken Salad
Mussel Salad Ravigote (French)
Sweet Corn, Tomato, and Salmon Ceviche Salad (Mexican)
Honey Hoisin Duck with Mixed Greens and Sprouts (Chinese)

Fattoush

The cuisine that gave us tabbouleh, the national dish of Lebanon and one of the great salads of the world, also gives us fattoush, a mixture of chopped fresh vegetables and crunchy toasted pita bits. The toasted bread, used exactly the same way we use croutons, should be added to the dressed salad at the last minute; I must confess, however, that I also enjoy the salad left over, when the bread has become soft and soppy with the savory sauce.

1 5-to-6-inch pita loaf
1 large tomato, coarsely chopped
1 medium cucumber, peeled and diced
1 medium green pepper, seeded and diced
1 medium red onion or 4–5 scallions, chopped
1 cup chopped crisp lettuce (iceberg or romaine hearts)
1 cup coarsely chopped flat-leaf parsley
1/3 cup finely chopped fresh mint leaves
1/4 cup olive oil
1/4 cup fresh lemon juice
1/4 teaspoon salt
Several good grinds black pepper
1 clove garlic, crushed

1. In a 400° F. oven, toast the pita for about 10 minutes, or until it is lightly browned and very crisp. Let cool, then crumble or break into coarse pieces.

2. In a bowl, combine all the chopped vegetables and herbs.

3. In a small bowl, combine the oil, lemon juice, salt, pepper, and garlic; whisk to blend thoroughly.

4. Pour the dressing over the vegetables and mix well. Let stand for 1/2–1 hour. Mix again and taste for salt.

5. Just before serving, mix the toasted pita into the salad.

Serves 4–6

Spinach and Mushroom Salad with Pine Nuts

Spinach finds a welcome place on the Italian table both cooked and raw, and fresh spinach is a popular salad green. This traditional salad has a very contemporary feel, with its sliced fresh mushrooms, sweet sautéed pine nuts, and tangy balsamic dressing.

10 ounces fresh spinach
6 tablespoons plus 2 teaspoons olive oil
3 tablespoons balsamic vinegar
2 cloves garlic, minced
¼ teaspoon salt
Several good grinds black pepper
3 tablespoons pine nuts (pignoli)
1–1½ cups sliced fresh mushrooms

1. Trim the ends off the spinach; wash the leaves thoroughly, then dry completely.
2. Combine the 6 tablespoons of oil, the vinegar, the garlic, the salt, and the pepper and whisk to blend thoroughly.
3. In a small skillet, sauté the pine nuts in the 2 teaspoons of oil over moderate heat, stirring constantly, until the nuts just begin to turn golden. (Be careful: they burn easily.) Remove from the heat and set aside.
4. In a large bowl, combine the spinach and the sliced mushrooms. Pour about half of the dressing over and toss lightly with the spinach. Taste and add more dressing as needed.
5. Just before serving, add the pine nuts and toss again.

Serves 4–6

Sesame-Ginger Spinach Salad

The distinctive flavors of Japanese cuisine enhance this salad of simple greens. Spinach is a traditional favorite, but a variety of mixed greens—romaine, chicory, arugula—can be substituted; more delicate greens should not be used, for they will not stand up to the dressing, which is very intensely flavored.

¼ cup Asian sesame oil
1 tablespoon seasoned rice vinegar
1 tablespoon fresh lemon juice
1 teaspoon soy sauce
1 teaspoon grated or very finely minced gingerroot
8–10 cups coarsely torn fresh spinach leaves, or
    other greens
1–2 tablespoons toasted sesame seeds, for garnish, if desired

1. In a small bowl or cup, combine the oil, vinegar, lemon juice, soy sauce, and gingerroot. Whisk to blend thoroughly.
2. Pour the dressing over the spinach leaves and toss to coat. Garnish the salad with toasted sesame seeds, if desired.

Serves 6

Spanish Chicory Salad with Orange and Red Onion

Here is a simple, refreshing salad that offers interesting contrasts of flavor and texture. Chicory is a robust and slightly bitter green that is available in most markets; frisée would be a satisfactory alternative.

8 cups fresh chicory, coarsely torn into bite-sized pieces
1 large navel or blood orange, peeled and thinly sliced
1 medium red onion, thinly sliced
1/3 cup olive oil
2 tablespoons red wine vinegar
2 tablespoons sherry vinegar
1/4 teaspoon salt
Several good grinds black pepper

1. In a large bowl, combine the chicory, the orange, and the onion.
2. In a small bowl, combine the oil, the vinegars, the salt, and the pepper. Whisk thoroughly to blend.
3. Pour about half of the dressing over the salad and toss lightly. Taste, and add more dressing as needed.

Serves 4–6

Hungarian Wilted Pepper Salad

Traveling in Hungary some years ago, my son, whose Hungarian-language skills are negligible, was a little frustrated when everything he ordered from restaurant menus turned out to be liver dumplings; he was therefore delighted to recognize finally something that appealed—*paprikasalata,* pepper salad. Imagine his surprise when he was served a whole uncut pepper and a cruet of vinegar! Now, there's a basic, no-frills salad. Hungarians are extremely fond of peppers, sweet and hot, raw and cooked. This is a refreshing and tasty salad, especially pretty if you use peppers of mixed colors. Be sure to cook the peppers just long enough to wilt them—they should not be browned or soft.

2 tablespoons olive oil
2 medium green peppers, seeded and cut into thin strips
1 medium sweet red pepper, seeded and cut into thin strips
1 medium yellow pepper, seeded and cut into thin strips
1/4 cup red wine vinegar
1/2 teaspoon sugar
1/4 teaspoon salt
1/2 teaspoon sweet or hot Hungarian paprika
1/2 teaspoon caraway seeds (optional)
1 medium sweet onion (Vidalia or Spanish), thinly sliced
2–3 tablespoons finely snipped fresh dill

1. In a medium skillet, heat the oil over moderate heat. Add the pepper strips and cook, stirring, for 3–4 minutes, just until the peppers are wilted but still fairly crisp.

2. Add all the remaining ingredients except the dill and mix thoroughly. Bring just to the simmer, then remove from the heat.

3. Pour the mixture into a serving dish, and stir in the dill. Let cool or chill, stirring occasionally, before serving.

Serves 4

Roasted Pepper Salad with Yogurt, Garlic, and Walnuts

Throughout the Middle East, Central Asia, India, the Balkans, and Greece, yogurt serves as a basic food, eaten by itself or as the primary ingredient in beverages, sauces, and soups. Seasoned with a variety of herbs and spices, it is frequently used in these cuisines as a dressing for salads, from the raita of India to the tsatsiki of the Greeks. We in America have not yet learned to appreciate the tart and refreshing flavor of traditional yogurts, unemulsified, unsmoothed, unsweetened—but they can be purchased in specialty stores or easily made at home.

> 2 cups roasted sweet red peppers, seeded and skinned
>   (see Note)
> 3–4 heaping tablespoons plain yogurt
> 3 cloves garlic, crushed
> 1/3 cup finely chopped freshly toasted walnuts
> Chopped dill or parsley, for garnish

1. Cut the peppers into small chunks or thick strips. Combine the peppers with the yogurt and the garlic and mix thoroughly.

2. Mix all but about 1 tablespoon of the chopped nuts into the salad. Sprinkle the remaining nuts over the salad, then garnish with a bit of chopped dill or parsley. Serve at room temperature.

Serves 4–6

NOTE: Commercially canned or jarred roasted peppers should not be used in this recipe; the citric acid in which they are preserved will cause the yogurt to curdle.

Mixed Vegetable Antipasto Salad

No prissy little salad this, but a robust chunky mixture tangy with vinegar and fragrant with garlic. It can be used as part of the traditional antipasto platter, along with anchovies, chunks of tuna, roasted peppers, salami, and cheese, and it makes an excellent foil for all kinds of cooked and cured meats, sausages, and cheeses.

2 carrots, sliced on the diagonal
2 cups cauliflower florets (about 1 small head)
2 cups thinly sliced fresh fennel
Good handful brined black or green olives
1 medium green pepper, seeded and cut into small chunks
1 medium sweet red pepper, seeded and cut into small
    chunks
¼ cup olive oil
¼ cup red wine vinegar
3 cloves garlic, crushed
¼ teaspoon salt
Plenty of freshly ground black pepper
½ teaspoon dried oregano
Good pinch crushed dried hot peppers (optional)

1. Cook the carrots and the cauliflower in boiling water for 2–3 minutes. Drain and set aside.

2. In a large bowl, combine the fennel, the olives, and the green and red peppers. Add the cooked drained vegetables.

3. Combine the oil, the vinegar, the garlic, the salt, the black pepper, the oregano, and the hot peppers, if desired. Whisk to combine thoroughly. Pour the dressing over the vegetables and mix well. Let stand for several hours at room temperature or, better yet, overnight in the refrigerator. Mix again and taste for salt.

Serves 4–6

NOTE: A variety of other vegetables, such as sliced cooked artichoke bottoms, cooked green beans, chickpeas, or red or white kidney beans, can be added or substituted.

Russian Mixed Vegetable Salad

In Northern Europe, where the fresh-vegetable harvest is short and limited, salads are often composed of a mixture of fresh, cooked, and pickled or preserved products that provide interesting varieties of texture and flavor. This hearty salad, with its tangy traditional dressing of sour cream, horseradish, and dill, can be made even more substantial with the addition of some diced ham or smoked turkey.

1 cup sauerkraut, rinsed, drained, and coarsely chopped
2 medium potatoes, cooked, peeled, and diced
2 medium cucumbers, peeled, seeded, and diced
½ cup diced pickled beets (canned work just fine)
¼ cup diced dill pickles
1 small onion, finely chopped
1 hard-cooked egg, separated
½ cup sour cream
2 tablespoons freshly grated horseradish
2 tablespoons pickled-beet juice
1 tablespoon fresh lemon juice
Several good grinds black pepper
⅓ cup finely snipped fresh dill

1. Combine all the vegetables and the diced egg white in a bowl.
2. Combine the sour cream, horseradish, beet juice, lemon juice, and pepper and mix thoroughly.
3. Pour the dressing over the vegetables and mix well; then stir in the dill.
4. Garnish the salad with finely crumbled egg yolk.

Serves 4–6

Asparagus Salad with Oyster Sauce

The Chinese have always preferred their vegetables cooked, if only briefly, so that salad-type dishes are frequently made from lightly cooked greens and other texturally interesting vegetables. A more authentic version of this salad would feature Chinese broccoli, with its long, tender green stalks. If you can get it, it is a delicious alternative to the asparagus.

1 pound fresh young asparagus (avoid very thick stalks)
2–3 scallions, slivered and cut into 2-inch lengths
1 small carrot, cut into julienne strips
½ sweet red pepper, seeded and cut into julienne strips
2 tablespoons Chinese oyster sauce
2 tablespoons rice-wine vinegar
½ teaspoon sugar
Good dash liquid hot-pepper sauce
Small handful chopped fresh coriander leaf

1. Trim the tough ends of the asparagus stalks, then cut the asparagus on the sharp diagonal into 2-inch pieces. Cook in boiling water for a couple of minutes, just until the asparagus is tender but still crisp. Drain thoroughly.

2. Combine the asparagus, the scallions, the carrot, and the sweet pepper.

3. Combine the oyster sauce, the vinegar, the sugar, and the hot-pepper sauce; whisk to blend thoroughly.

4. Pour the dressing over the vegetables and mix well. Stir in the chopped coriander. Serve the salad at room temperature. (You can let the salad marinate at room temperature for up to 1 hour, but if it stands longer than that the asparagus will begin to yellow.)

Serves 4

Greek Salad of Beets and Beet Greens

For those of you who were brought up exclusively on pickled beets and Harvard beets, this traditional Greek way will come as a refreshing surprise. The natural sweetness of the beets is highlighted by the tangy lemon and aromatic oregano, and the cooked beet greens add interesting dimensions of color and texture. When you buy your beets, choose a bunch with leaves that are fresh and green, not bruised or blackened. This salad is very good with tiny baby beets, if you can find them.

1 bunch beets, about 4–5 medium, with leaves
3 tablespoons olive oil
3 tablespoons fresh lemon juice
½ teaspoon salt
Several good grinds black pepper
1 teaspoon dried oregano

1. Pinch off the beet leaves, discarding any that are bruised or blackened. Wash the leaves thoroughly, then cook in a little boiling water for a few minutes, until they are wilted. Drain thoroughly.

2. Cut the beet stems about 1 inch from the top and discard. Wash the beets, then cook in boiling water for about 20–30 minutes, or until tender when pierced with a sharp knife. Drain the beets, then let cool and peel.

3. Slice the beets and place in a bowl. Squeeze the liquid out of the greens, chop them coarsely, and add them to the sliced beets.

4. Combine the oil, the lemon juice, the salt, the pepper, and the oregano. Whisk to blend thoroughly. Pour the dressing over the beets and mix well. Let stand at room temperature for 1–2 hours, then taste for salt and lemon.

Serves 4–6

Sesame Beansprout Salad

This crunchy salad is one of the traditional accompaniments to the Korean barbecue; it is a good addition to almost any Asian meal. To keep the beansprouts as fresh and crisp as possible, toss them with the dressing at the last minute. Peeled, seeded strips of cucumber can be added to the mixture, if desired.

10 ounces fresh beansprouts
4–5 scallions, cut in 1-inch lengths and slivered
2 tablespoons rice-wine vinegar
2 tablespoons Asian sesame oil
Good dash salt, or more to taste
Good dash ground hot red pepper

1. Combine the beansprouts and the scallions in a bowl.

2. Combine the vinegar, the oil, the salt, and the hot pepper and mix thoroughly. Pour the dressing over the beansprouts and toss lightly (your hands are best for this).

Serves 4

Japanese Eggplant and Double Ginger Salad

The Japanese have a true passion for pickles, pickled condiments, and tangy salads like this one, flavored with both fresh and pickled gingerroot and a piquant sweet-and-sour sauce. It makes an excellent accompaniment to grilled or stewed dishes, served, of course, with plenty of steamed rice.

1½ tablespoons soy sauce
1½ tablespoons rice vinegar
1½ teaspoons sugar
2 tablespoons peanut oil
1 tablespoon finely minced gingerroot
4 scallions, chopped (separate white and green parts)
3 10–12-inch Asian eggplants, cut in thin rounds
   (about ⅜ inch thick)
Good pinch crushed dried hot peppers, or Japanese
   sansho pepper
1 tablespoon shredded Japanese pickled sweet-and-sour
   gingerroot

1. Combine the soy sauce, the vinegar, and the sugar. Mix well and set aside.

2. In a heavy skillet or wok, heat the oil over high heat. Add the gingerroot, the white parts of the scallions, and the eggplant rounds. Stir-fry until the eggplant begins to brown and just to become soft. Sprinkle the eggplant with the hot peppers while frying.

3. Add the sauce mixture to the eggplant, stirring to coat it evenly. Cook briefly until all the liquid has been absorbed and the eggplant is nicely glazed.

4. Remove from the heat and place the eggplant in a shallow serving dish. Stir in the pickled gingerroot and mix well. Garnish the salad with the chopped green parts of the scallions. Serve at room temperature.

Serves 4

Moroccan Eggplant Salad

Salads are an important part of the Moroccan table. Made from a large variety of raw and cooked vegetables, they are brightly seasoned with the mix of ingredients from the Mediterranean, the Middle East, and Central Asia that makes the flavor of Moroccan food unique. This eggplant salad can serve as an appetizer, with bread or crackers, or as the salad accompaniment to the main course. It should be served at room temperature.

¼ cup olive oil
1 large onion, thinly sliced
1 medium to large eggplant, peeled and cut into thin strips
1 medium sweet red pepper, seeded and cut into strips
1 medium yellow pepper, seeded and cut into strips
2 medium zucchini, cut into strips
1 teaspoon paprika
1 teaspoon ground coriander
1 teaspoon ground cumin
½ teaspoon salt
Plenty of freshly ground black pepper
2 tablespoons fresh lemon juice
Good handful coarsely chopped fresh coriander leaf
Harissa (Moroccan fresh hot red chile pureed with
    olive oil) or liquid hot-pepper sauce, to taste
Sliced cucumber, tomato wedges, and oil-cured black olives,
    for garnish

1. Pour the oil into a large skillet or pot, then add all the vegetables and mix well. Cook over moderate heat, uncovered, stirring occasionally, until the vegetables become limp, about 15–20 minutes.

2. Add the paprika, coriander, cumin, salt, and pepper, mix well, and cook for another 10 minutes.

3. Remove from the heat and stir in the lemon juice, coriander, and hot sauce to taste. Let cool to room temperature, then taste for lemon and salt.

(continued)

4. Serve the salad garnished with the cucumber slices, tomato wedges, and black olives.

Serves 4–6

Spicy Szechuan Eggplant Salad

The southwestern province of Szechuan regards itself as the gastronomic center of China, if not the world, and the joys of the table are endlessly discussed and constantly enjoyed. Flavor and texture are modulated with consummate skill, and simple, inexpensive ingredients are turned into mouth-filling delights, like this eggplant dish with its characteristic blend of sweet, sour, aromatic, and pungent.

2 tablespoons soy sauce
2 tablespoons rice-wine vinegar
2 teaspoons sugar
3 tablespoons ketchup
1 teaspoon Chinese chile paste with garlic
1½ teaspoons cornstarch
2 tablespoons peanut oil
1 medium onion, finely chopped
1 tablespoon finely minced gingerroot
4 large cloves garlic, minced
1 teaspoon crushed dried hot peppers
2 large eggplants, peeled and diced
6 scallions, finely chopped
Good handful chopped fresh coriander leaf
1 tablespoon Asian sesame oil

1. In a small bowl, combine the soy sauce, the vinegar, the sugar, the ketchup, the chile paste, and the cornstarch. Mix thoroughly and set aside.

2. Heat a wok or skillet over high heat. Pour in the peanut oil and swirl it around. Add the onion, the gingerroot, the garlic, and the hot peppers, and stir-fry for a few minutes, until the mixture becomes aromatic.

3. Add the eggplant cubes and stir-fry until the eggplant is tender.

4. Mix the reserved sauce again, then add it to the eggplant and stir-fry until the mixture is slightly thickened and clear.

5. Remove from the heat and stir in the scallions, the coriander, and the sesame oil. Serve the salad at room temperature.

Serves 6–8

Burmese Spiced Green Bean Salad

The Burmese are extremely fond of salads, which they make from both raw and cooked vegetables, and season, as do so many people, with salt and acid. In Southeast Asia, the salt is frequently in the form of fish sauce, fish paste, or soy sauce, and the sourness is provided by lemon or lime juice, tamarind, or vinegar.

1 pound green beans, of uniform thickness, cut on a sharp
    diagonal into 1-inch pieces
1 tablespoon peanut oil
1 tablespoon fish sauce
2 tablespoons fresh lime juice
1 teaspoon shrimp paste or anchovy paste
1/4 teaspoon (or more to taste) cayenne pepper
3 tablespoons finely chopped roasted peanuts

1. Cook the beans in boiling water for about 5 minutes, until just tender but still crisp. Drain thoroughly.

2. In a small bowl or cup, combine all the remaining ingredients except for 1 tablespoon of the chopped peanuts. Whisk the sauce to blend well.

3. Pour the sauce over the drained beans and mix thoroughly.

Taste for hotness and add a bit more cayenne to taste, if desired. Garnish the beans with the remaining 1 tablespoon of peanuts before serving.

Serves 4

Middle Eastern Tomato and Cucumber Salad

I never met a salad I didn't like, but this is one of my favorites, a very simple peasant dish that has all the refreshing flavor and texture of good salads everywhere. No flavored vinegars or infused oils—indeed, no oil at all—just some basic lemon juice and salt to highlight and enhance the fresh flavors of tomato, cucumber, onion, and coriander. It is good with all kinds of other foods, or just by itself with some fresh pita bread.

2 medium tomatoes, cut in small chunks or wedges
2 medium cucumbers, peeled and cut in small chunks
1 small onion, thinly sliced
Good handful coarsely chopped fresh coriander leaf
2–3 tablespoons fresh lemon juice
1/4 teaspoon salt
Several grinds black pepper

1. Combine the vegetables and the coriander in a bowl. Toss with the lemon juice, the salt, and the pepper, then let stand at room temperature for about 1/2 hour. Mix again, taste for salt and lemon, add more if necessary, and serve.

Serves 4

Cool as a Cucumber

A cucumber should be well sliced, and dressed with pepper and vinegar, and then thrown out, as good for nothing.

Samuel Johnson

Dr. Johnson was a man of strong opinions, but his dim view of cucumbers is not shared by most of the world. The cucumber is one of the most ancient cultivated salad vegetables, thought to have originated in India many thousands of years ago. It spread throughout Asia and then to the Middle East; it is one of the few vegetables mentioned in the Bible as a favorite food of the children of Israel. Cucumbers were highly esteemed by both ancient Greeks and Romans; The Roman cookbook writer Apicius gives a recipe for cucumbers dressed with honey, vinegar, and *liquamen* (fish sauce) that sounds uncannily similar to the salads of Southeast Asia with their sweet-and-sour fish-sauce dressings. There are many reasons for the cucumber's widespread appeal: it is an easy grower in both temperate and tropical climates, and its crisp, sweet flesh and high water content make it an ideal ingredient for cool and refreshing salads. To this day, in many cuisines it is combined with yogurt or sour cream, herbs, and spices, to provide a refreshing foil for highly spiced, sauced, or oily dishes. There are many varieties of cucumber and large differences in flavor and texture. The overgrown waxed green monsters that are routinely available have much less flavor and crispness than small, young, fresh cucumbers; in general, the smaller the size, the better the vegetable. The best cucumbers I ever ate were in the Middle East, where they had a crisp yet tender flesh, a delicate flavor, and a pronounced perfume.

My Grandma's Unburnt Cucumber Salad

Grandma was a burner; she routinely blackened all the food she cooked, years before redfish was even a gleam in Paul Prudhomme's eye. The one salad she served escaped the ravages of her incendiary touch only because it never had a chance to get anywhere near the stove. It was traditionally served as part of a light "dairy" meal, with bagels and fresh rye bread, eggs (burnt), and smoked fish. I have added only the pepper and the chives, which Grandma would likely have disdained as mere frills.

2 medium cucumbers, peeled and cut into small chunks
½ cup thinly sliced radishes
6 scallions, coarsely chopped
3–4 heaping tablespoons sour cream
Plenty of freshly ground black pepper
2 tablespoons finely snipped chives
Salt to taste, if desired

Combine the vegetables in a bowl. Add the sour cream, the pepper, and the chives, and mix thoroughly. Chill before serving. Let diners add salt to taste, if desired.

Serves 4

NOTE: Small chunks of firm ripe tomato can be added to the mixture; add more sour cream as needed.

Tomato and Red Onion Salad with Avocado Vinaigrette

The vinaigrette is a simple mixture of oil and vinegar; in this recipe, the liquid oil is replaced with pureed avocado, a fruit that is rich in delicately flavored oil. The tangy, velvety sauce is an excellent enhancement for juicy summer beefsteak tomatoes and sliced red onion.

2–3 large beefsteak tomatoes, thickly sliced
1 medium red onion, thinly sliced
1 medium perfectly ripe avocado, peeled
¼ cup white wine vinegar
1 clove garlic, crushed
¼ teaspoon salt
Several good grinds black pepper

1. Arrange the tomato slices on a serving plate; top the tomatoes with the sliced onion.
2. In a small bowl, mash the avocado thoroughly, then stir in the vinegar, the garlic, the salt, and the pepper. Mix until smooth.
3. Spoon dollops of the sauce around and over the tomatoes, or pass the sauce separately. Serve at room temperature.

Serves 4–6

Mediterranean Layered Salad

This is an adaptation of a Turkish salad, a vertical *salade composée*, best presented in a clear glass or trifle bowl so that the many colorful layers of vegetables and herbs can be admired before they are devoured. It's great for the buffet table, because it can be prepared ahead of time, looks beautiful, and can feed a lot of people. The secret for good flavor is to toss each vegetable component with dressing before it is layered into the bowl. This recipe is just a guide for a basic salad; you can vary it with all kinds of different vegetables, such as sliced cooked beets, finely sliced fresh fennel, shredded carrot and celery root, or cooked chickpeas. Always put the potatoes at the bottom, so that any excess juice or sauce will be gracefully absorbed.

½ cup olive oil
⅓ cup fresh lemon juice
1 clove garlic, crushed
1 teaspoon salt
Plenty of freshly ground black pepper
3 medium potatoes, cooked, peeled, and sliced
1 medium red onion, finely chopped
¼ cup finely chopped flat-leaf parsley
1 medium sweet red pepper, seeded and diced
1 medium yellow pepper, seeded and diced
2 cucumbers, peeled, seeded, and sliced
¼ cup finely snipped fresh dill
2 tomatoes, cut in half and sliced
2 tablespoons chopped fresh oregano, or 2 teaspoons
    crushed dried
¼ cup crumbled feta cheese
12 Kalamata olives

1. Combine the oil, the lemon juice, the garlic, the salt, and the pepper. Whisk to blend thoroughly.
2. Combine the potatoes and onion; pour on about ¼ cup of the

dressing and toss to blend thoroughly. Layer the potatoes and onion in the bottom of the serving bowl. Sprinkle the parsley over them.

3. Toss the peppers with a couple of tablespoons of the dressing; layer the peppers over the parsley.

4. Toss the cucumbers with a couple of tablespoons of the dressing; layer the cucumbers over the peppers. Sprinkle the dill over the cucumbers.

5. Mix the tomato slices with a couple of tablespoons of the dressing; layer the tomatoes over the dill.

6. Sprinkle the oregano over the tomatoes, then sprinkle on the feta and the olives.

Serves 6–8

Really Red Slaw

Cabbage is a hardy, nutritious, easily grown vegetable, and cabbage salads are common all over the world. Our familiar cole slaw is an Americanization of the Dutch *kool sla* (cabbage salad), an adaptation of one of the most traditional of Northern European salads. Unfortunately for many of us, cole slaw has come to mean little plastic tubs of limp, flabby cabbage mired in a quicksand of mayonnaise. A good slaw is crisp and fresh, with just enough dressing to coat the shredded vegetables with a creamy, sweet, and tangy flavor. Here is a little variation on the theme, with red cabbage, slivered beets, and sweet red onion combining to provide vivid color and zesty flavor.

> 4 cups finely sliced or shredded red cabbage
>   (about half of a small head)
> 2 cups slivered or julienne-cut cooked beets
> 1 medium red onion, finely sliced
> 1/3 cup mayonnaise
> 1/3 cup raspberry vinegar
> 1/2 teaspoon celery seeds
> 1 teaspoon sugar
> 1/2 teaspoon salt
> Several good grinds black pepper
> 1 shallot, finely minced

1. In a bowl, combine the cabbage, the beets, and the onion.

2. Combine the mayonnaise, the vinegar, the celery seeds, the sugar, the salt, the pepper, and the shallot. Whisk to blend thoroughly.

3. Pour the dressing over the vegetables and toss lightly to blend. Chill, then taste, and adjust seasoning if necessary.

Serves 6–8

Beefsteak Tomatoes with Anchovy, Lemon, and Basil

The dressing for this salad, a traditional favorite from the Mediterranean, may well have been the inspiration for the Caesar salad that has become so popular in recent years. This one lacks the raw egg and the Parmesan cheese; it is excellent on thick slices of summer beefsteak tomatoes, garnished with fresh basil and capers.

½ of a 2-ounce can anchovies, packed in olive oil
2 cloves garlic, crushed
Several good grinds black pepper
3 tablespoons fresh lemon juice
3–4 large beefsteak tomatoes, thickly sliced
Small bunch fresh basil leaves
1–2 tablespoons capers, drained

1. Mash the anchovies, with about 1 tablespoon of the oil, and the garlic into a smooth paste.
2. Stir in the pepper and the lemon juice and mix until smooth.
3. Dribble the sauce over the sliced tomatoes, then top each slice with a couple of whole basil leaves.
4. Garnish the tomatoes with capers.

Serves 6–8

Turkish White Bean Salad

Like so many other peoples of the Mediterranean, Turks enjoy a wide variety of marinated vegetables and salads at almost all meals and particularly for the *mezze,* a savory assortment of appetizers. Eggplant, peppers, tomatoes, and olives all feature prominently in this tradition, as do a variety of beans and legumes. This white-bean salad is typical of the region and works to good advantage at a picnic or barbecue.

1 cup small dried white beans (pea, navy, etc.)
1 medium onion, cut in half (no need to peel)
1–2 bay leaves
4 tablespoons red wine vinegar
½ teaspoon salt
1 medium onion, peeled and finely chopped
1 medium green pepper, seeded and finely chopped
1 large tomato, coarsely chopped
3 cloves garlic, finely chopped
¼ cup olive oil
Plenty of freshly cracked black pepper
Good handful finely chopped flat-leaf parsley
Black olives and hard-cooked egg wedges, for garnish

1. Soak the beans in cold water to cover overnight. Drain, then cover with fresh cold water. Add the halved onion and bay leaves, bring to the simmer, and cook, uncovered, for about 1–1½ hours, until the beans are tender.

2. Drain the beans; discard the onion and bay leaf. Place the hot beans in a bowl and stir in 2 tablespoons of the vinegar and the salt. Mix well and let stand at room temperature for 1–2 hours.

3. Add the chopped onion, green pepper, tomato, and garlic to the beans.

4. In a small bowl, combine the oil, the remaining 2 tablespoons of vinegar, and the pepper. Whisk to blend thoroughly, then pour the dressing over the beans and mix well. Stir in the parsley, then taste for salt, and add some more if necessary. Let the salad stand at room temperature for 1–2 hours before serving. Serve at room temperature, garnished with olives and hard-cooked egg wedges.

Serves 6

Spiced Lentil and Golden Orzo Salad

In many cultures that depend heavily on plant foods, grains and legumes—peas, beans, and lentils—are combined in a variety of dishes to provide an appropriate balance of amino acids, as well as exciting experiences of flavor, texture, and color. This hearty salad, with its typical North African and Near Eastern ingredients, can serve as a light main course or a salad accompaniment.

1 cup lentils
½ teaspoon turmeric
½ cup orzo
¼ cup olive oil
6 tablespoons fresh lemon juice
½ teaspoon salt
1 teaspoon ground freshly roasted cumin
¼ teaspoon liquid hot-pepper sauce
⅓ cup chopped fresh dill
2 tablespoons finely chopped fresh mint
4 scallions, chopped
Tomato wedges and sliced cucumber, for garnish

1. Cook the lentils in 2 cups of boiling water for 20–30 minutes, until just tender. Drain and set aside.

2. Add the turmeric to 2 cups boiling water. Add the orzo, stir well, then cook, uncovered, over moderate heat for about 10 minutes, or until just tender but still slightly chewy. Drain. Combine the drained lentils and the orzo in a bowl.

3. Combine the oil, lemon juice, salt, cumin, and hot-pepper sauce. Whisk to blend thoroughly. Pour the dressing over the lentils and orzo and mix thoroughly.

4. Add the dill, the mint, and the scallions and mix in well. Let stand at room temperature for 1 hour.

5. Taste the salad for salt and lemon. Mound the salad on a serving dish and garnish with tomato wedges and cucumber slices.

Serves 4–6

Multicolored Potato and Pepper Salad with Sun-Dried Tomatoes and Basil

A great legacy to the world from the ancient people of the Andes is the potato, hybridized into a multitude of varieties, colors, and textures. Potato salads are a genuine American tradition, prepared initially according to the taste of some of our earlier settlers, with bacon fat and vinegar from Germany, mayonnaise from Holland and France. With a growing acceptance and appreciation of other cuisines, however, Americans are creating a whole new world of potato salads; this one, with its decided Italian flavor, is very beautiful, using to good advantage a number of colorful potatoes and peppers that have recently become widely available.

1 medium onion, coarsely chopped
1–2 large cloves elephant garlic, thinly sliced
1 each medium sweet red, green, and yellow pepper, seeded
    and cut in small chunks
4 tablespoons olive oil
2 medium purple potatoes
2 medium gold-fleshed potatoes
⅓ cup coarsely chopped sun-dried tomatoes
½ cup coarsely chopped fresh basil leaves
3 tablespoons red wine vinegar
1 teaspoon salt
Plenty of freshly ground black pepper
Handful of black olives and some additional basil leaves,
    for garnish

1. In a skillet, sauté the onion, garlic, and peppers in 2 tablespoons of the oil, stirring, just until the vegetables begin to turn limp, but before they brown. Remove from the heat.

2. Cook the potatoes in boiling water until they are just tender when pierced with a sharp knife. Drain, then peel and cut into small cubes.

3. In a bowl, combine the pepper mixture, the potatoes, the sun-dried tomatoes, and the basil.

4. In a small bowl or cup, combine the remaining 2 tablespoons of oil, the vinegar, the salt, and the pepper. Whisk to blend thoroughly.

5. Pour the dressing over the vegetables and mix well. Let stand at room temperature for 1 hour or so, then mix again and taste; adjust seasoning if necessary. Serve the salad at room temperature, garnished with black olives and additional basil leaves.

Serves 4–6

Portuguese-Style Redskin Potato Salad with Tomatoes and Garlic

The Portuguese, like the Spanish, took enthusiastically to the South American potato and developed a repertoire of hearty potato dishes. In this preparation, thinly sliced potatoes are cooked in the *tomatada,* the classic Portuguese sauce of olive oil, tomatoes, and garlic. It can be eaten hot, but, served at room temperature with the addition of vinegar, it makes an unusual and delicious salad.

1 medium onion, thinly sliced
4 large cloves garlic, finely chopped
3 tablespoons olive oil
2 cups coarsely chopped tomatoes
4–5 medium redskin potatoes (no need to peel),
    thinly sliced
½–1 teaspoon salt
¼ teaspoon freshly ground black pepper
2 tablespoons red wine vinegar
Good handful finely chopped fresh coriander leaf

1. In a large skillet, sauté the onion and the garlic in the oil over moderate heat, stirring, until the onion wilts and begins to turn golden, about 4–5 minutes.

2. Add the tomatoes, mix well, then add the potatoes, ½ teaspoon of the salt, and the pepper, and mix well. Cover and cook over low heat for about 15 minutes, or until the potatoes are just tender.

3. Uncover the pan and quickly cook the sauce down until it is thick and most of the liquid has cooked away. Stir in the vinegar and the coriander and remove from the heat. Cool slightly, then taste for salt; you will probably need some salt at this point. Serve at room temperature.

Serves 3–4

Pouring Oil on Troubled Greens

Those of us who were not washed away in the flood of balsamic vinegar some years ago are having trouble keeping afloat in the recent deluge of extra-virgin olive oil. Who would have thought the world to have so many virgin olives in it? As with so much else, the label and the price tag are not guarantees of quality: I have had extra-virgin oils that tasted more like machine oil from Pennsylvania than the liquid sunshine of the Mediterranean. Buy a number of varieties in small quantities, do a lot of tasting, then select the oil for its appropriate culinary task. A rich, fruity oil may be too heavy for very delicate greens, but so-called light oils frequently have no flavor at all. A supermarket peanut oil is fine for frying or cooking, but in salad dressings or sauces, where a true peanut flavor is important, a high-quality cold-pressed oil is worth the extra pennies. Delicate oils like walnut and avocado must be carefully stored away from heat and light and used to complement appropriate foods; their subtle flavors would be wasted on bitter or peppery greens and pungent herbs. The same cautions apply to vinegars, which come in a remarkable variety and are essential not only for salads but for cooking and seasoning of all kinds. Develop your own palate and let it be your guide—it is a unique and singular organ that will serve you more truly than any book or teacher or label or trend.

Salad of Shrimp and Sugar Snap Peas with Ginger Peanut Vinaigrette

This delightful salad is firmly rooted in the traditional foods and flavors of Asia, particularly the savory peanut-sauced fruit-and-vegetable salads of Indonesia. The nectarine adds a surprising bite of tart-sweet flavor that goes wonderfully with the shrimp and snap peas. Try this salad for a light, satisfying summer meal.

½ cup peanut oil (a high-quality, cold-pressed, flavorful
   variety is best)
⅓ cup rice-wine vinegar
1 teaspoon sugar
1 teaspoon grated gingerroot
¼ teaspoon salt
2 teaspoons peanut butter, at room temperature
⅛ teaspoon cayenne pepper
1 pound sugar snap peas
1 pound cooked shrimp, peeled and deveined
1 nectarine, fully ripe but firm, pitted and thinly sliced
3–4 scallions, coarsely chopped
Mixed greens
2 tablespoons finely chopped peanuts

1. Combine the oil, the vinegar, the sugar, the gingerroot, the salt, the peanut butter, and the cayenne. Whisk to blend thoroughly.

2. Blanch the snap peas in boiling water for 1 minute. Drain.

3. In a bowl, combine the shrimp, the snap peas, the sliced nectarine, and the scallions. Pour the sauce over the salad and toss lightly but thoroughly.

4. Spoon the salad onto a serving plate on a bed of greens. Sprinkle with chopped peanuts.

Serves 4–6

Spanish Squid and Rice Salad

Rice salads are common throughout the Mediterranean and the Near East; with bits of ham, fish, or seafood added, they can serve as light but satisfying summer meals. This Spanish variety is full of flavor, with its garlic, saffron, and vinegar. The trick with the squid is to cook it as briefly as possible, so that it does not become tough or rubbery.

1 medium onion, finely chopped
6 cloves garlic, minced
4 tablespoons olive oil
1 cup long-grain rice
2 cups chicken stock
½ teaspoon saffron threads
Several good grinds black pepper
12–16 ounces cleaned squid, cut in thin strips or rings
Salt and freshly ground pepper to taste
2 tablespoons red wine vinegar
⅓ cup finely chopped flat-leaf parsley
1 cup cooked fresh or frozen peas
Additional chopped parsley, for garnish

1. In a medium saucepan, sauté the onion and 4 of the minced garlic cloves in 2 tablespoons of the oil over moderate heat, stirring, until the onion wilts.

2. Stir in the rice and sauté a few minutes more.

3. Add the stock, the saffron, and the pepper, bring to the simmer, then cook, covered, over low heat for about 20 minutes, until all the liquid has been absorbed. Let cool completely.

4. In a medium skillet, sauté the remaining 2 cloves of minced garlic in the remaining 2 tablespoons of oil over moderate heat for a few minutes.

5. Turn the heat up to high, add the squid, and stir-fry for about 1 minute. Remove from the heat, salt and pepper lightly, and stir in the vinegar. Let cool.

6. Add the squid mixture to the rice, mix well, then stir in the chopped parsley and the peas. Let stand, covered, in the refrigerator for an hour or so. Mix again, then taste for salt and vinegar; you may need some more of both at this point. Garnish the salad with additional chopped parsley.

Serves 4

Salade Niçoise

The Niçoise is a traditional old favorite from the south of France and still one of the best salads around, always a good choice for a festive summer lunch or light supper. A classic "composed" salad, it consists of a mixture of cooked green beans and diced potatoes, dressed with a robust vinaigrette, surrounded and garnished with a variety of Mediterranean goodies—olives, capers, anchovies, tuna. You can use canned tuna, but if you do, choose a French or Italian variety packed in olive oil; the flavor is much better than those packed in water or other oils.

2 medium potatoes (all-purpose or firm, waxy-fleshed type)
½ pound green beans, cut in 1-inch lengths (about 2 cups)
½ cup olive oil
⅓ cup white wine vinegar
1 tablespoon Dijon mustard
1 clove garlic, crushed
¼ teaspoon salt
Several good grinds black pepper
2 tomatoes, cut in small wedges
Good handful oil-cured black olives
1–2 tablespoons capers
4–6 ounces grilled fresh tuna (page 18), sliced or cut into
    small chunks, or 1 can tuna (6–7 ounces) packed in olive oil
1 small can anchovies
2–3 tablespoons chopped fresh chervil (you can also use
    chopped fresh tarragon and/or parsley)

1. Cook the potatoes until just tender; peel and dice.
2. Cook the green beans until just tender but still crisp. Drain.
3. In a small bowl, combine the oil, vinegar, mustard, garlic, salt, and pepper. Whisk to blend thoroughly.
4. Combine the green beans and the potatoes. Pour over them about ⅓ cup of the dressing, mix well, and let stand at room temperature for about ½ hour. Taste, and add more dressing if necessary.
5. Mound the salad on a serving platter; surround and decorate

with the tomatoes, olives, capers, tuna, and anchovies. Drizzle a little more dressing over the garnishes. Sprinkle the platter with the chopped herbs.

Serves 4–6

Vietnamese-Style Jicama, Beansprout, and Chicken Salad

Salads are an important part of Vietnamese cuisine, frequently made with bits of meat—strips of roast beef or chicken, crabmeat, or shrimp. They are very flavorful and light and thus very much in tune with contemporary tastes. Jicama is not a traditional Asian ingredient—it comes originally from Mexico—but its subtle flavor and crisp texture make it an ideal vegetable for salads like this, perfect for a light summer lunch.

1 cup jicama, peeled and cut into julienne strips
1 cup fresh beansprouts
1 carrot, cut into julienne strips
2–3 scallions, slivered
½–¾ cup shredded or slivered cooked chicken
3 tablespoons fresh lemon juice
1 tablespoon fish sauce
2 cloves garlic, minced
¼ teaspoon crushed dried hot peppers, or liquid
    hot-pepper sauce to taste
½ teaspoon sugar
3 tablespoons finely chopped roasted peanuts
⅓ cup coarsely chopped fresh coriander leaf
Salt or additional fish sauce, to taste

(continued)

1. Place the jicama, beansprouts, carrot, scallions, and chicken in a bowl. Toss lightly to combine.

2. In a small bowl or cup, combine the lemon juice, fish sauce, garlic, hot peppers, and sugar. Whisk to combine thoroughly.

3. Pour the dressing over the salad, then add the peanuts and coriander, and mix gently but thoroughly. Taste for salt, and add some, or some extra fish sauce, if desired.

Serves 4

Mussel Salad Ravigote

The word "ravigote" means "delightful or refreshing to the palate," and it usually refers to a tangy vinaigrette flavored with capers and a variety of fresh herbs. It is excellent with all kinds of cold seafood, and particularly good with mussels. Serve this dish as a light main-course summer salad, or individually plated in smaller portions as a first course.

4–5 pounds fresh mussels, steamed and shelled
3 tablespoons minced shallot
2 tablespoons finely chopped scallion
2 tablespoons finely snipped fresh dill
2 tablespoons finely chopped flat-leaf parsley
2 tablespoons chopped tarragon or chervil
1 tablespoon capers, coarsely chopped
1/4 cup olive oil
2 tablespoons white wine vinegar
1 teaspoon Dijon mustard
1/4 teaspoon salt
Plenty of freshly ground black pepper
Coarsely torn mixed greens or baby greens

1. In a bowl, combine the cooked, shelled mussels and the shallot, scallion, herbs, and capers.

2. Combine the oil, the vinegar, the mustard, the salt, and the pepper. Whisk to blend thoroughly.

3. Pour the dressing over the mussels and mix gently but thoroughly. Serve the mussels on a bed of mixed greens.

Serves 4, more as an appetizer

Sweet Corn, Tomato, and Salmon Ceviche Salad

The technique of "cooking" fish or seafood in acidic liquids is used throughout the world but is most familiar to us in the Mexican ceviche, with its tangy lime-and-chile marinade. In this recipe, a ceviche of fresh salmon is combined with two ancient Mexican foods, corn and tomatoes, to make a refreshing summer salad. It serves very nicely as an appetizer or a first course.

⅓ pound boneless fresh salmon
3–4 limes
2 cups fresh corn kernels (about 3 ears' worth)
1 cup diced fresh tomatoes
3–4 scallions, chopped
12 pimento-stuffed green olives, coarsely chopped
Small handful finely chopped fresh cilantro
2 tablespoons olive oil
¼ teaspoon salt
Several good dashes liquid hot-pepper sauce
Coarsely torn greens and sliced avocado, for garnish

1. With a sharp knife, cut the salmon into paper-thin slices. Place the salmon in a glass or ceramic dish and squeeze on enough lime juice to cover. Place in the refrigerator for 3–4 hours.

2. Blanch the corn kernels in boiling water for 1 minute. Drain.

3. Combine the corn, the tomatoes, the scallions, the olives, and the cilantro. Combine the oil, the salt, the pepper sauce, and 4 additional tablespoons of lime juice. Whisk to blend thoroughly.

4. Pour the dressing over the vegetables and mix well.
5. Drain the salmon slices, then mix them gently into the salad.
6. Serve the salad with some greens and sliced avocado, for garnish.

Serves 4–6

Honey Hoisin Duck with Mixed Greens and Sprouts

Salads composed of vegetables or greens with more substantial ingredients added are no modern invention; the English have an old tradition of salmagundi, a salad of mixed meats, cheese, and hard-cooked eggs, combined with cooked and raw vegetables and served with a creamy dressing—the original chef's salad? Here is a delicious Asian duck salad, with a sweet-and-tangy hoisin dressing. It can be individually plated for an elegant first course or served on a large platter.

1 boneless duck breast (about 1 pound), grilled, broiled, or
    sautéed to desired doneness, and allowed to cool
2 tablespoons hoisin sauce
1 tablespoon honey
2 tablespoons rice-wine vinegar
2 tablespoons peanut oil
½ teaspoon grated gingerroot
⅛ teaspoon salt
Several good dashes liquid hot-pepper sauce
4–6 cups mixed torn greens (include some arugula and
    some radicchio for color)
1–2 cups snow-pea shoots or other fresh green sprouts
    (onion sprouts are particularly good)
Peanut oil

Lemon juice

Salt

Freshly ground black pepper

1. Cut the cooked, cooled duck into thin slices.

2. Combine the hoisin, the honey, the vinegar, the peanut oil, the gingerroot, the salt, and the hot-pepper sauce. Whisk to blend thoroughly.

3. Spoon about 2 tablespoons of the sauce over the sliced duck and let stand at room temperature while preparing the greens.

4. Combine the greens and the sprouts in a bowl. Drizzle on 2–3 tablespoons of peanut oil, a couple of good squeezes of lemon juice, a little salt, and some freshly ground black pepper. Toss the greens; they should be very lightly coated with dressing, not drenched.

5. Arrange the greens on individual plates or a large serving platter. Arrange the duck slices over the greens. Drizzle the remaining hoisin dressing over the salad.

Serves 4–6

Chapter Eight

The Condimental Extra

Woe to the cook whose sauce has no sting.

Geoffrey Chaucer

One facet of the universal human food experience has always been paramount, and that is the search for a good and proper flavor, for food that satisfies our mouths with familiar and agreeable sensations as well as filling our bellies with a nutritious meal. What tastes good to you may not taste good to me, of course, especially if your taste buds were honed on raw fish seasoned with soy sauce and horseradish and mine on hot dogs with pickle relish and mustard. The details of the seasoning enterprise vary widely, from area to area and from cuisine to cuisine, but no matter who we are or what tribe we belong to, we are all doing the same thing—modifying, transforming, enhancing the flavor of our food.

Flavor comes from many sources. Most basic is the flavor of the food itself: pork tastes very different from lamb, and both are clearly distinguishable from chicken or liver. Then there are the flavors produced by the cooking techniques applied: smoked ham has a flavor very unlike roast pork, though both meats come from the same animal; raisins dried in the sun do not taste very much like the sweet, juicy grapes from which they are made. Last, and perhaps the most important, are the flavors produced by the deliberate addition of seasoning ingredients, which we humans have elaborated into a truly remarkable variety and range of flavoring substances.

We don't know who first began to fool around with the flavor of food or when it occurred, but it was certainly very early in our history. It may well have been the women who, scouring the areas around the campsite for valuable plant foods while the men were out on a hunt, gathered wild seeds and nuts and dug up starchy roots and tubers, plucked flowers and berries and leaves, scraped bits of bark, sniffed and tasted all manner of herbs and grasses and wild greens. It was, surely, the women who were the traditional healers and nurturers, concocting from the most ancient times all sorts of medicinal teas, infusions, restorative broths, and healing potions, and who experimented with, and passed on the knowledge about, the seasoning and medicinal properties of plants.

However it began, it endures. We all go to quite extravagant lengths to achieve a good and proper flavor for our food, and have done so, apparently, from our earliest appearance as the cooking animal, the creature who sticks her finger in the pot and says, "A little more garlic, maybe?" But in addition to seasoning our food, we go even further: we design substances, themselves separately cooked and prepared, to heighten and intensify the flavor experience, to complement or enhance the already seasoned food. We manufacture condiments—sauces, relishes, pastes, spreads—whose only function is to embellish the rest of our food. My hot dog, already seasoned and cooked, is made richer and more appealing by the addition of mustard and pickle relish, two substances I would be loath to consume by themselves. As one of the Marx Brothers once observed, "Mustard's no good without roast beef!"

Imagine a world in which there was no mustard for your ham-and-cheese, no tartar sauce for your crab cakes, no horseradish for your gefülte fish, no ketchup for your burger and fries. How much less tempting is a taco without salsa, a dumpling without its vinegary soy dip, sushi without pickled ginger and wasabi, a gumbo without hot sauce. How boring life would be without chutneys and sambals, sour pickles and red-hot chiles. The condiment is pure embellishment, designed for the sole purpose of tickling our taste buds and making the rest of the food more pleasing.

However their ingredients and flavors may vary from cuisine to cuisine, most condiments share a similar underlying design. They tend to be intense in flavor and to play on our basic tastes for sour, salty, sweet, and less commonly, bitter. They frequently contain ingredients that irritate the palate and thus intensify the flavor experience. They provide concentrated little dollops of stimulation, not necessarily pleasant by themselves but titillating as accessories to the rest of the meal. They work by exciting the mouth with complement and contrast, perking up bland food with pungent flavors, refreshing fatty foods with cleansing acidic tastes, highlighting salty or smoky flavors with sweetness.

Condiments are fascinating because they reveal that uniquely human inclination for aesthetic experience. They may contain some nutrients, but their function has nothing to do with nourishment, unless it is to make our basic and sometimes boring sustenance more palatable. We do not eat them by themselves, and yet we become addicted to them; without their intense flavors, our food seems undressed and uninteresting. One can hardly imagine a lion who pauses to anoint his freshly killed meal with a good dash of Worcestershire, or a horse who cannot swallow his hay without a spoonful of rémoulade. Our species is involved in a never-ending quest for novelty, excitement, and stimulation, though almost always within the constraints of familiar ingredients and recognizable traditions. The condiment is the finishing touch, the stylish little extra that no one needs and everyone wants.

RECIPES

Cranberry Habañero Chutney (American)
Kumquat Chutney (Indian)
Fresh Mint and Coriander Chutney (Indian)
Ginger Coconut Raita (Indian)
Himalayan Hot Sauce
Hilbeh (Yemeni Fenugreek and Coriander Sauce)
Turkish Tarator
A Trio of Salsas (Mexican, Turkish, Indian)
Smoky Eggplant Salsa (Nouvelle Mexican)
Peanut Coconut Sambal (Indonesian)
Spicy Mushroom Sambal (Indonesian)
Tapenade with Tomatoes (French)
Saffron and Tomato Ali-Oli (Spanish)
Olive, Walnut, and Garlic Pesto (Mediterranean)
Roasted Eggplant, Garlic, and Pepper Puree (Mediterranean)
Mixed Vegetable Caponata (Italian)
Spiced Rhubarb Sauce (Central Asian)
Sweet and Spicy Onion-Tomato Jam (American)
Caramelized Sweet Pepper Relish (American)
Roasted Green Pepper and Avocado "Mayonnaise" (Tex-Mex)
Atjar (Indonesian Mixed Vegetable Pickle)
Tangy Beet and Horseradish Relish (Northern European)
Dilled Mustard-Horseradish Sauce (Eastern European)
Mango Ketchup (American)

Cranberry Habañero Chutney

Chutneys, both fresh and cooked, are one of India's great contributions to the world of condiments. Cooked chutneys are part of an extensive repertoire of pickled and preserved fruits and vegetables and are the precursors of such familiar products as ketchup and pickle relish. This chutney recipe uses somewhat more American ingredients than the traditional Indian ones but produces very much the same sort of piquant, sweet, and tangy condiment that first titillated Western palates some three hundred years ago. It is excellent with curries and other spiced foods, and makes a welcome addition to the Thanksgiving table.

1 12-ounce bag cranberries
1 1-pound can crushed pineapple, packed in juice
2 Habañero chiles (or Scotch bonnets), seeded and minced
¼ cup cider vinegar
½ cup sugar
1 teaspoon cinnamon
1 teaspoon ground ginger
½ cup coarsely chopped walnuts

1. In a heavy pot, combine all the ingredients except the walnuts. Bring to the simmer and cook, uncovered, over low to moderate heat, stirring occasionally, for about 30 minutes.

2. Stir in the walnuts, then remove from the heat and let cool. Store the chutney in a covered container in the refrigerator. Let stand at least 3 or 4 days before serving.

Makes about 3 cups

Kumquat Chutney

Kumquats, the tiny tangy citrus fruits that came originally from China, are at their best in relishes and preserves that use their combination of sweet and tart most effectively. This spicy-sweet chutney goes well with curries, kabobs, and most grilled or roast meats.

4–4½ cups fresh kumquats

2 cups white distilled vinegar

1 cup water

2 cups sugar

1 large onion, coarsely chopped

4 large cloves garlic, minced

½ teaspoon crushed dried hot red peppers

1 cup golden raisins

¼ cup finely chopped crystallized ginger

1 teaspoon ground ginger

1. Wash the kumquats, then drain thoroughly. Cut the kumquats in half. With a sharp, small knife, flick out and discard any obvious seeds.
2. Put the kumquats in a heavy pot with the vinegar, water, sugar, onion, garlic, and hot peppers. Bring to the simmer, then cook, uncovered, over moderate heat, stirring occasionally, for about 45–50 minutes, until the kumquats are soft and the mixture is syrupy.
3. Add the raisins and the crystallized and ground ginger, mix well, and cook, stirring occasionally, for another 10–15 minutes. Let cool thoroughly, then store in a covered container in the refrigerator. Let stand for a couple of days before serving.

Makes about 1 quart

Fresh Mint and Coriander Chutney

Unlike cooked or preserved fruit and vegetable condiments, this chutney is made from raw ingredients and should be eaten soon after it is prepared; it will keep for only a day or so covered in the refrigerator. It has a wonderful, intense flavor from the fresh herbs and seasonings and goes well with curries, kabobs, and spicy foods.

1 cup fresh mint leaves, tightly packed
½ cup fresh coriander leaves, tightly packed
1 small onion, chopped, or 4 scallions, chopped
1 small fresh hot green chile, seeded
3 tablespoons fresh lime juice
2 teaspoons sugar

Combine all the ingredients in a food processor and process into a smooth sauce.

Makes about ⅔ cup

Ginger Coconut Raita

The raita is an Indian condiment that is a kind of cross between a relish and a salad, combining yogurt with a number of different seasonings and vegetables to provide a refreshing foil for curries and other highly seasoned and spicy foods. This is an unusual and complex raita, with an intriguing blend of sweet and sour, hot and cool, astringent and aromatic.

1 small onion, coarsely chopped
2 teaspoons chopped gingerroot
1 tablespoon fresh lime juice
3 tablespoons dried flaked unsweetened coconut
3–4 tablespoons fresh coriander leaf
1 small fresh hot green chile (serrano is good), seeded
1 cup plain yogurt
½ teaspoon sugar

1. In a food processor, combine the onion, the gingerroot, the lime juice, the coconut, the coriander, and the chile pepper. Process into a coarse paste.
2. Combine the paste with the yogurt and the sugar and mix thoroughly. Let stand at room temperature for at least ½ hour before serving to blend the flavors.

Makes about 1½ cups

Himalayan Hot Sauce

From Tibet comes this intriguing hot sauce, clearly a relative of the Indian yogurt-based raita. Native Tibetans prefer this sauce much hotter than I have made it; you can add more cayenne if your taste buds can take it. This goes well with grilled meats and kabobs, but it can also be used as a dip with pita bread and vegetables. The sauce must be left to stand, refrigerated, for at least 6–8 hours or, better yet, overnight, to allow its proper flavor to develop.

1 small onion, coarsely chopped
1 tablespoon finely chopped gingerroot
3 cloves garlic
2 medium plum tomatoes, coarsely chopped
1 teaspoon ground fenugreek
½ teaspoon cayenne pepper
¼ teaspoon salt
Good handful fresh coriander leaves
1 cup plain yogurt

1. In a food processor, combine the onion, the gingerroot, the garlic, and the tomatoes. Process into a coarse paste.
2. Add the fenugreek, cayenne, salt, and coriander and process briefly. The mixture should not be pureed completely but should retain some texture.
3. Stir the vegetable mixture into the yogurt and mix well. Cover and refrigerate for at least 6–8 hours, or overnight. Taste for salt and hotness.

Makes about 2 cups

Hilbeh

(Yemeni Fenugreek and Coriander Sauce)

This spicy sauce from Yemen is an exotic relative of other, more familiar sauces, like the pesto of Italy and the romesco of Spain, in which nuts or seeds are ground with aromatic herbs and seasonings into savory sauces and condiments. In this case, fenugreek seeds, more commonly known as a ground spice in curry mixtures, are soaked and then combined with hot peppers and fresh coriander leaf. The thick sauce is used as a relish with kabobs, as a spicy flavor enhancer for chopped fresh-vegetable salads, or as a spread or dip for Arabic bread. Fenugreek seeds are available in Indian or Middle Eastern groceries.

1 tablespoon fenugreek seeds
¼ cup lukewarm water
2 tablespoons fresh lemon juice
2 small fresh hot chile peppers, seeded
3 cloves garlic
¼ teaspoon salt
½ cup fresh coriander leaf

1. Soak the fenugreek seeds in the water at least 8 hours, or overnight. Drain.
2. Combine the drained seeds with all the remaining ingredients in a food processor. Process into a paste; there is no need to puree completely. Let stand at room temperature for a couple of hours, then taste for salt and chile.

Makes about ½ cup

Turkish Tarator

The tarator is a popular sauce that exists in a number of varieties throughout the Near and Middle East. It contains some kind of nut—walnuts, almonds, hazelnuts, or pine nuts; in Lebanon, it is made with sesame seeds and called "taratour bi tahini," the base for the familiar hummus and baba ghanouj. Garlic, parsley, and lemon or vinegar complete the seasoning, and in Turkey yogurt is a frequent addition. The tarator is kin to other savory nut pastes or sauces, highly seasoned and very versatile. It is excellent as a sauce for fried or grilled fish, or raw or cooked vegetables, and as a dip for Arabic bread.

½ cup freshly toasted hazelnuts, skins removed
1 slice firm-type white bread, crusts removed
3 cloves garlic
½ cup olive oil
1 tablespoon red wine vinegar
¼ teaspoon salt
Several good grinds black pepper
⅓ cup finely chopped flat-leaf parsley
½ cup plain yogurt

1. In a food processor, process the nuts until they are finely chopped.
2. Soak the bread in water for a few minutes, then squeeze out the water with your hands.
3. Add the bread, the garlic, the oil, the vinegar, the salt, and the pepper to the nuts. Process into a smooth paste.
4. Spoon the paste into a bowl; stir in the parsley and the yogurt and mix well.

Makes about 1½ cups

Painful Pleasure

Many of our most popular and traditional condiments have an irritant component, an ingredient that pricks or stings the mucous membranes of the mouth and palate, producing sensations that are akin to, but not quite, pain. These many different compounds, found in a variety of foods such as pepper, mustard, horseradish, ginger, and raw onions, seem to function universally as powerful enhancements to the eating experience, contributing their own flavors as well as highlighting or intensifying other flavors already present. When Columbus landed in the Americas in 1492, looking for the black pepper of the Indies that Europeans so craved, he found the native people enjoying the most powerful irritant food ever discovered—the chile pepper, actually a whole family of different peppers with a wide range of flavor and pungency. The chiles contain capsaicin, an irritant chemical concentrated in the inner membranes and, to a lesser extent, the seeds and the flesh. In only five hundred years, chiles have become the most widely used spice in the world, second only to salt as a seasoning agent. The pattern of acceptance of chiles throughout the world makes clear that the pungency, the burn in the mouth, helps to give zest and excitement to bland and boring foods, particularly the starchy and mealy plant foods on which so many people depend. No matter who we are or where we live, however, we all seem to relish some kind of sting or bite to perk up our food and light up our mouths.

A Trio of Salsas

The tomatoes and the chile peppers are among Mexico's most valuable gifts to the world of food, two ingredients that have had an astonishing impact on cuisines across the globe. Their age-old alliance finds its most popular expression in salsa, the bright and tangy sauce that enlivens everything from tacos to meat loaf, and that has been adopted and refashioned in kitchens from Turkey to India. The original Mexican "salsa cruda," or uncooked sauce, was a simple mixture of tomatoes, chile, and salt, elaborated with the addition of ingredients like citrus and cilantro, which were introduced by the Spanish after the Conquest. There are, of course, dozens of salsas in Mexican cuisine; this one is very simple and basic, and still one of the best.

The Mexican Original

1 large tomato, finely chopped
1 small onion, finely chopped
2 serrano chiles, seeded and minced (use jalapeños if
     you want a less pungent sauce)
Juice of 1 lime
Good handful finely chopped fresh cilantro
Good dash salt, or to taste

Combine all the ingredients and mix well.

Makes about 1½ cups

The Turkish Version

Like our own ketchup, this popular condiment is always present on Turkish tables, but it never finds its way into cookbooks. Its name, "aci ezme," reveals its relationship to the New World original: "ezme" means "pounded" or "chopped," and "aci," meaning "hot," is derived from "aji," the word for "chile" first encountered by Columbus in the Caribbean. As in Mexico, there are many varieties of this sauce, but the tomato and the chile are constant ingredients.

(continued)

1 large tomato, finely chopped
1 medium green pepper, seeded and finely chopped
1 small onion, finely chopped
2–3 small fresh hot chile peppers, seeded and minced
2 tablespoons red wine vinegar
Good dash salt, or to taste
Small handful finely chopped flat-leaf parsley

Combine all the ingredients and mix well.

Makes about 2 cups

The Indian Version

Only a slight shift in seasoning results in a product whose flavor is characteristically Indian. In India, this is called a relish or a chutney, but its parallel to the Mexican original is clear, in terms of its basic ingredients and its use. Instead of corn chips or tortillas, it is eaten with pappadums or chapatis, or used as a garnish for savory snack foods like samosas or pakhoras.

1 large tomato, finely chopped
1 small onion, finely chopped
2–3 small fresh hot chile peppers, seeded and minced
1 teaspoon grated gingerroot
Juice of 1 lime
2 tablespoons finely chopped fresh mint, or 2 teaspoons
    crumbled dried
2 tablespoons finely chopped fresh coriander leaf
Good dash salt, or to taste
2 heaping tablespoons plain yogurt

Combine all the ingredients and mix well.

Makes about 1½ cups

Smoky Eggplant Salsa

"Salsa" is one of those fascinating phenomena of the modern global melting pot—a Spanish word for a condiment of Mexican origin that made its impact on the American table through the cuisines of the Southwest, and is now used throughout the world as a generic term for piquant relishes and condiments of every description. Here's a good one that retains much of the character of the original, to use as a sauce or as a dip with corn chips and vegetables.

2 large eggplants
1 chipotle chile (smoked jalapeño)
2 tablespoons fresh lime juice
2 tablespoons olive oil
½ teaspoon dried oregano
½ teaspoon salt
1 large tomato, finely chopped
1 small onion, finely chopped
½ cup finely chopped fresh cilantro

1. Roast the eggplants in a hot (450° F.) oven (see page 256) or grill over hot coals, until they are very tender when pierced with a sharp knife. Remove and cool, then peel off the skin.

2. While the eggplants are cooking, soak the chipotle in the lime juice for at least ½ hour.

3. Combine the peeled eggplant, the chipotle with the lime juice, the oil, the oregano, and the salt in a food processor. Blend until smooth.

4. Add the tomato, the onion, and the cilantro to the eggplant puree and mix well. Taste for salt.

Makes about 2 cups

Peanut Coconut Sambal

The sambal is Indonesia's "hot stuff," a spicy condiment, sauce, or relish whose defining ingredient is hot chile. There are dozens of sambals, from the simplest preparations of ground fresh chile peppers fried in oil to complex mixtures of fruit, vegetables, seafood, and meat. This peanut-coconut sambal is a very appealing and versatile garnish that gives a spicy-sweet crunch to rice, noodles, salads, or curries.

> 2 shallots, minced
> 1 teaspoon crushed dried hot peppers
> 2 tablespoons peanut oil
> 1 cup coarsely chopped dry-roasted salted peanuts
> 1 tablespoon sugar
> 1 teaspoon ground coriander
> ½ cup dry shredded unsweetened coconut
> ⅛ teaspoon salt

1. In a medium skillet, fry the shallots and the hot peppers in the oil over high heat, stirring, until the shallots become golden and the mixture is aromatic.

2. Turn the heat down to moderate, then add the peanuts, the sugar, and the coriander, and mix well. Cook, stirring, for a couple of minutes, until the peanuts start to brown.

3. Add the coconut and the salt, mix well, and cook, stirring, for another couple of minutes, just until the coconut turns golden. Remove from the heat and let cool completely. The sambal will keep well for months in a tightly covered jar.

Makes about 1½ cups

Spicy Mushroom Sambal

Mushrooms are not a common ingredient in Indonesian cuisine, but they turn up occasionally in wonderful spicy sauces to serve as accompanying dishes in the rijstafel. This one has a fine complex flavor that is sweet, pungent, and aromatic; it makes a good foil for rice, noodles, or satay.

1 medium onion, finely chopped
3 cloves garlic, minced
1 teaspoon finely minced gingerroot
1 teaspoon crushed dried hot peppers
2 tablespoons peanut oil
2 cups sliced fresh mushrooms
1 large tomato, finely chopped (about 1 cup chopped)
2 tablespoons soy sauce
1 teaspoon brown sugar
1 teaspoon ground coriander
2 teaspoons finely chopped fresh lemon grass, or
   ½ teaspoon lemon-grass powder
½ teaspoon caraway seeds
⅛ teaspoon salt, or to taste

1. In a medium skillet, cook the onion, the garlic, the gingerroot, and the hot peppers in the oil over moderate heat, stirring, until the mixture becomes aromatic and starts to turn golden.

2. Add the mushrooms, and then all the remaining ingredients except the salt; mix well, bring to the simmer, and cook, uncovered, over low heat, stirring occasionally, for about 20 minutes, until the mixture is dark and thickened. Stir in the salt and mix well. Serve warm or at room temperature as a relish.

Makes about 2 cups

Fat for Thought

Though we tend to think of condiments in terms of the flavors they provide—salty, tangy, sweet-and-sour, piquant—we cannot overlook the fact that many are found in the form of fats and oils. These oil- or fat-based products are used in two ways: first, to convey or provide flavor, and second, to add richness and textural enhancement. Fat is valuable because it contains its own complex flavor compounds and also enhances and expands the flavors in other foods. In terms of texture, fats and oils contribute rich silky coating or enrobing qualities, adding smooth, unctuous characteristics, a sensual "mouth-feel" that signals gastronomic as well as nutritional enrichment. Think of the unique flavors of Asian sesame oil, extra-virgin olive oil, delicate walnut oil, or cold-pressed peanut oil. Combine these with additional seasonings and the system grows ever more complex, resulting in products like piri-piri, the spicy garlic-flavored olive oil of the Portuguese, the hot chile oils of China, the rich spice- and herb-infused oils that have recently become so popular. Another popular fat-based condiment is mayonnaise, the classic egg-and-oil emulsion that adds flavor, moisture, and richness to sandwiches, salads, and spreads. Many cultures use animal fats and dairy products as condimental agents, enriching their cooked foods with a pat of butter, a dollop of sour cream, or a sprinkle of grated cheese. Whether you are eating a BLT with mayo or a soupe au pistou, a baked potato with butter or sour cream or fish cakes with tartar sauce, you are dressing up the food with a condiment based on oil or fat—food for thought if you're counting calories or cholesterol!

Tapenade with Tomatoes

The tapenade is a popular sauce from the south of France; its name derives from an ancient Provençal word for "caper," one of the critical ingredients. This recipe omits the pounded olives that are frequently included, and mixes the tapenade with chopped tomatoes to make an intense and highly flavored sauce to serve with cold meat, as a spread for fresh crusty peasant bread, or as a delicious quick sauce for hot pasta.

2 tablespoons capers, drained
1 2-ounce can anchovies, packed in olive oil
3 cloves garlic, crushed
1 cup finely chopped fresh ripe tomatoes
Small handful finely chopped flat-leaf parsley
2 tablespoons olive oil

1. Mash the capers and the anchovies, with their oil, into a coarse paste. Stir in the crushed garlic and mix well.
2. Add the anchovy mixture to the chopped tomatoes, then stir in the parsley and the olive oil and mix well.

Makes about 1½ cups

Saffron and Tomato Ali-Oli

The Mediterranean is a hotbed of garlic sauces, from the agliata of Italy to the aioli of southern France to the ali-oli of Spain to the skorthalia of Greece. They are based on a variety of ingredients—bread, potatoes, nuts, and eggs—but the two constants are garlic and olive oil, both used in generous amounts. This Spanish version contains almonds, tomato, and saffron, which give it its rich ruddy color. It is traditionally eaten with simple boiled vegetables like potatoes, carrots, onions, and artichokes, and it is particularly good with steamed mussels and shrimp, or as a sauce for grilled or fried fish or squid.

2 tablespoons fresh lemon juice
1/2 teaspoon saffron threads
1 hard-cooked egg yolk
1 medium tomato, coarsely chopped
4 cloves garlic
1/4 cup slivered almonds
1/4 teaspoon salt
Good dash cayenne pepper
1/2 teaspoon sherry vinegar
1/2 cup olive oil

1. Combine the lemon juice and the saffron and let stand for 15–20 minutes.

2. In a food processor, combine the egg yolk, the tomato, the garlic, the almonds, the salt, the cayenne, and the vinegar. Process into a paste.

3. Add the lemon and saffron and process until smooth. With the machine running, slowly add the oil in a steady stream until it is completely blended in.

Makes about 1 cup

Olive, Walnut, and Garlic Pesto

Traditional Mediterranean ingredients are blended into an extremely rich and versatile seasoning sauce. Serve it with crackers, or spread it on thin slices of baguette and heat in the oven for a few minutes. Like the more familiar basil-and-pine nut pesto, this can be served as a sauce for cold meats, spooned into hot soup as a last-minute flavor enhancement, or tossed with hot cooked pasta.

½ cup (about 12–15) brine-cured black olives, pitted
⅓ cup freshly toasted walnuts
4 cloves garlic
1 tablespoon fresh lemon juice
Small handful flat-leaf parsley
¼ cup olive oil

1. In a food processor, combine the olives, the walnuts, the garlic, and the lemon juice. Process into a coarse paste, then add the parsley and process lightly.
2. With the machine running, add the olive oil in a small, steady stream until it is well blended.

Makes about 1 cup

Roasted Eggplant, Garlic, and Pepper Puree

The simplest of vegetables, roasted in their skins for rich, mellow flavor, then pureed to make a savory dip that tastes of the Mediterranean, the Balkans, and the Middle East. Serve this at room temperature as a spread for bread or crackers, as a dip for raw and cooked vegetables, or as a relish for cold meats.

1 medium to large eggplant
4 sweet red peppers
1 head garlic
2 tablespoons olive oil
1 tablespoon red wine vinegar
½ teaspoon salt
Plenty of freshly ground black pepper
Additional olive oil, for garnish

1. To roast the vegetables: Preheat the oven to 450° F. With a sharp knife, make several slits in the eggplant. Place the eggplant and the peppers on a baking tray. Cut a slice about ¼ inch thick off the top of the head of garlic; wrap the garlic loosely with aluminum foil.

2. Roast the vegetables for about 30–40 minutes. Turn the peppers occasionally so that they blacken on all sides; test the eggplant for softness by poking it with a sharp knife.

3. Let the eggplant cool completely, then peel off the skin and discard. Remove the peppers from the oven and place in a paper or plastic bag; let stand for 15–20 minutes, then slip off the skins and remove the seeds from inside the peppers. Let the garlic cool completely, then squeeze out the soft pulp from the skin.

4. In a food processor, combine the skinned roasted eggplant, the skinned peppers, the garlic puree, the oil, the vinegar, the salt, and the pepper. Puree until smooth. Taste for salt.

5. Serve the puree at room temperature; drizzle a little olive oil over the top.

Makes about 2 cups

Mixed Vegetable Caponata

The caponata is a Sicilian stewed vegetable relish that always contains eggplant, olive oil, and vinegar; depending on availability or the cook's whim, a number of other vegetables can be added. It is hard to make a small amount of caponata, but it keeps well, covered, in the refrigerator, and makes a fine addition to the buffet table or a backyard barbecue.

1 large onion, chopped
1 large eggplant, peeled and diced (about 4 cups diced)
2 sweet red and/or green peppers, seeded and diced
2 ribs celery, diced
1 small knob fresh fennel, diced (about 1 cup)
1 medium zucchini, diced (about 1 cup)
2 cups coarsely chopped or sliced mushrooms
2 peperoncini (Italian long hot green peppers),
    finely chopped
1 cup coarsely chopped fresh or canned tomatoes
6 cloves garlic, minced
1/3 cup olive oil
1/3 cup balsamic vinegar
1 teaspoon salt
1/4 teaspoon freshly ground black pepper
2 tablespoons capers, drained
1/2 cup oil-cured black olives, preferably Sicilian
Good handful coarsely chopped fresh basil

1. In a very large pot, combine the vegetables, the garlic, the oil, and the vinegar. Cook, uncovered, over low to medium heat, stirring occasionally, for about 1–1¼ hours, until the mixture is soft and most of the liquid has cooked away.

2. Stir in the salt, pepper, capers, olives, and basil. Mix well, then taste, and adjust the seasoning if necessary. Serve the caponata at room temperature with bread or crackers, or as a relish or vegetable side dish.

Makes about 6 cups

Spiced Rhubarb Sauce

In the highlands of Central Asia, there persists a tradition of cooking and saucing savory dishes with a variety of fruits—apple, plum, pomegranate, and quince. Garden rhubarb, thought to have originated in Siberia, is cooked in meat stews, called "koresh" in Iran, and made into rich sauces to serve with grilled meats and kabobs. Try this tangy red sauce as a glaze and sauce for roast duck, ham, or sausages.

1 pound rhubarb
1 medium onion, finely chopped
¼ cup fresh lemon juice
¼ cup water
1 teaspoon paprika
2 tablespoons sugar
2 teaspoons cinnamon
¼ cup grenadine (pomegranate) syrup
Small handful finely chopped fresh coriander leaf

1. Wash and trim the rhubarb, then dice. You should have about 3 cups diced fruit.
2. In a heavy pot, combine the rhubarb, the onion, the lemon juice, the water, and the paprika. Bring to the simmer, then cook, uncovered, over low heat, stirring from time to time, about 15–20 minutes, or until the mixture is very soft and thick.
3. Add the sugar, the cinnamon, and the grenadine and mix well. Stir over low heat for a few more minutes. Remove from the heat and stir in the coriander. The sauce will keep well, covered, in the refrigerator.

Makes about 2 cups

Sweet and Spicy Onion-Tomato Jam

Less pungent than typical Indian chutneys and more complex than our familiar ketchup, this thick, rich, sweet, and spicy jam is but one member of a whole family of onion-tomato sauces cooked down into vividly colored, intensely flavored relishes. Use it as a condiment for grilled and roasted meat or sausage, as a flavor enhancement for soups and sauces, or as a spread on sandwiches, crisp crackers, or thin slices of hot crusty bread.

2 tablespoons olive or vegetable oil
3 cups finely chopped onion
1/4 cup minced elephant garlic
3 cups finely chopped fresh tomatoes
2 tablespoons brown sugar
1/4 cup cider vinegar
1/2 teaspoon salt
Good dash cayenne pepper, or more to taste

1. In a heavy pot or skillet, combine the oil and the onion. Cook over low heat, stirring occasionally, for about 30 minutes, or until the onion is very soft and a rich golden color.

2. Add all the remaining ingredients, mix well, then bring to the simmer and cook, uncovered, over low heat, stirring from time to time, for about 1 hour, until the mixture is very thick and soft and all the liquid has cooked away.

3. Cool completely, then store in a covered jar in the refrigerator. Tightly covered, it will keep for many weeks.

Makes about 3 cups

Caramelized Sweet Pepper Relish

This is a delicious and versatile mixture; you can use it as a relish to serve with meat or poultry, as a spread for crackers or French bread, or as a sensational sandwich garnish. It is important to choose thick, fleshy peppers (the yellow ones are particularly good here), and to cook them very slowly in the oil, so that the natural sugar in them is fully caramelized.

1 large onion, coarsely chopped
6–8 large fleshy sweet peppers, mostly red and yellow, but a
    few green for color, seeded and cut into small chunks
¼ cup olive oil
1–2 teaspoons balsamic vinegar
Salt and freshly ground pepper to taste

1. In a large skillet, combine the onion, the peppers, and the oil. (It may seem like a great quantity of peppers at first, but they will cook down.) Cook over low heat, stirring occasionally, for about 40–50 minutes, until the peppers are richly browned and very soft.

2. Add the vinegar and quickly scrape up all the browned bits at the bottom of the skillet. Cook for a few more minutes, stirring, then add salt and pepper to taste. The relish will keep well, covered, in the refrigerator for a week or two.

Makes about 3 cups

Roasted Green Pepper and Avocado "Mayonnaise"

Just as roasting brings out the sweet rich flavor of red peppers, so too does it enhance the unique flavor of green peppers and chiles. This sauce, based on the traditional foods and flavors of Mexico, is not a true mayonnaise because it does not contain eggs; the creamy texture is provided by avocado. Try the sauce as a sandwich spread (great with grilled eggplant), as a condiment for cold or grilled meats, or as a dip for corn chips and vegetables.

2 medium green peppers, or 2 poblano chiles
1–2 jalapeños
½ small ripe avocado
3 cloves garlic
3–4 tablespoons fresh cilantro
1 teaspoon fresh lime juice
¼ cup olive oil
½ teaspoon salt

1. Roast the green peppers and the jalapeños on a tray in a hot (450° F.) oven. Remove the jalapeños when they are just beginning to brown; continue roasting the peppers until they are blackened on all sides, about 30 minutes. Or char the peppers and the chiles over a gas flame or on a charcoal grill. Place the hot roasted peppers in a paper or plastic bag to steam.

2. When the green peppers are cool, remove and discard the skin, the stem, and the seeds. With a sharp knife, scrape the seeds from the jalapeños.

3. In a food processor, combine the roasted green peppers, the jalapeños, the avocado, the garlic, the cilantro, and the lime juice. Puree until smooth. With the machine still running, slowly pour in the olive oil in a small stream, until completely blended and smooth. Stir in the salt and mix well.

Makes about 1 cup

Atjar
(Indonesian Mixed Vegetable Pickle)

Pickling is a nearly universal practice, and there are few cultures that do not produce pickles of some kind—fruits and vegetables preserved with salt and acid and flavored with sugar, spices, and aromatics. Many of our popular pickles, like half-sours and garlic dills, come from Europe, but many others have their origin in the rich pickle tradition of Asia; familiar favorites like chowchow and piccalilly are clearly related to products like this Indonesian vegetable pickle, tinted yellow with turmeric and flavored with ginger and hot pepper.

½ pound green beans, flat beans, or Chinese long beans, cut into 1-inch lengths
2 large carrots, thickly sliced on the diagonal
2 cups small cauliflower florets
1 cup coarsely shredded or sliced cabbage
1 cup white vinegar
¼ cup sugar
1 teaspoon turmeric
2 tablespoons julienne strips fresh gingerroot
1–2 fresh hot chiles, seeded and cut into julienne strips
¼ teaspoon cayenne or other hot-pepper powder
1 large clove elephant garlic, thinly sliced
1 large onion, cut into eighths, then separated into leaves
1 large red or green sweet pepper, seeded and cut into chunks
2 medium cucumbers, peeled, seeded, and cut into medium strips

1. In a large pot, cook the beans and the carrots in boiling water for 3–4 minutes. Add the cauliflower and cabbage and cook for 1 minute more. Drain the vegetables and set aside.
2. In the same pot, combine the vinegar, the sugar, the turmeric, the gingerroot, the fresh chiles, the cayenne, and the garlic. Bring to the simmer and cook for a few minutes.

3. Add the onion, the peppers, and the cucumbers, mix well, and bring just to the simmer. Stir in the reserved blanched vegetables and mix well.

4. Remove from the heat and let cool. Store, covered, in the refrigerator for a day or two before serving, turning the vegetables in the marinade once or twice. These vegetables will keep well, covered, in the refrigerator.

Makes about 4 cups

Tangy Beet and Horseradish Relish

In Northern Europe, climate and a short growing season dictate a dependence on hardy root vegetables—onions, potatoes, turnips, carrots—as well as other cool-weather crops, like cabbage. Beets are an ancient staple, featured in hearty soups, such as borscht, and in a variety of salad and vegetable dishes. They have a long and close relationship with horseradish, another root vegetable of the mustard family, which has a pungent flavor and sinus-clearing aroma. The popularity of horseradish as a condiment indicates that even where people do not have access to such stimulating seasonings as black pepper or chile, they find ingredients to provide excitement for their basic fare.

2 cups diced cooked beets
1 small onion, finely chopped
3–4 tablespoons freshly grated horseradish
¼ cup cider vinegar
1 tablespoon sugar
Good dash salt, or to taste

Combine all the ingredients and mix thoroughly. Let stand, covered, in the refrigerator for a day or two before serving. The relish will keep for weeks, covered, in the refrigerator.

Makes about 2 cups

Dilled Mustard-Horseradish Sauce

From the mustard-and-horseradish cultures of Northern and Central Europe comes this delightfully pungent condiment, commonly used as a sauce or spread for meats, cold cuts, and sandwiches. It also goes nicely with cold poached salmon and smoked fish. For an attractive brunch dish, arrange a platter with a variety of smoked fishes, sliced cucumber, tomato, sliced cooked potato, and hard-cooked eggs; garnish with sprigs of fresh dill and serve the sauce on the side.

½ cup sour cream
¼ cup finely grated fresh horseradish
3 tablespoons Dijon mustard
¼ cup finely snipped fresh dill

Combine all the ingredients and mix thoroughly. If the mixture seems too thick, it can be thinned with a little light cream. The sauce will keep well, tightly covered in the refrigerator, for a week or two.

Makes about 1 cup

Mango Ketchup

America's entry in the condiment sweepstakes is an all-time winner, the offspring of the union between an English tradition of tangy sauces called "ketchups" and an indigenous New World fruit, the tomato, with its substantial body and unprecedented brilliant red color. English ketchups were originally made from a variety of fruits, berries, vegetables, even walnuts, and frequently took the form of thin, dark, strained liquids. This mango ketchup has the same smooth thick consistency as its tomato cousin, with a rich golden color and a bright fruity flavor.

3–4 large fully ripe mangoes
1 cup cider vinegar
½ cup sugar
1 medium onion, coarsely chopped
3–4 cloves garlic, chopped or sliced
½ teaspoon crushed dried hot peppers
½ teaspoon cinnamon
½ teaspoon ground ginger

1. Cut the mango flesh off the pit; peel the flesh and cut it into chunks.

2. Combine the mango and all the other ingredients in a heavy saucepan. Bring to the boil, then simmer, uncovered, over low heat, stirring occasionally, for about 20 minutes, until the mango is very soft.

3. Remove from the heat and let cool slightly. In a blender or food processor, puree the mixture until it is smooth.

4. Store the ketchup in tightly covered jars in the refrigerator. It will keep for months. Excellent with ham, sausage, or any grilled or roasted meat and poultry.

Makes about 4 cups

Chapter Nine

Layered, Spread, Sandwiched, and Stuffed

Sink your teeth into a forkful of lasagne and savor its luscious layers of tender pasta, creamy cheese, and rich, chunky sauce. Wrap your mouth around a chicken-salad club and take off on a textural adventure of crisp toast, crunchy bacon, creamy chicken, and juicy tomato. Take a bite of a crispy golden fried spring roll, filled with tender vegetables and seafood and dipped into a tangy sweet-and-sour sauce. Nowhere is human culinary ingenuity and playfulness more evident than in these stuffed and layered foods, complex constructions of many different elements. This kind of cooking is surely a rather recent development in culinary history, because it presumes a wide variety of ingredients and equipment and a number of separately prepared foods deliberately orchestrated into elaborate compositions of color, flavor, and texture. Despite clear differences in ingredients and style, these products turn up in remarkably similar forms in cuisines throughout the world, evidence once again of the astonishing consistency of the cooking animal. And although they may not be the earliest of our kitchen accomplishments, many are venerable, and all are hugely enjoyed.

The ancient Greeks relished a dish of simmered squid stuffed with ground meat; imperial Romans, legendary stuffers of both foods and themselves, enjoyed such exotica as dormice stuffed with spiced meat and pine nuts, and pastry eggs stuffed with tiny birds called fig-peckers, a special delicacy. Medieval Europe delighted in the practice of stuffing large animals and birds with a variety of ingredients, including smaller animals and birds, while at the same time developing an elaborate tradition of dough-wrapped and stuffed foods—pies, pastries, breads, savory tarts, and turnovers.

In Asia, particularly in China, there is a long history of stuffed and wrapped foods, all sorts of buns, pancakes, dumplings, and rolls, steamed, boiled, or fried, and filled with every kind of vegetable, bean, meat, and seafood. India maintains an ancient tradition of spiced filled pastries, both savory and sweet; and the Middle East is an age-old hearth of stuffed fruits and vegetables—vine leaves, cabbage, eggplant, onions. When the foods of the New World became available to the Old, a wealth of novel vegetable containers—peppers, tomatoes, potatoes, squash—added delicious new dimensions to the established tradition.

There is a real sense in which a wonton is a ravioli is a kreplach, just as an empanada is the same as a spring roll or a samosa, and a quiche equivalent to (horrors!) a tamale pie. Despite differences in ingredients, these wrapped, stuffed, and layered products are very much alike, manifesting a similar structure, a similar culinary strategy, and a similar aesthetic. Many of them undoubtedly have a common history: the Romanian musaca is related to the Greek and Turkish moussaka, and all three may have originated in the same tradition that produced lasagne and eggplant parmigiana. But others are clearly separate and unique: it is very unlikely that Japanese sushi and Greek dolmathes have a common origin, yet they are very much alike in their structure and their appeal.

Something in the human mind takes immense pleasure in putting known things together in new and exciting ways, in playing with food to create dishes that, though innovative, turn out remarkably alike all over the world. There is clearly something very attractive and satisfying about these compound products, making them such a popular part of the universal food experience and allowing them, more than other preparations, to cross cultural boundaries. The reasons for their appeal are many—novelty, surprise (remember the four-and-twenty blackbirds baked in a pie?), pleasing simultaneous experiences of flavor and texture, and the fact that many of these dishes are pick-uppable savory snacks, quick, easy, and fun to eat.

Here in America, we are heirs to this rich legacy of stuffed, spread, and sandwiched food, and we continue to elaborate it in a complex tradition unique to these shores. We are the undisputed masters of the sandwich, a form that came to us from England as slices of meat or cheese enclosed between two slices of bread, and that burgeoned here into the extraordinary variety of hoagies, clubs, Reubens, muffulettas, and Big Macs that are the well-loved stuff of our daily diets. Hot dogs, ham and cheese on rye, bagels and cream cheese, tofu and sprouts in pita pockets—all are as American as apple pie, though they, like the pie, have their origins in distant lands and different times.

A knish for you, a quesadilla for me—who could ask for anything more?

RECIPES

Enchilada Casserole with Green Chile–Tomatillo Sauce (Mexican)
Afghani Meat and Noodle Casserole
Baked Vegetable Lasagne (Italian)
Chicken Biryani (Indian)
Romanian Vegetable and Noodle Musaca
Onion Kulcha (Indian)
Ham and Cheese on Rye in Casserole (Anglo-American)
Rosemary Focaccia with Olives, Garlic, and Pepper (Italian)
Chinese Scallion Pancakes
Lahmajun (Armenian Meat Pies)
Panuchos (Mexican)
Taverna Shrimp (Greek)
Mushroom and Black Bean Burritos with Chile Cream Sauce
    (Mexican)
Garlic Potato Knishes (Eastern European Jewish)
Vegetable Samosas (Indian)
Grilled Vegetable Quesadillas (Mexican)
Spiced Eggplant Wrapped in Phyllo (Middle Eastern)
Coulibiac of Fresh Salmon with Leeks and Dill (Russian)
Afghani Leek Dumplings with Minted Yogurt
Fragrant Shrimp-Basil Rolls (Thai)
Southwestern-Style Shepherd's Pie
Four-Onion and Cheese Tart (French)
Pastel de Camarones (Creole Shrimp and Corn Pie)
Lettuce Leaf Rolls with Spiced Chicken and Chinese Sausage (Chinese)
Peppers Stuffed with Chicken, Rice, and Walnuts (Middle Eastern)
Indian Potato-Stuffed Peppers
Balkan Vegetable-Stuffed Cabbage Rolls
Chinese Stuffed Cabbage
Norimake with Smoked Salmon (Japanese)

Enchilada Casserole with Green Chile–Tomatillo Sauce

In the Mexican tradition, "enchilada" means anything garnished or sauced with chiles, which, of course, is practically everything; the term is used more specifically for dishes in which tortillas are cooked with chile sauce. The tortillas can be rolled or folded or, as in this case, layered with a tasty chicken-and-vegetable filling, green-chile-and-tomatillo sauce, and melted cheese.

For the filling

2 tablespoons vegetable oil

1 medium onion, thinly sliced

2 cloves garlic, minced

1 medium sweet red pepper, seeded and cut into thin strips

1 medium green bell pepper, seeded and cut into thin strips

1 medium zucchini, cut into strips

2 cups cooked chicken, coarsely shredded or cut into strips

½ teaspoon salt

½ teaspoon dried oregano

For the sauce

1 medium onion, chopped

3 cloves garlic, minced

1 serrano chile, seeded and minced

1 poblano chile or 1 large green pepper, seeded and chopped

2 tablespoons vegetable oil

½ pound fresh tomatillos, husked and quartered
   (about 2 cups)

½ cup water

½ teaspoon dried oregano

¼ teaspoon salt

Good handful chopped fresh cilantro

10 corn tortillas

2 cups (8 ounces) shredded jack or mild Cheddar cheese

(continued)

1. Make the filling: In a large skillet, heat the oil and sauté the onion, garlic, peppers, and zucchini over moderate heat, stirring, until the onions are just wilted. Add the chicken, salt, and oregano and mix well. Remove from the heat.

2. Make the sauce: In a medium saucepan, sauté the onion, garlic, and chiles in the oil over moderate heat, stirring, until the vegetables are limp and the onion is beginning to turn golden.

3. Add the tomatillos, water, and oregano, bring to the simmer, then cook, uncovered, over low heat for about 10 minutes, or until the tomatillos are soft.

4. Let the sauce cool slightly, then puree coarsely in a blender or food processor. Stir in the salt and the chopped cilantro.

5. Preheat the oven to 400° F. Lightly grease a 13 × 9 × 2-inch baking pan or casserole. Spoon about ½ cup of the sauce evenly over the bottom of the pan. Place 5 tortillas, torn to fit, in a layer over the sauce. Spread the chicken-vegetable mixture evenly over the tortillas. Top the chicken layer with the remaining tortillas.

6. Spoon the remaining sauce evenly over the tortillas. Sprinkle the cheese evenly over the top.

7. Bake the casserole for about 30 minutes, until the cheese is bubbly.

Serves 6

NOTE: The green chile–tomatillo sauce is also excellent as a dip for other foods, like Costa Rican Chicken-Tortilla Nuggets (page 173). The recipe makes about 2 cups sauce.

Afghani Meat and Noodle Casserole

Layers of fat noodles, spiced meat with tomato sauce, sautéed leeks, and tangy yogurt go into this traditional dish from Afghanistan, which bears a striking resemblance to layered baked casseroles from all over the world. Serve it with a green salad or a cooked green vegetable.

2 cups plain yogurt
2 large leeks, mostly white parts, coarsely chopped
3 tablespoons butter
1 pound lean ground beef or lamb
2 large onions, coarsely chopped
2 cups tomato sauce
1/2 teaspoon salt
1 teaspoon ground coriander
1 teaspoon ground cumin
Several good grinds black pepper
1/4 teaspoon cayenne pepper
12 ounces pot-pie noodle squares, or coarsely broken
    lasagne noodles
3 cloves garlic, crushed
1 tablespoon crushed dried mint

1. Line a strainer or colander with cheesecloth. Spoon the yogurt into the strainer and let stand for 1–2 hours to drain out excess liquid.

2. In a medium skillet, sauté the leeks in 2 tablespoons of the butter over moderate heat, stirring occasionally, until the leeks are soft. Remove the leeks from the pan and set aside.

3. In the same pan, brown the ground meat over high heat, breaking up the meat as it cooks. When all the pink color has disappeared, remove the meat from the pan with a slotted spoon and set aside. Pour off and discard all the fat in the pan.

4. In the same pan, sauté the onions in the remaining 1 tablespoon of butter over moderate heat, stirring, until the onions are soft and just beginning to turn golden.

(continued)

5. Add the reserved meat, tomato sauce, salt, coriander, cumin, black pepper, and cayenne pepper, and mix well. Bring to the simmer, then cook over low heat, uncovered, for about 20–30 minutes, until the mixture is thick. Taste for salt and cayenne, and adjust the seasoning if necessary.

6. Cook the noodles in boiling salted water according to package instructions until just tender but still firm. Drain, rinse in cold water, then drain again.

7. Combine the drained yogurt and the garlic and mix thoroughly.

8. Preheat the oven to 350° F. Lightly butter a 13 × 9 × 2-inch baking pan or lasagne pan. Spread half of the yogurt over the bottom of the pan. Layer half of the noodles over the yogurt. Spoon half of the meat sauce over the noodles. Spoon the reserved leeks over the meat sauce. Repeat with another layer each of yogurt, noodles, and meat sauce. Sprinkle the crushed mint all over the final layer of meat sauce.

9. Cover the casserole with foil and bake for 30–35 minutes. Let stand for 5–10 minutes before serving.

Serves 4–6

Baked Vegetable Lasagne

Of the great variety of layered ethnic dishes, lasagne is probably the most familiar, loved for its toothsome layers of pasta, cheese, and savory sauce. The possibility for variation is great; this one substitutes a number of vegetables for the traditional meat and sausage—fresh spinach and basil in the ricotta layer, mushrooms and zucchini in the tomato sauce. Like most layered dishes, this one requires a good deal of preparation, but it can be done early in the day and the assembled lasagne popped into the oven just before dinner.

1 medium onion, coarsely chopped
2 tablespoons olive oil
3 cloves garlic, minced
3 cups canned crushed tomatoes

1½ teaspoons salt

½ teaspoon dried oregano

Several good grinds black pepper

2 cups sliced mushrooms

1 cup sliced zucchini

3–4 tablespoons minced flat-leaf parsley

2 eggs

6–8 ounces fresh spinach, trimmed, washed, and dried

1 cup loosely packed fresh basil leaves

2 cups ricotta cheese

¼ cup freshly grated Parmesan cheese

¼ teaspoon grated nutmeg

12–16 ounces lasagne noodles

3 cups (12 ounces) shredded mozzarella

1. In a medium saucepan, sauté the onion in the oil over moderate heat, stirring, until the onion becomes translucent. Stir in the garlic and cook for a few minutes more.

2. Add the tomatoes, ½ teaspoon of the salt, the oregano, and some pepper, bring to the simmer, then cook, uncovered, over low heat for about 15 minutes. Add the mushrooms and zucchini, mix well, and cook for another 10 minutes. Stir in the parsley and remove from the heat.

3. In a food processor, combine the eggs, the spinach, and the basil, and process coarsely. Add the ricotta, the Parmesan, the remaining salt, the nutmeg, and some more pepper, and process until smooth. Preheat oven to 375° F.

4. Cook the noodles in boiling salted water for 10–12 minutes, until just tender but still firm. Drain, rinse in cold water, then drain again.

5. Grease a lasagne pan or 13 × 9 × 2–inch baking dish. Spoon in just enough tomato sauce to film the bottom of the pan lightly.

6. Make a layer of slightly overlapping noodles. Spoon half of the ricotta mixture evenly over the noodles.

7. Make another layer of noodles; spoon half the tomato sauce over the noodles, then sprinkle half of the mozzarella over the tomato sauce.

(continued)

8. Repeat with another layer of noodles, then the remaining ricotta, a fourth layer of noodles, and the remaining sauce. Sprinkle the rest of the mozzarella over the sauce.

9. Cover the pan with foil, and bake for 30 minutes. Uncover the pan and bake for 15–20 minutes more. Remove the lasagne from the oven, let stand for 5 minutes, then cut in squares to serve.

Serves 6

Chicken Biryani

The biryani is a festive Indian layered dish of flavored rice and spiced meat, extravagantly garnished with nuts, fruit, and other costly ingredients. In this one, two layers of coconut-saffron rice surround a rich chicken curry, all embellished with raisins and buttered cashews.

½ cup plus 2 tablespoons cashew butts (coarsely broken
    and halved nuts)
1 tablespoon butter

For the rice

1 medium onion, finely chopped
2 tablespoons butter or ghee
1½ cups basmati rice
1 cup unsweetened coconut milk
1 cup chicken stock
1 teaspoon saffron threads
¼ teaspoon salt
½ cup golden raisins

For the chicken curry

1 medium onion, finely chopped
1 tablespoon finely minced gingerroot

½ teaspoon crushed dried hot peppers
2 tablespoons vegetable oil
2 teaspoons ground coriander
1 teaspoon ground cumin
1 teaspoon paprika
½ teaspoon cinnamon
½ teaspoon ground cardamom
½ teaspoon salt
Several good grinds black pepper
1½ pounds boneless chicken, cut into ½-inch pieces
1 tablespoon fresh lime juice
½ cup plain yogurt

½ cup chicken stock
Chopped fresh coriander, for garnish, if desired

1. In a small skillet, sauté the cashews in the butter, stirring, until the nuts are just lightly browned. Remove from the heat and set aside.

2. In a medium saucepan, sauté the onion in the butter until the onion becomes translucent. Add the rice and stir it into the onions for a few minutes.

3. Add the coconut milk, the 1 cup of stock, the saffron, the salt, and the raisins. Cover and cook over low heat for 15–20 minutes, until all the liquid has been absorbed. Stir in all but 2 tablespoons of the nuts. Let the rice stand, covered, while you prepare the chicken curry.

4. In a large skillet, sauté the onion, gingerroot, and hot peppers in the oil until the onions wilt and the mixture becomes aromatic. Stir in the spices, salt, and pepper, and stir for a few minutes.

5. Add the chicken pieces and stir them into the spice mixture, turning to brown lightly. Add the lime juice and yogurt, mix well, and cook for a few minutes. Preheat the oven to 375° F.

6. Butter a deep 2½–3-quart casserole. Spoon half of the rice into the casserole, then spoon all the chicken and sauce over the rice.

(continued)

Top the chicken with the remaining rice, making a smooth layer. Pour in the additional ½ cup of stock.

7. Cover the casserole and bake for about 45 minutes. Garnish the top with the remaining 2 tablespoons nuts, and with some chopped coriander, if desired.

Serves 6

Romanian Vegetable and Noodle Musaca

The musaca (or moussaka) is a traditional dish that exists in countless forms throughout Greece, the Balkans, and Turkey. It can contain meat, vegetables, pasta, and sauce, but it is always prepared and baked in layers, frequently with a cheese- or milk-based topping. This Romanian version makes a well-seasoned and satisfying vegetarian meal.

1 medium onion, coarsely chopped

1 medium green pepper, seeded and diced

1–2 fresh hot green chile peppers, seeded and minced

4 cloves garlic, minced

2 tablespoons olive oil

1 small eggplant, peeled and diced (about 2 cups diced)

1 carrot, diced

1 cup finely chopped cabbage

1 medium zucchini, diced

2 cups coarsely chopped mushrooms

1 28-ounce can crushed tomatoes

1 teaspoon salt

¼ cup finely snipped fresh dill

⅛ teaspoon freshly ground black pepper

1 pound fine egg noodles

2 tablespoons butter

8 ounces farmer cheese

2 eggs

½ cup milk

3 tablespoons freshly grated Parmesan

3 tablespoons crumbled feta cheese

Paprika

1. In a large skillet or pot, sauté the onion, the sweet and hot peppers, and the garlic in the oil over moderate heat, stirring occasionally, until the onion turns limp and translucent.

2. Add the eggplant and sauté, stirring, until it is just lightly browned.

3. Add all the other vegetables and the tomatoes, then bring to the simmer and cook, uncovered, over low heat for about 45 minutes, stirring from time to time, until the vegetables are soft and most of the liquid has cooked away. Stir in ½ teaspoon of the salt, the dill, and the pepper and mix well. Taste for salt and adjust seasoning, if necessary.

4. Cook the noodles in boiling salted water for 1–2 minutes, until just tender. Drain, then return to the pot and toss while still hot with the butter and about ¼ teaspoon of salt.

5. Spoon the noodles evenly into a buttered 13 × 9 × 2-inch baking pan or lasagne pan. Spoon the vegetable mixture over the noodles. Preheat the oven to 350° F.

6. In a blender or food processor, combine the farmer cheese, the eggs, the milk, the Parmesan, the feta, about ¼ teaspoon of salt, and several good grinds of black pepper. Blend until smooth.

7. Spoon the cheese mixture evenly over the vegetables; gently poke a few holes with a spoon to let some of the sauce penetrate the layers. Sprinkle the cheese layer with paprika.

8. Bake the musaca for 50–60 minutes, until it is firm and lightly browned.

Serves 6–8

Onion Kulcha

India is the center of an old and elaborate bread tradition, one that includes the simplest griddle-cooked chapatis, the tandoori-baked nan and roti, and a great variety of stuffed, rolled, and spiced products. The kulcha is a flat round or oval loaf, enriched with butter and yogurt, and garnished with buttery onions and kalongi, black onion seeds, which have a unique flavor and are available in Middle Eastern and Indian groceries. If you can't get the kalongi, you can substitute poppy or sesame seeds. The kulcha is best hot from the oven, with kabobs, salads, and curries.

1 teaspoon sugar
1 cup warm water
1 envelope active dry yeast
2 tablespoons butter or ghee
½ cup plain yogurt
2 teaspoons salt
3½–4 cups flour
3 tablespoons (about) softened butter
1 large onion, finely chopped
2–3 teaspoons kalongi seeds
Coarse (kosher) salt (optional)

1. In a mixing bowl, stir the sugar into the warm water; sprinkle the yeast over the water and let proof for 5–10 minutes.
2. In a small saucepan, combine the 2 tablespoons of butter or ghee, the yogurt, and the salt. Heat, stirring, just until the butter melts. Let cool slightly, then mix into the yeast mixture.
3. Add 2 cups of the flour to the liquid and mix thoroughly. Add in additional flour and knead to make a soft but nonsticky, elastic dough.
4. Form the dough into a ball and place in a lightly oiled bowl. Cover with a towel and let rise in a warm place for 1–1½ hours, or until doubled in bulk.
5. Punch the dough down, then divide into 6 equal balls. Let rest for about 15–20 minutes, lightly covered. Preheat the oven to 450° F.; if you are using baking tiles or stones, place them in the oven before heating.

6. On a floured board, roll each ball into a 6-inch round or oval loaf. Spread each loaf with about 1½ teaspoons of the softened butter. Sprinkle each loaf with some of the chopped onions and about ½ teaspoon of the seeds. With your fingers, lightly press the onions into the dough.

7. Bake the loaves on preheated stones or trays for about 8–10 minutes, until lightly golden brown. Sprinkle the hot breads with a bit of coarse salt, if desired.

Makes six 6-inch loaves

Ham and Cheese on Rye in Casserole

Hot baked dishes, constructed of layers of bread or pasta with savory sauces and bits of meat and vegetables, are produced in kitchens throughout the world. This hearty casserole, nice for a Sunday brunch or supper, comes from the English bread-pudding tradition and translates our favorite sandwich into a flavorful sit-down meal. Serve it with cole slaw or a crisp green salad.

2 extra-large eggs
1½ cups milk
1½ tablespoons Worcestershire sauce
¼ teaspoon cayenne pepper
1 teaspoon dry mustard
½ teaspoon grated nutmeg
½ teaspoon salt
8 slices stale firm-type rye or pumpernickel bread
1 cup slivered or coarsely chopped smoked ham
1 large tomato, sliced
Freshly ground black pepper to taste
2 cups shredded sharp Cheddar cheese

1. In a medium bowl, whisk the eggs thoroughly, then add the milk, Worcestershire, cayenne, mustard, nutmeg, and salt. Mix well.

(continued)

2. Generously butter a 1½–2-quart deep casserole. Place 4 slices of the bread in the bottom of the casserole; cut or tear the bread to fit, if necessary. Pour about a third of the egg mixture over the bread.

3. Sprinkle the ham evenly over the bread, then top with the tomato slices. Lightly salt and pepper the tomato. Cover the tomato layer with half of the shredded cheese.

4. Make another layer with the remaining bread. Pour the rest of the egg mixture over the bread. Sprinkle with the remaining cheese.

5. The casserole can be baked at this point, but it is better covered and refrigerated for 4–6 hours, or even overnight. Bring it to room temperature before baking. Bake in a preheated 350° F. oven for about 40–45 minutes, until it is puffed and nicely browned.

Serves 4

Rosemary Focaccia with Olives, Garlic, and Pepper

The American love affair with Italian food has produced some startling products and transformations. The classic bruschetta, long designated here as "garlic bread"—thick slices of soft white bread slathered with margarine and granulated garlic—is becoming bruschetta once again, although now in far more extravagant incarnations. Similarly, focaccia, originally a simply garnished rustic hearth-baked flatbread, is beginning more and more to resemble pizza, with its myriad of savory toppings. Here is a simple focaccia, crusty and full of traditional flavor. If you have a baking stone, now is the time to use it.

1 teaspoon sugar
1 cup warm water
1 envelope active dry yeast
1 teaspoon salt
1 tablespoon finely chopped fresh rosemary leaves
½ cup whole-wheat flour

2½ cups (about) all-purpose flour

1 tablespoon olive oil

3 cloves garlic, crushed

¼ teaspoon cracked black pepper

6–7 large Italian or Greek brine-cured black olives,
    pitted and coarsely chopped

1. In a large mixing bowl, mix the sugar into the water; sprinkle the yeast over the water and let proof for 5–10 minutes.

2. Stir in the salt, the rosemary, the whole-wheat flour, and 1 cup of the all-purpose flour, and mix thoroughly. Add in additional flour and knead to make a firm, nonsticky, elastic dough.

3. Form the dough into a ball, then place in a lightly oiled bowl. Cover and let rise for 1–1½ hours, or until doubled in bulk.

4. Punch the dough down, then spread it evenly in a 9- or 10-inch cake or baking pan.

5. Combine the olive oil and the garlic, and brush the mixture evenly over the dough. Sprinkle on the cracked pepper, then the olives. With your fingers, lightly press the olives into the dough. Preheat the oven to 400° F. If you are using a baking stone, place it in the oven to preheat.

6. Let the bread rise, lightly covered, for about ½ hour. Bake for 20–25 minutes, until nicely browned.

7. Remove the bread from the pan and let cool on a rack. Cut into wedges to serve.

Makes one 9-inch or 10-inch loaf

Chinese Scallion Pancakes

In the world's repertoire of spread and garnished breads, the Chinese scallion pancake is surely one of the most appealing—flaky, flavorful rounds fried to a golden crisp, to be eaten as a savory snack or as part of the appetizer course of a meal. Lard produces the flakiest pastry, but solid vegetable shortenings can be substituted, if desired.

3 cups flour
1 teaspoon salt
1 teaspoon sugar
1 cup warm water
6 tablespoons (about) lard (or Crisco), at room temperature
Coarse (kosher) salt
1½ cups (about) finely chopped scallions
Vegetable oil, for frying

1. In a mixing bowl, combine the flour, the salt, and the sugar and mix well. Add the water and knead to make a firm, nonsticky, elastic dough. Cover with a towel and let rest for ½ hour.

2. Divide the dough into 6 equal pieces. Roll each piece into a ball in your hands. On a floured board, roll each ball into a thin pancake, about 10 inches in diameter.

3. Spread each pancake with about 1 tablespoon of the lard. Sprinkle lightly with coarse salt. Sprinkle 3–4 tablespoons of the scallions over the pancake, to within about ½ inch of the edge.

4. Starting from the edge closest to you, roll up a pancake into a tight cylindrical roll. Squeeze and pinch the edges and the ends to seal. Roll the cylinder between your palms to form a long thin rope.

5. Holding the rope up by one end, twist it with your other hand until the whole rope is twisted. Form the twisted rope into a flat, tight coil on the table—it will look like a large snail. Roll the coil out into a 6–7-inch flat pancake.

6. Roll, twist, coil, and roll out the other 5 pancakes (see steps 4 and 5).

7. In a heavy skillet, heat about ⅓ cup of vegetable oil over moderate heat. Fry the pancakes 1 at a time, turning once, until golden brown on both sides. Drain on paper towels, then serve warm, cut in wedges.

Makes 6 pancakes

Lahmajun
(Armenian Meat Pies)

What pizza is to Italy, lahmajun is to Armenia—baked round flatbread spread with a savory ground-meat sauce. It can serve as a meal, as a snack, or as an hors d'oeuvre; in the Armenian community, it is one of the traditional foods served at festive occasions and communal events.

1 recipe Armenian Meat Sauce (page 155; but see step 1 below for variation)
1 teaspoon sugar
1 cup very warm water
1 envelope active dry yeast
1 tablespoon vegetable oil
3 cups flour
1 teaspoon salt
Plain yogurt and hot sauce, for garnish

1. Prepare the meat sauce as directed, but decrease the tomatoes from 2 cups to 1 cup. Cook the sauce until it is very thick and no liquid remains.

2. In a large mixing bowl, dissolve the sugar in the water. Sprinkle the yeast over the water and let proof for 5–10 minutes.

3. Add the oil to the yeast mixture, then stir in the flour and the salt. Knead thoroughly to form a smooth, nonsticky, elastic dough.

(continued)

4. Place the dough in a lightly greased bowl and let rise, covered, for 1–2 hours, or until it is doubled in bulk.

5. Punch the dough down, then form into two even portions. Roll each portion into a cylinder, and cut each one into 6 equal parts. Preheat the oven to 450° F.

6. On a floured board, roll each piece of dough into a round pancake about 5–6 inches in diameter. Place the rolled rounds onto a lightly greased baking sheet.

7. Place about 2 heaping tablespoons of meat filling on each round, then spread the filling evenly and press lightly into the dough. Continue with the remaining dough and filling.

8. Bake the lahmajun for 12–15 minutes, until nicely browned around the edges. Serve warm or at room temperature, with yogurt and hot sauce for garnish. For hors d'oeuvres cut each piece into quarters.

Makes twelve 5–6-inch pies

NOTE: The baked lahmajun can be frozen and reheated.

Panuchos

In the tradition of tacos, tostadas, and a whole host of stuffed, wrapped, and rolled finger foods made from tortillas are one of my all-time favorites, panuchos. They are little corn cakes made from masa harina (tortilla flour), filled with mashed black beans, then fried and topped with savory shredded pork and marinated sweet-and-sour onions. They are somewhat time-consuming to prepare, but well worth the effort.

For the onions

1 large onion, thinly sliced

⅓ cup cider vinegar

2 tablespoons sugar

For the meat (see Note)

1 medium onion, coarsely chopped

3 cloves garlic, minced

2 tablespoons vegetable oil

1 pound boneless pork butt or shoulder, cut into cubes

2 teaspoons ground achiote

¼ teaspoon ground cloves

½ teaspoon cinnamon

1 teaspoon dried oregano

½ cup orange juice

2 tablespoons fresh lemon juice

½ cup water

1 whole chipotle pepper (smoked jalapeño)

½ teaspoon salt

For the beans

1 small onion, chopped

1 tablespoon lard or vegetable oil

2 cups cooked or canned black beans, drained

Good dash salt, or to taste

½ teaspoon epazote (optional but good)

For the corn cakes

1 cup masa harina

½ cup warm water

Vegetable oil, for frying (about ½ cup)

1. Combine the sliced onion with the vinegar and sugar and mix well. Let stand for 3–4 hours, mixing occasionally.

2. In a heavy saucepan or skillet, sauté the medium chopped onion and the garlic in the oil over moderate heat, stirring, until the onion just begins to turn golden. Stir in the pork and the achiote, mix well, and cook, stirring, for a few minutes.

3. Add all the remaining meat ingredients, bring to the simmer, then cover and cook over low to moderate heat for about 1–1½ hours, or until the meat is very tender. If the mixture dries out too much during the cooking, add a little water.

4. When the meat is very tender, shred it coarsely with a knife and fork. Continue to cook it until most of the liquid has cooked away but the meat still has a little sauce. Remove and discard the chipotle.

5. In a small skillet, sauté the small chopped onion in the lard or oil until the onion turns golden. Mash the beans coarsely into the onion, then add the salt and the epazote. (You can also puree the beans in a food processor, if desired.)

6. Combine the masa harina with the water; knead lightly into a firm, nonsticky dough. Cover and let stand for ½ hour. Divide the dough into 12 equal pieces. The masa dough tends to dry out, so keep the dough and the rolled cakes lightly covered while you are working.

7. Roll each piece of dough into a ball with your hands, then roll out the ball between 2 pieces of waxed paper into a thin cake about 3 inches in diameter. Peel off the top layer of waxed paper. With your fingers, pinch up a small rim (about ¼ inch) all around the cake to form a small shell.

8. Spread about a tablespoon of the mashed beans evenly into the shell.

9. Heat the oil in a heavy frying pan. Fry the bean-filled shells over moderate heat for a few minutes, until the bottoms are golden brown and crisp. Remove the shells from the pan and drain on paper towels.

10. Top each panucho with some shredded pork, then garnish with the drained sweet-and-sour onions. Or serve the bean-filled corn cakes on a platter and pass bowls of the meat and onions for guests to add themselves.

Makes about 12 panuchos (serves 6)

NOTE: For the meat part of this dish, you can substitute the recipe for Mexican Carnitas (page 168).

Taverna Shrimp

Here is a Greek version of the open-face sandwich, shrimp in a rich oregano-scented tomato sauce spooned over slices of crusty bread and topped with partially melted feta cheese. Serve it on a warm summer evening with glasses of chilled retsina and life will taste good!

1 medium onion, finely chopped
4 cloves garlic, minced
2 tablespoons olive oil
2 cups canned crushed tomatoes
2 tablespoons fresh lemon juice
1 teaspoon crumbled dried oregano
1/4 teaspoon salt
Several good grinds black pepper
1 pound raw shrimp, peeled and deveined
1/2 cup crumbled feta cheese
4 large or 8 small slices crusty bread, cut 1/2 inch thick
Olive oil
Chopped parsley, Kalamata olives, and lemon wedges,
  for garnish

1. In a medium skillet, sauté the onion and the garlic in the oil over moderate heat, stirring, until the onion just softens and begins to turn golden.

2. Add the tomatoes, lemon juice, oregano, salt, and pepper, and mix well. Bring to the simmer, then cook, uncovered, over low heat, stirring occasionally, for 10–15 minutes.

3. Place the shrimp in the sauce and cook over low heat for a few minutes, just until the shrimp turn pink. Do not overcook. Sprinkle the crumbled feta over the mixture, then cover and remove from the heat.

4. Brush both sides of the bread slices lightly with olive oil. Place on a baking sheet and bake in a 400° F. oven for 5–7 minutes, or until just lightly golden and crisp.

(continued)

5. Spoon the shrimp with sauce and cheese over the bread; garnish with a little chopped parsley, and serve with olives and lemon wedges.

Serves 4

Mushroom and Black Bean Burritos with Chile Cream Sauce

Of the world's wealth of wrapped and rolled foods, perhaps none has had such a strong impact on the American table in the last decade or so as the stuffed-tortilla tradition of Mexico, refashioned through the cooking of California and the Southwest. Indeed, there are so many versions of the filled tortilla—tacos, enchiladas, quesadillas, burritos, chimichangas—that it is sometimes hard to distinguish among them. The burrito is generally considered to be a wheat-flour tortilla wrapped around a stuffing of meat or beans, then either deep-fried or baked with a sauce. This is a baked and sauced version, a rich and piquant Southwestern equivalent of Italian manicotti or French rolled crêpes.

For the stuffing

1 medium onion, finely chopped
3 cloves garlic, minced
2 tablespoons olive oil
2 cups finely chopped fresh mushrooms
2 cups cooked or canned black beans, thoroughly drained
1/4 teaspoon salt
Several good grinds black pepper
1/4 teaspoon dried oregano
1/2 cup sour cream
1 cup shredded jack cheese

8 small (fajita-size) flour tortillas

For the sauce

1 small onion, finely chopped

1–2 serrano chiles, seeded and minced

2 medium green frying peppers, seeded and minced

2 tablespoons olive oil

2 tablespoons flour

1 cup chicken stock

¼ cup light cream

3 tablespoons chopped fresh cilantro

Good dash salt

1. In a skillet, sauté the onion and the garlic in the oil until just soft; add the mushrooms and sauté, stirring, over moderate heat, until the mushrooms are soft and all the liquid has cooked away.

2. Add the beans, salt, pepper, and oregano, and cook, stirring, for a few more minutes. The mixture should be fairly dry.

3. Remove from the heat and stir in the sour cream and the cheese.

4. Preheat the oven to 350° F. Spoon 2 tablespoons or so of the filling onto each tortilla. Roll up the stuffed tortillas and place seam side down in a lightly buttered baking dish or casserole. Continue wrapping and rolling until all the filling and tortillas are used.

5. Cover the baking dish with foil and bake for 25–30 minutes.

6. While the burritos are baking, make the sauce: Sauté the onion, the chiles, and the frying peppers in the oil over moderate heat, stirring, until the vegetables are soft and the onion is beginning to turn golden.

7. Stir in the flour to make a roux; cook, stirring, for 2–3 minutes.

8. Whisk the stock into the roux and continue to cook, stirring, until the sauce becomes thickened and smooth. Stir in the cream and the chopped cilantro and heat to the simmer. Taste for salt and add as necessary.

9. Remove the burritos from the oven and spoon the hot sauce over them.

Makes about 8 burritos (serves 4)

Garlic Potato Knishes

Knishes are the special creation of the Ashkenazi, Jews who migrated from the Middle East and the Mediterranean into Central and Eastern Europe. No one seems to know the origin of the word "knish," but the product and the technique are thought to derive from two possible sources: the pâtés en croûte of Alsace, and the dough-wrapped savories, like pierogi, of Eastern Europe. In any case, the knish has become a traditional favorite in its own right, rich, savory, and fun to eat.

3 medium potatoes, peeled and halved
1 large onion, finely chopped
2 tablespoons butter
2 tablespoons olive oil
1–2 large cloves elephant garlic, minced (about ¼ cup)
3–4 tablespoons milk
½ teaspoon salt, or more to taste
¼ teaspoon freshly ground black pepper
2 eggs
2 tubes refrigerator biscuits (10 per tube)—you will need
    about 15 biscuits
2 teaspoons water
Paprika

1. Cook the potatoes in boiling water until they are very tender.
2. While the potatoes are cooking, cook the onion in the butter and oil in a skillet over moderate heat, stirring occasionally, until the onion is richly golden-browned (this will take about 15 minutes). Stir the garlic into the mixture and cook for another few minutes.
3. Drain the potatoes and mash them with the milk. Add the salt, the pepper, and the onion mixture and mix well. Taste for salt and add more to taste if necessary.
4. Separate one of the eggs and reserve the yolk. Add the other egg and the egg white to the potato mixture and mix well. Preheat the oven to 400° F.
5. On a floured board, roll each biscuit into a round approxi-

mately 6 inches in diameter. Spoon a heaping tablespoon of potato in a rectangle to within about ½ inch of the sides. Fold the short sides over the filling, then roll up the filled circle to make a cylinder. Place the knishes, seam side down, on a lightly greased baking sheet.

6. When all the knishes are filled and rolled, lightly beat the reserved egg yolk with 2 teaspoons water. Brush the knishes with egg glaze, then sprinkle them with paprika. Bake for about 15–20 minutes, or until nicely browned. The knishes can be served whole or cut into smaller pieces.

Makes about 15 knishes

NOTE: These knishes freeze well.

Food and Flavor

Though much of what we eat is remarkably similar in terms of both form and technique, it is also strikingly different in some very significant ways. Knishes and egg rolls, samosas and empanadas may look alike, in the pot and on the plate, but there's no confusing them once we get a whiff or a taste. If we humans prepare and construct our food in ways that are very much alike, we also take great pains to make it taste different, to imbue it with a unique and distinctive flavor and aroma. We do this primarily by selecting, from an almost limitless array of ingredients, those seasonings that from long use and tradition make our food taste good, that provide a familiar and appealing flavor. A noodle is a noodle, prepared and garnished and enjoyed in much the same fashion all over the world, but the Chinese variety is likely to be flavored with soy sauce, gingerroot, and sesame oil, whereas the Italian version features tomato, olive oil, garlic, and basil. Polish noodles are flavored with onions and butter and sour cream, Thai with fish sauce and coconut and chile. Whatever the cuisine and whatever the dish, we all seek out consistent sets of seasoning ingredients that we use over and over again to give our food its characteristic flavor. And in this regard, though we are all doing the same thing, we are all doing it differently, deliberately choosing the sensory attributes that make what we eat distinguishable from what other people are eating, individualizing our food where it has its most powerful and intimate impact—in the mouth and in the nose.

Vegetable Samosas

Samosas are probably the best known of India's rich repertoire of stuffed pastries and pancakes, tasty little turnovers made from a yogurt-enriched dough with a variety of spicy fillings and fried to a golden crisp. Serve these with a sweet-and-tangy fruit chutney.

For the filling

2 medium potatoes, peeled and diced
    (about 1½ cups diced)
1 medium carrot, diced
1 cup finely chopped or diced cauliflower
2 tablespoons vegetable oil
½ teaspoon black mustard seeds
1 medium onion, finely chopped
1 tablespoon finely minced gingerroot
¼ teaspoon crushed dried hot peppers
2 cloves garlic, minced
2 teaspoons ground cumin
1 teaspoon ground coriander
1 teaspoon ground fenugreek
1 teaspoon turmeric
½ teaspoon salt, plus more to taste if necessary
Several good grinds black pepper
⅓ cup fresh or frozen peas
1 teaspoon fresh lime juice
3–4 heaping tablespoons plain yogurt

1. Cook the potatoes and the carrot in boiling water for about 5 minutes, until tender. Add the cauliflower and cook for another minute or two. Drain the vegetables and set aside.

2. In a skillet, heat the oil over moderate to high heat. Add the mustard seeds and cook, stirring, until the seeds begin to pop.

3. Turn the heat down, then add the onion, the gingerroot, and the hot peppers. Cook, stirring, until the onion wilts and the mixture becomes aromatic. Add the garlic, the spices, the salt, and the pepper and stir around in the oil for a few minutes.

4. Add the drained cooked vegetables and the peas to the spice mixture. Stir in the lime juice and the yogurt and cook, stirring, for a few minutes. Taste for salt. The mixture should be fairly thick and cohesive. Remove from the heat and let cool while preparing the pastry.

For the pastry

1½ cups flour

½ teaspoon salt

2 tablespoons butter, melted

¼ cup plain yogurt

2–3 tablespoons water

About 1 cup vegetable or peanut oil, for frying

1. Combine the flour and salt in a bowl. Stir in the butter, the yogurt, and the water and mix until well blended. The dough will be fairly dry and lumpy. Form the dough into a ball and let it rest, covered, for ½ hour.

2. Pinch off pieces of dough about the size of a small walnut. Roll each piece between your palms into a small ball, then roll the ball on a floured board into a circle about 3–4 inches in diameter.

3. Place a heaping tablespoon of cooled filling on each dough round. Brush the upper edge of the round with water, then fold up to make a semicircle. Press the edges of the samosa to seal, then score the edge with the tines of a fork. Repeat with the remaining dough and filling.

4. Heat about 1 cup of vegetable or peanut oil in a deep skillet or fryer over moderate to high heat. Fry the samosas 4–5 at a time (do not crowd the pan), turning once, until they are golden brown on each side. Drain the fried pastries on paper towels, then serve with a good fruit chutney.

Makes about 12–15 samosas

NOTE: You can substitute prepared buttermilk-biscuit dough for the pastry if you want to save some time. Roll each biscuit on a floured board into a 3–4-inch circle; fill and fry as directed. It's not as good as the real thing, but it works.

Grilled Vegetable Quesadillas

Queso—cheese—is the defining ingredient in quesadillas, originally a simple preparation of tortillas layered or stuffed with melted cheese. The product has become much more elaborate, with a wide variety of fillings, like these tasty grilled turnovers with their savory stuffing of onion, eggplant, and peppers. They make a nice addition to the outdoor barbecue or the cocktail buffet.

1 medium onion, coarsely chopped
2 cloves garlic, minced
1–2 jalapeños, seeded and minced
1 small eggplant, peeled and diced (about 2 cups diced)
1 large sweet red pepper, seeded and diced
3–4 tablespoons olive oil (more if necessary)
½ teaspoon salt
Several good grinds black pepper
Small handful chopped fresh cilantro
12–15 small (fajita-size) flour tortillas
1½–2 cups shredded jack or pepper-jack cheese
1 egg, lightly beaten
Additional olive oil, for grilling

1. In a skillet, combine the onion, the garlic, the chiles, the eggplant, the sweet pepper, and the oil. Cook over moderate heat, stirring occasionally, for about 15 minutes, until the mixture is soft. Add a bit more oil if necessary to keep the eggplant from sticking.
2. Stir in the salt, the pepper, and the cilantro, and remove from the heat.
3. Soften the tortillas slightly in a hot skillet or the microwave. Place a heaping tablespoon of the vegetable filling on the lower half of each tortilla, then add about 2 tablespoons of the shredded cheese.
4. Brush the upper edge of the tortilla with the egg wash, and fold up the tortilla to make a semicircle. Pinch the edges to seal. Keep the filled quesadillas covered with a clean towel.
5. When all the quesadillas have been made, brush them lightly

on both sides with olive oil. Grill them over hot coals for a couple of minutes on each side, turning once.

6. Serve the quesadillas hot, with a good tangy salsa.

Makes 12–15 quesadillas

Spiced Eggplant Wrapped in Phyllo

Of the many doughs used to wrap foods, none are so delicate or delicious as the flaky, many-layered types produced by a variety of cuisines—the strudels of Eastern and Central Europe, the lard-layered doughs of China, the buttery puff pastry and mille-feuilles (thousand leaves) of the French, the phyllo of the Near and Middle East. They make wonderful crisp, flaky wrappings for a variety of savory foods, to serve as elegant appetizers or hors d'oeuvres.

1 medium onion, finely chopped
2 tablespoons olive oil
1 medium eggplant, peeled and diced
    (about 2–2½ cups diced)
½ teaspoon salt
Several good grinds black pepper
½ teaspoon cinnamon
¼ teaspoon ground allspice
1 cup canned crushed tomatoes
1 tablespoon fresh lemon juice
3 tablespoons currants
½ cup cooked rice
2 tablespoons lightly toasted pine nuts
16 phyllo pastry sheets (9 × 13 inches each)
⅓ cup (about) olive oil or melted butter
2 teaspoons bread crumbs

1. In a medium skillet, sauté the onion in the oil over moderate heat until the onion begins to turn golden.

2. Add the diced eggplant and sauté for about 5 minutes, stirring frequently.

3. Stir in the salt, pepper, cinnamon, and allspice and sauté for another few minutes.

4. Add the tomatoes, the lemon juice, and the currants and simmer, uncovered, over low heat for 20–30 minutes, or until the mixture is thick and soft and all the liquid has cooked away. Remove from the heat, stir in the rice and the pine nuts, and mix well. Taste for salt, and adjust seasoning if necessary. Let cool.

5. Keep the phyllo sheets covered with a damp cloth. Remove 1 sheet at a time and place it, long side across, in front of you. Brush the sheet lightly but completely with oil or butter. Place another sheet on top of it and brush again with the oil. Repeat, using 8 sheets in all.

6. Sprinkle the last of the oiled sheets with about 1 teaspoon of the bread crumbs. Spoon half of the eggplant filling across the center of the sheet, to within 1 inch of both short sides. Fold the long side closest to you up over the filling, then brush that surface completely with oil. Fold the short sides in, then brush them with oil. Fold the other long side over the filling and brush with oil.

7. Place the rolled pastry, seam side down, on a baking sheet. Brush the top side thoroughly with oil. With a very sharp knife, lightly score the roll into 4 even sections, for easier slicing after baking. Preheat the oven to 375° F.

8. Repeat the process with the second 8 sheets of phyllo and the remaining filling to make a second roll.

9. Bake the rolls for about 35–45 minutes, until they are a light golden brown. Let stand for 5 minutes, then slice each roll along prescored lines into 4 pieces. Serve warm or at room temperature.

Makes two 10-inch rolls (8 slices)

Coulibiac of Fresh Salmon with Leeks and Dill

*The kulebyaka must make your mouth water, it should be volup-
tuous. . . . As you cut yourself a piece of it . . . your heart overflowing
with delight, you let your fingers pass over it. . . . Then you start eating
it, and the butter drips like large tears, and the stuffing is succulent,
luscious. . . .*

Anton Chekhov

The coulibiac is a traditional Russian delicacy, originally a kind of
fish pie that became "Frenchified" in the nineteenth century with
the use of a rich brioche-like dough to enclose the succulent filling.
It makes an elegant appetizer or first course, or it can be served, in
the Russian fashion, with soup.

For the dough

½ cup warm water
2 teaspoons sugar
1 envelope active dry yeast
1 egg, lightly beaten
2 tablespoons butter, melted
1½–2 cups flour
1 teaspoon salt

For the filling

1 medium potato, peeled and quartered
1 large leek, mostly white part, finely chopped
2 tablespoons butter
½ teaspoon salt
Several good grinds black pepper
3–4 tablespoons finely snipped fresh dill
2 tablespoons snipped fresh chives
3–4 tablespoons sour cream
2 cups cooked fresh salmon, cut into bite-sized pieces or
    coarsely flaked (about 1 pound raw)

1 egg, lightly beaten

Melted butter with fresh lemon juice, for garnish, if desired

1. To make the dough: Mix the water and sugar in a mixing bowl. Sprinkle the yeast over the water and let proof for 5–10 minutes.

2. Add the beaten egg, the melted butter, 1 cup of the flour, and the salt. Beat until well blended and smooth.

3. Add enough additional flour to make a light dough. Knead until the dough is elastic and nonsticky. Place the dough in a lightly greased bowl, cover, and let rise in a warm place for about 1 hour, or until doubled in bulk.

4. Make the filling: Cook the potato in boiling water until very tender. Drain and set aside.

5. In a medium skillet, sauté the leek in the butter over moderate heat, stirring, until the leek is soft. Stir in the salt, pepper, dill, chives, and sour cream. Remove from the heat.

6. Mash the cooked potato into the leek mixture; mix thoroughly. Gently fold the salmon into the potato mixture. Taste for salt and pepper and adjust seasoning if necessary. Set aside.

7. Punch the dough down and roll it out on a floured board into a rectangle about 10 × 16 inches. Spoon the salmon mixture down the middle of the rectangle, to within about 1 inch of the short sides and about 2 inches of the long sides. (Or fit the dough into a lightly buttered 10 × 5-inch loaf pan, fill with salmon mixture, and bring up the sides of the dough to cover.)

8. Fold one long side up over the filling, then bring the other long side over and pinch lightly to seal. Fold the short sides in and pinch lightly to seal.

9. Place the coulibiac seam side down on a lightly buttered baking sheet. With a sharp knife, make 3 or 4 slashes in the top of the roll. Cover lightly and let rise for about ½ hour. Preheat the oven to 375° F.

10. Before placing in the oven, brush the coulibiac thoroughly with the lightly beaten egg. Bake for about 30 minutes, until it is a rich golden brown. Let stand for 5 minutes before cutting into slices. Serve warm, as is, or drizzled with a little melted butter to which some fresh lemon juice has been added.

Serves 6

Afghani Leek Dumplings with Minted Yogurt

These spicy leek dumplings, called *aushak* in Afghanistan, are an ancient and beloved food; they are sometimes fried but are more frequently boiled and served with yogurt and a keema, or meat sauce, as a main course. I like them better as a first course or appetizer, with a bit of yogurt to spoon over them. You can make the simple flour-and-water dough from scratch if you like, but the ready-made Chinese round pot-sticker wrappers make a perfect envelope. Though the half-moon dumplings are easily filled and pleated by hand, you can also use one of those clever little plastic dumpling makers that cost less than a dollar and do a fine job.

4 cups finely chopped leeks
2 tablespoons olive oil
1/4 teaspoon salt
1/8 teaspoon cayenne pepper
1 package (about 40) round pot-sticker wrappers or
    wonton wrappers
1 cup plain yogurt, for garnish
1 tablespoon crushed dried mint, for garnish

1. In a heavy skillet, cook the leeks in the oil over low to moderate heat, stirring from time to time, for about 10 minutes, until the leeks are wilted and soft and just beginning to turn golden.
2. Stir in the salt and the cayenne and mix well. Let cool slightly.
3. Place about a teaspoonful of leek on a wrapper. Moisten the edges of the wrapper with cold water, then fold the filled wrapper in half to form a semicircle. Pinch or pleat the edges to close completely. Keep the filled dumplings covered with a towel or plastic wrap while filling the remaining wrappers.
4. Combine the yogurt and the crushed mint. Mix well and set aside.
5. Cook the dumplings in plenty of boiling salted water for 7–8 minutes. Remove from the pot with a slotted spoon and place on a serving plate. Serve the dumplings warm, garnished with the minted yogurt.

Makes about 30 dumplings

Fragrant Shrimp-Basil Rolls

In much of Southeast Asia, the wrappers for delicate spring rolls and other savories are often made from rice flour. The rice "papers" come dried, wrapped in plastic, and can be stuffed and then fried, steamed, or, as in this case, simply softened in water and then rolled around the filling. Rice papers are a useful item to keep in your pantry to serve as a quick and easy wrapper for hors d'oeuvres; they can be bought round, in semicircles, or in squares, but I think the square ones are easiest to work with.

2 tablespoons fish sauce
1 teaspoon lemon-grass powder or 2 teaspoons finely
    chopped lemon grass
2 cloves garlic, crushed
1 teaspoon sugar
1 tablespoon fresh lime juice
1/4 teaspoon crushed dried hot peppers
1 cup water
1 pound medium to large shrimp
1 package spring-roll (rice-paper) wrappings, square or
    round
1 bunch fresh basil
1/2 cup finely chopped roasted peanuts

For the dipping sauce

1/4 cup fish sauce
2 tablespoons rice vinegar
2 teaspoons sugar
2 cloves garlic, crushed
1/4 cup hoisin sauce

1. In a medium saucepan, combine the fish sauce, lemon grass, garlic, sugar, lime juice, hot peppers, and water. Bring to the boil, then simmer over low heat for about 5 minutes.

(continued)

2. Add the shrimp, mix well, cover, and cook over very low heat for a few minutes, just until the shrimp turn pink. Remove from the heat; let stand covered for 10–15 minutes. Drain the shrimp, then shell and devein.

3. Soak the rice papers 2 or 3 at a time in warm water for a few minutes, until they are pliable.

4. On each wrapper, place a couple of basil leaves, then top with 2–3 shrimp. Sprinkle the shrimp with a small amount of chopped peanuts. Roll the stuffed wrappers, tucking in the short ends as you roll. Keep the filled rolls covered with a towel or plastic wrap while you prepare the rest.

5. Combine all the sauce ingredients and mix thoroughly. Any leftover chopped peanuts can be added to the sauce. Serve the sauce as a dip for the shrimp rolls.

Makes about 15–20 rolls

Southwestern-Style Shepherd's Pie

It is from the English that Americans inherited their love of pies— foods cooked in, and topped with, pastry crusts that were picturesquely called "coffins" in medieval England. A derivative tradition developed of food cooked in pots or casseroles without the bottom crust but topped with pastry or biscuit dough; the Pennsylvania Dutch are famous for one topped with large boiled noodle squares and called, appropriately, "slippery" pot pie. From potato cultures there evolved the shepherd's pie, chunks of leftover meat and vegetables cooked in a savory sauce and topped with a mashed-potato crust. This recipe is a Southwestern version, with a spicy red-chile filling and a green-chile-laced mashed-potato topping.

½ pound green beans, cut into 1-inch lengths

2 tablespoons vegetable oil

1 medium onion, coarsely chopped

3 cloves garlic, minced

1 medium sweet red or green pepper, seeded and coarsely
   chopped

2 carrots, cut in small chunks

¼ teaspoon crushed dried hot peppers

2 cups canned crushed tomatoes

1 tablespoon ground ancho chile

½ teaspoon dried oregano

½ teaspoon ground cumin

½ teaspoon salt

1 medium zucchini, cut into small chunks

2 cups cooked chicken or turkey, cut into small chunks

3 medium potatoes, peeled and cut into quarters

2 tablespoons butter

1 medium green frying pepper or green bell pepper,
   seeded and finely chopped

1–2 jalapeño peppers, seeded and minced

⅓ cup milk

½ teaspoon salt, or more to taste

1. Cook the green beans in boiling water for 3–5 minutes, until just tender but still crisp. Drain and set aside.

2. In a saucepan, heat the oil over moderate heat. Add the onion, garlic, sweet pepper, carrots, and hot peppers, and sauté, stirring, until the onion just begins to turn golden.

3. Stir in the tomatoes, ancho chile, oregano, cumin, salt, and zucchini. Bring to the simmer and cook for about 5 minutes.

4. Add the reserved green beans and the chicken or turkey; simmer for a few minutes more. Taste for salt and seasoning.

5. Cook the potatoes in boiling water until very tender; drain.

6. Heat the butter over moderate heat, then sauté the green peppers and the chile peppers for a few minutes, stirring, until soft. Add the milk and heat through, then remove from the heat.

7. Add the potatoes and mash thoroughly; mix in the salt and then taste. You may need some more salt.

8. Spoon the red-chile mixture into a buttered 2-quart casserole; spoon the mashed potatoes on top, in a thick border around the edge of the casserole. Bake in a preheated 350° F. oven for 25–30 minutes, until bubbly.

Serves 4

Four-Onion and Cheese Tart

Four members of the *allium* family—onions, leeks, scallions, and chives—give their unique flavors to this savory tart that comes from the French tradition of pastry shells baked with rich fillings of cream, cheese, and eggs.

Pastry for 8- or 9-inch quiche or fluted tart pan
2 cups finely chopped onions
2 cups finely chopped leeks
2 tablespoons butter
1 cup finely chopped scallions
3 tablespoons finely snipped garlic chives or regular chives
1 teaspoon salt
1/4 teaspoon freshly ground black pepper
2 eggs
1 cup light cream
1/8 teaspoon grated nutmeg
1/8 teaspoon cayenne pepper
2 teaspoons Dijon mustard
2 cups shredded Gruyère, Emmenthaler, or other
  full-flavored, "nutty" Swiss cheese

1. Fit the pastry into the quiche pan and set aside.
2. In a medium skillet, sauté the onions and the leeks in the butter over moderate heat, stirring occasionally, for 10–12 minutes, until the onions are soft and a nice golden-brown color.
3. Stir in the scallions and the chives and cook, stirring, for an-

other few minutes. Add ½ teaspoon of the salt and half of the pepper and mix well. Remove from the heat. Preheat the oven to 375° F.

4. Whisk the eggs thoroughly, then stir in the cream, the nutmeg, the cayenne, the remaining ½ teaspoon of salt, and the remaining pepper. Mix well.

5. Spread or brush the mustard evenly over the bottom of the pastry. Spoon the onion mixture evenly into the shell. Sprinkle the shredded cheese evenly over the onions. Pour the egg mixture carefully into the shell.

6. Bake the tart for 30–40 minutes, until it is set and lightly browned. Let stand for 5 minutes before cutting into wedges to serve.

Serves 4 as a main course, 6–8 as an appetizer

Pastel de Camarones
(Creole Shrimp and Corn Pie)

The word "creole" means "mixed together," and creole cooking refers to the traditions developed in the Caribbean and the Gulf Coast out of an invigorating mixture of many foods from different cultures. This chunky, highly seasoned pie shows French, Spanish, English, and Native American influences; it makes a good appetizer or first course, or it can serve as a lunch or light supper entrée.

Pastry for 8- or 9-inch quiche or fluted tart pan
6 scallions, finely chopped
1 medium sweet red pepper, seeded and diced
1 large rib celery, diced
2 tablespoons olive oil
1 cup tomato sauce
½ teaspoon liquid hot-pepper sauce
1 teaspoon dried thyme
1 teaspoon salt
¼ teaspoon freshly ground black pepper
1½ cups corn kernels (fresh off the cob are best, but frozen
    can be used), about 2–3 ears
1½ cups small-to-medium cooked shrimp, peeled and
    deveined
Small handful flat-leaf parsley, finely chopped
2 eggs
⅔ cup light cream or half-and-half
⅛ teaspoon cayenne pepper
⅛ teaspoon grated nutmeg
1 cup shredded jack or mild Cheddar cheese

1. Fit the pastry into the pan and set aside.
2. In a medium skillet, sauté the scallions, the sweet pepper, and the celery in the oil over moderate heat, stirring, until the vegetables are limp. Preheat the oven to 375° F.

3. To the sautéed vegetables add the tomato sauce, the hot-pepper sauce, the thyme, ½ teaspoon of the salt, and half of the pepper. Bring to the simmer and cook over low heat, uncovered, for about 10 minutes, stirring occasionally. The sauce should be fairly thick.

4. Add the corn, mix well, and continue to cook, stirring occasionally, for about 5 minutes. Remove from the heat and stir in the shrimp and the parsley.

5. Whisk the eggs thoroughly, then stir in the cream, the cayenne, the nutmeg, the remaining ½ teaspoon of salt, and the remaining pepper.

6. Spoon the shrimp mixture evenly into the prepared pastry shell. Pour the egg mixture over the shrimp. Sprinkle the cheese evenly over the top.

7. Bake the pie for about 30–40 minutes, until it is set and lightly browned. Let it stand for about 5 minutes before cutting into wedges to serve.

Serves 4 as a main course, 6–8 as an appetizer

Vegetable Containers

We don't know who first thought of stuffing a cabbage or a vine leaf, but it is an idea that very likely derived from the ancient practice of wrapping food in protective vegetation in order to cook it. Long before people developed cooking pots that could be placed directly over the fire or in the hot coals—vessels made of pottery or ceramic or, much later, of metal—they used natural plant materials to cook their food. These wrappings—banana leaves in Asia, corn husks in the New World, seaweed in coastal areas—are still used by many cultures today to steam-cook food and protect it from the direct heat of the fire; the plant wrappings contain enough natural moisture to protect the stuffing and prevent it from burning. It would take but a small leap of the imagination to go from a vegetable wrapping used as a cooking container to an edible wrapper filled with stuffing and cooked in a savory liquid or sauce, a dish that provided a whole meal in a single package, with delightful new elements of flavor and texture. The cuplike leaves of the common cabbage fairly beg to be stuffed with something, as do the hollowed-out shells of eggplants, squashes, and peppers, and these vegetables turn up stuffed and sauced with a variety of ingredients and seasonings in cuisines throughout the world. From the tiniest vine leaf to the fattest pumpkin, whether as leaves or cases or shells, stuffed vegetables are an ingenious and widespread preparation.

Lettuce Leaf Rolls with Spiced Chicken and Chinese Sausage

A delicious exemplar of the Asian dedication to wrapped and rolled savory snacks, this one uses not the customary dough wrapping but a simple lettuce leaf, filled by the diner with a spicy mixture of chicken, sausage, and Chinese cabbage. Boston lettuce is the best choice for individual wrapping, but an interesting variation is Belgian endive, which makes a nice presentation for a cocktail party or buffet; the long leaves can be spread with the filling ahead of time and arranged attractively on a serving plate.

2 tablespoons soy sauce
1 tablespoon rice-wine vinegar
2 tablespoons hoisin sauce
1 teaspoon sugar
1 teaspoon Chinese chile paste with garlic
1½ teaspoons cornstarch
2 tablespoons peanut oil
½ cup chopped scallions
1 tablespoon finely minced gingerroot
3 cloves garlic, finely minced
3 ounces diced Chinese sausage (about ½ cup diced)
6 ounces boneless, skinless chicken, cut in pea-sized pieces
    (easiest to do if the chicken is partially frozen)
2 cups diced bok choy
Small handful fresh coriander leaf, finely chopped
16–20 leaves Boston lettuce or Belgian endive

1. In a small bowl, combine the soy sauce, the vinegar, the hoisin, the sugar, the chile paste, and the cornstarch. Mix thoroughly and set aside.

2. Heat a wok or skillet over high heat. When the pan is very hot, pour in the oil and swirl it around a bit. Add the scallions, the gingerroot, and the garlic and stir-fry for a few minutes, until the mixture becomes aromatic.

(continued)

3. Add the sausage and the chicken and stir-fry another few minutes, just until the chicken loses its pink color.

4. Add the bok choy and stir-fry a few minutes more.

5. Mix the reserved sauce, then stir it into the pan. Cook, stirring, until the sauce boils and thickens.

6. Remove from the heat and stir in the chopped coriander. Let the mixture cool, then use as a filling for lettuce leaves.

Makes about 3 cups filling (16–20 rolls)

NOTE: The chicken-sausage mixture can also be eaten hot, with rice or noodles.

Peppers Stuffed with Chicken, Rice, and Walnuts

The appeal of stuffed foods is surely aesthetic, a playful exercise in varieties of flavor and texture, but the practice may well have originated in the determination of thrifty cooks everywhere to recycle leftover food. Stale bread, cooked pasta, and whole grains commonly function as the basis for the stuffing, with other ingredients added for flavor and variety. This simple Middle Eastern chicken-and-rice stuffing, with its savory tomato sauce, plays well against the flavor of the baked sweet-pepper shells.

 2 very large green peppers, seeded and cut into quarters, or
    4 medium green peppers, seeded and cut in half
    lengthwise (through the stem end)

For the stuffing

 2 cups cold cooked rice
 2 cups diced cooked chicken
 1/2 cup coarsely chopped freshly toasted walnuts
 3–4 tablespoons finely snipped fresh dill

½ teaspoon salt
¼ teaspoon freshly ground black pepper
1 cup plain yogurt

For the sauce
2 tablespoons olive oil
1 large leek, mostly white part, finely chopped
2–2½ cups tomato sauce
1 tablespoon fresh lemon juice
1 teaspoon cinnamon
¼ teaspoon ground allspice
½ teaspoon salt
Several good grinds black pepper

1. Seed and cut peppers, large ones in quarters, medium in half lengthwise through stem end.

2. Make the stuffing: In a bowl, combine the rice, chicken, walnuts, dill, salt, pepper, and yogurt. Mix gently but thoroughly.

3. With a spoon or, better yet, your fingers, stuff the mixture into the prepared pepper cases, mounding it generously. Place the stuffed peppers in a single layer in a lightly greased shallow casserole or baking dish.

4. Make the sauce: In a small saucepan, heat the olive oil over moderate heat. Add the leek and sauté, stirring, until the leek begins to turn golden.

5. Add the tomato sauce, lemon juice, cinnamon, allspice, salt, and pepper. Mix well, then bring to the simmer and cook, uncovered, over low heat, stirring occasionally, for about 5 minutes. Preheat the oven to 350° F.

6. Spoon the sauce over and around the stuffed peppers. Cover the casserole, then bake for about 50–60 minutes. Uncover the casserole for the last few minutes of cooking. If the sauce seems too thick, you can add some chicken stock or water.

Makes 8 stuffed peppers; serves 4

Indian Potato-Stuffed Peppers

In the highly vegetarian cuisine of India, vegetables stuffed with vegetables rather than meat or other animal foods provide delicious and satisfying meals. The potato is always a great favorite, as it is in so many other parts of the world, because it is cheap, filling, nutritious, and amenable to a wide variety of spices and seasonings. These savory stuffed peppers can serve as the main course, as a side dish, or as part of a larger Indian meal.

3 medium all-purpose potatoes
1 medium onion, finely chopped
1 tablespoon finely minced gingerroot
2 tablespoons vegetable oil
3 cloves garlic, minced
1 teaspoon freshly ground toasted cumin
1 teaspoon freshly ground toasted coriander
1 teaspoon freshly ground toasted fenugreek
1 teaspoon turmeric
1/2 teaspoon crushed dried hot peppers
3–4 heaping tablespoons plain yogurt
1 tablespoon fresh lime juice
1/2 teaspoon salt
Several good grinds black pepper
1/3 cup fresh or frozen peas
3–4 tablespoons chopped fresh coriander leaf
4–5 small-to-medium sweet red or green peppers, cut in
    half lengthwise (through the stem) and seeded
Additional coriander leaves, for garnish

1. Boil the potatoes in their skins until very tender. Drain, then peel, and set aside.

2. In the same pot, sauté the onion and the gingerroot in the oil until the onion is limp. Add the garlic and cook for another few minutes.

3. Stir in the spices and the hot peppers, then add the cooked

potatoes, the yogurt, the lime juice, the salt, and the pepper. Mash
the potatoes thoroughly but do not puree; the mixture should have
a good mashed-potato texture.

4. Preheat the oven to 350° F. Stir the peas and the chopped
coriander into the potatoes and mix well. If the mixture seems a little dry, you can add some more yogurt.

5. Spoon the potato mixture lightly into the pepper halves. Place
the stuffed peppers in a single layer in a large shallow casserole or
baking dish. Pour a little water into the bottom of the casserole.
Bake, covered, for about 30–35 minutes. Serve the peppers warm or
hot, garnished with additional coriander leaves.

Serves 4–6 as a side dish

Balkan Vegetable-Stuffed Cabbage Rolls

A delicious vegetarian dish from a part of the world where savory stuffed vegetables are a familiar and well-loved preparation, combining ingredients and seasonings from the Middle East, the Mediterranean, and Europe into a unique and distinctive tradition.

For the stuffing

1 large eggplant, peeled and diced
1 medium onion, coarsely chopped
1 large sweet red or green pepper, seeded and diced
4 cloves garlic, minced
1/4 cup olive oil
1/2–3/4 teaspoon salt
Several good grinds black pepper
1/4 teaspoon crushed dried hot peppers
2 tablespoons chopped fresh dill
1 cup cooked rice
2–3 tablespoons crumbled feta cheese
10–12 outer leaves from a large head of cabbage

For the sauce

1 medium onion, coarsely chopped
3 cloves garlic, minced
2 tablespoons olive oil
2 cups canned crushed tomatoes
1 tablespoon fresh lemon juice
3 tablespoons chopped fresh dill
1/4 teaspoon salt
Several good grinds black pepper

Sour cream or plain yogurt, for garnish (optional)

1. Make the stuffing: In a large skillet, combine the eggplant, the onion, the sweet peppers, the garlic, and the oil. Cook over moderate heat, stirring from time to time, until the eggplant is very soft, about 20–30 minutes.

2. Remove from the heat and stir in the salt, black pepper, hot peppers, dill, rice, and feta. Let cool slightly, then taste for salt.

3. Blanch the cabbage leaves in boiling water for 3–4 minutes. Drain thoroughly, then cool.

4. Make the sauce: In a large, heavy pot, sauté the onion and the garlic in the oil over moderate heat, stirring, just until the onion wilts. Add the tomatoes, lemon juice, dill, salt, and pepper. Bring to the simmer.

5. Place a heaping tablespoon of filling on each cabbage leaf. Fold in the sides of the leaf to make a package and secure with a toothpick. Repeat with the remaining filling and cabbage leaves.

6. Place the cabbage rolls in the simmering sauce, then cover and cook over low heat for about 45 minutes. Turn the rolls gently once or twice during cooking. Remove the cover for the last few minutes of cooking to thicken the sauce slightly.

7. Serve the cabbage rolls and sauce garnished with sour cream or yogurt, if desired.

Makes 10–12 rolls; serves 4–6

Chinese Stuffed Cabbage

In contrast to the more familiar ground-beef-stuffed cabbage with tomato sauce, the Chinese use their favored meat, pork, as a savory filling for the more delicately flavored Napa cabbage. Try this for a pleasant change of pace and as a useful do-ahead addition to a Chinese meal.

1 medium to large head Napa cabbage

For the filling

1 pound lean ground pork
6 scallions, chopped
3 cloves garlic, minced
1 tablespoon finely minced gingerroot
2 tablespoons finely snipped (Chinese) garlic chives
½ teaspoon sugar
¼ teaspoon salt
¼ teaspoon white pepper
1 tablespoon soy sauce
1 tablespoon Asian sesame oil
1–1½ cups finely chopped cabbage (after 10–12 outer
  leaves have been removed)

For the sauce

1½ cups chicken stock
3–4 slices gingerroot
1 tablespoon soy sauce
2 tablespoons rice wine
½ teaspoon sugar
1 tablespoon cornstarch, dissolved in 1 tablespoon
  cold water
1 tablespoon Asian sesame oil
Additional chopped scallions, for garnish

1. Remove 10–12 outer leaves from the cabbage. Blanch the leaves in boiling water for 2–3 minutes, until they are just limp. Drain the leaves and set aside to cool.

2. Make the filling: Combine the ground pork with the scallions, garlic, gingerroot, chives, sugar, salt, pepper, soy sauce, sesame oil, and chopped cabbage. Mix thoroughly.

3. Place about 2 tablespoons of filling on each cabbage leaf; fold up the edges to make a package and secure with a toothpick.

4. In a large pot or deep skillet, combine the stock, sliced ginger, soy sauce, rice wine, and sugar. Mix well. Place the stuffed cabbage rolls in the liquid, bring to the simmer, then cover and cook over low heat for about 40–50 minutes. (If there is any additional meat filling left over, shape it into small meatballs and add them to the sauce.)

5. Remove the cabbage rolls (and any meatballs) from the sauce with a slotted spoon and place on a rimmed serving dish or shallow bowl.

6. Bring the sauce to a full boil, then stir in the cornstarch paste and whisk until the sauce is smooth, clear, and slightly thickened. Stir in the sesame oil.

7. Pour the hot sauce over the cabbage rolls and garnish with chopped scallions.

Serves 4–6

Norimake with Smoked Salmon

Vegetables and dough function as food wrappers in many different cuisines, but the Japanese kitchen has developed its own unique envelope—dried seaweed, or laver, roasted and pressed into thin 8-inch square sheets called nori, sold ready-to-use in convenient plastic packages. These seaweed sheets, rolled up with vinegared rice and bits of fish and seafood, make a tasty and decorative appetizer or hors d'oeuvre; if you have never made sushi and have reservations about using the traditional raw fish, try this smoked-salmon version. Japanese tradition uses a little bamboo mat to roll the norimake, but a clean kitchen towel works very well.

2½ cups water
2 tablespoons mirin (sweet rice wine for cooking)
2 cups medium- or short-grain rice
2 tablespoons rice vinegar
2 teaspoons sugar
1 teaspoon salt
5–6 sheets dried roasted nori
6–8 ounces thinly sliced smoked salmon
6 scallions, cut in long slivers, or Chinese garlic chives
Pickled gingerroot and wasabi (Japanese horseradish
    paste), for garnish

1. In a medium saucepan, combine the water and the mirin. Bring to the boil, then stir in the rice, mix well, cover, and cook over low heat for 15–20 minutes, until all the liquid has been absorbed.
2. Stir in the vinegar, the sugar, and the salt; mix thoroughly, then cover and let stand for 20–30 minutes.
3. Place a sheet of nori on a folded kitchen towel. Spoon on enough rice (about 1 cup) to cover the sheet completely except to within about ½ inch from the top edge. Smooth the rice into an even layer.
4. Place 2 or 3 strips of salmon horizontally on the rice, making sure the strips come just to the side edges. Place 3 or 4 slivers of scal-

lion or garlic chives horizontally around the salmon strips, making sure the slivers come to the side edges as well.

5. Using the towel as a guide, carefully roll up the spread sheets from the bottom edge closest to you. Lightly moisten the top edge of the nori with a little water. Squeeze the roll gently to close tightly. Place the rolled norimake on a plate. Continue with the remaining sheets and filling to make 5 or 6 rolls.

6. With a sharp serrated knife, cut each roll into 8 pieces. If not serving immediately, cover with plastic wrap and place in the refrigerator. The norimake should be eaten the same day they are made.

7. Serve the norimake with pickled gingerroot and wasabi.

Makes 40–48 pieces

Chapter Ten

Sweet Elaborations

By tradition, the organization of most cookbooks echoes the structure of most meals, beginning with the soups or appetizers, proceeding through the meats, the vegetables, the salads, and concluding finally with the sweet course, known to us all as dessert. Dessert! It is for many of us the apogee of the meal, the best part reserved for the last, the reward for so many forkfuls of spinach shoveled down as little more than an exercise in carotene consumption. It is, in the end, the end for which we strive, gobbling our brisket while thoughts of sugarplums dance in our heads—unctuous cheesecakes, fudgy brownies, frozen creams that seduce the palate with their silky chill.

But this passion for rich and elaborate sweets as appropriate finales for a meal is not shared by most of the rest of the world. Indeed, for many people, if there is a dessert course at all, it may consist simply of fresh fruit or a hot beverage like tea or even, as is common in China, a hot savory broth. The Dutch and the French frequently end their meals with cheese; Brillat-Savarin declared that "dessert without cheese is like a pretty girl with only one eye." So we Americans are somewhat unique in regarding a full load of sugar, fat, and calories as a proper conclusion to the meal; it may well be that this particular indulgence is part of the eating patterns that have brought us to the brink of nutritional overkill, the more serious implications of "death by chocolate."

But though our patterns of consumption may be unique, our taste for sweet things is not, for this is probably the most widespread and fundamental of human taste preferences. Research has indicated that we are born already equipped with a positive response to sweet tastes, and for good reason. Sweetness points to an immediate quick source of energy, of calories, in an easily digested, safe form, and for our earliest ancestors, like their primate forebears, the ability to detect and exploit such foods would have been an enormous advantage. In addition, our very first food, mother's milk, is sweet (and human milk is significantly sweeter than other mammalian milks), and it makes good sense for the helpless human infant to come into the world already prepared to enjoy the taste of its first food.

So as a species we all love sweet things, and this innate preference has joined with the culinary imperative in humans to produce the wide variety of sweet delicacies and sugary confections that are so dear to us all. We may consume them in different ways and at different times, endow them with all kinds of symbolic and ritual importance, but it is their sweetness that makes them unique, transforming our familiar savory food into special treats.

The same substances that form our daily fare turn up as sweet elaborations. The grains and vegetable foods that serve as basic sustenance are refashioned from the savory to the sweet; rice, bread, cornmeal, noodles are sweetened, newly garnished and enriched with fruits and nuts and dairy products, and flavored with sweet and aromatic spices like cinnamon, ginger, nutmeg, and cardamom. Nuts and seeds, chopped or ground into savory pastes and sauces, like the Genovese pesto or the Middle Eastern tahini, are compounded with sugar or honey into sweet confections like halva or nougat. Cuisines that rely heavily on eggs and dairy products turn those foods into sweetened concoctions—puddings, pies, custards, and creams—that are highly esteemed and dearly loved.

Not only do we use many of our common foods to fashion our sweet treats, but we also prepare and structure them in very similar ways. We simmer foods in sweet syrups instead of savory meat stocks; we make refreshing salads from fruits instead of vegetables; we construct texturally exciting layers of different ingredients, wrapping or stuffing them in envelopes or shells of dough; we concoct garnishes and condimental sauces, from the simplest sprinkling of chopped nuts or chocolate jimmies to more elaborate whipped creams and meringues, fruit coulis and crunchy crumb toppings. And always, in this sweet undertaking, we combine the best and the costliest ingredients—butter and cream, fruits and nuts, chocolate and vanilla, honey and sweetened liqueurs—with our most elaborate and extravagant techniques to produce dishes that are as delicious to the eye as they are to the mouth.

However different the sweet elaborations of our varying traditions may be, the delight in this kind of food is universal, spanning the globe and the generations. We are no longer dependent for basic nourishment and simple energy on the chance find of ripe fruit or a dripping honeycomb, and perhaps because sweets are no longer so important as food, their preparation reveals us at our most playful and most imaginative. We eat them because we love them, not because we need them. This is food for fun, food for art, food for indulgence—the sweetest food of all.

RECIPES

Honey-Balsamic Mixed Berry Salad (America)
Compote of Dried Fruits and Nuts (Central Asia)
Fruity Bread Pudding (England)
Cinnamon Apple Spoonbread (America)
Orange Blossom Rice Pudding (Middle East)
Lemon Curd Cheesecake (America)
Hazelnut Crème Brûlée with Dried Sour Cherries (France)
Strawberry Soufflé (France)
Biscuit Tortoni (Italy)
Cranberry Fool (England)
Karidopita (Greek Walnut Cake)
Fruited Almond Tea Loaf (England)
Applesauce Cake with Mixed Nut–Honey Topping (America)
Almond Raspberry Cake (Northern Europe)
Harvest Vegetable Spice Cake (America)
Flourless Chocolate Cake with Praline Whipped Cream (America)
Chocolate-Glazed Shortbread Squares (America)
Yellowjacket Tart (America)
Toasted Coconut–Banana Cream Pie (America)
Pear Tart with Hazelnut Praline Topping (America)
Blueberry Spice Pie with Whipped Ginger Cream (America)
Layered Apple Crisp Torte (America)

Honey-Balsamic Mixed Berry Salad

Fruit salads, like their vegetable counterparts, are greatly enhanced by a touch of acid, although one provided in a sweeter, less pungent form, like orange or pineapple juice. In this simple summer salad, balsamic vinegar adds a bit of tartness and a rich, mellow flavor. You don't have to break the bank for an expensive aged balsamic; an ordinary supermarket variety will do nicely.

2 cups mixed fresh berries (blackberries, raspberries,
    blueberries, etc.)
2 cups seedless green grapes
2 tablespoons honey
2 tablespoons balsamic vinegar
2–3 small ripe cantaloupes, cut in half and seeded
Sprigs of mint, for garnish

1. Combine the berries and the grapes in a bowl.

2. Combine the honey and the vinegar and mix thoroughly. Pour the sauce over the fruit and mix gently. Chill the mixture briefly.

3. Spoon the fruit mixture into the cantaloupe halves. Garnish with sprigs of mint.

Serves 4–6

Compote of Dried Fruits and Nuts

Who's to say that dried or preserved foods are not as interesting or as valuable as their fresh counterparts? Drying is an ancient means for preserving food for times of scarcity and produces a wealth of new cooking and eating possibilities. Central Asia is the hearth of many of our familiar dried fruits and nuts, which are still used there to add richness and flavor to both sweet and savory dishes. This old-fashioned compote is a delicious mixture, good by itself, with yogurt or ice cream, or as a filling for strudel (recipe follows).

2 cups dried apricots
1 cup pitted prunes (try the lemon-flavored ones)
½ cup dark raisins
½ cup golden raisins
3 cups water
½ cup sugar
1 teaspoon cinnamon
½ cup coarsely broken walnuts
¼ cup shelled unsalted pistachios

1. In a heavy pot, combine the apricots, the prunes, the raisins, and the water. (If you don't use the lemon-flavored prunes, add a few strips of lemon peel.) Simmer over low heat, uncovered, for 15–20 minutes, stirring occasionally, until the fruit is tender but not mushy.
2. Add the sugar and the cinnamon, mix well, then cook for another 5 minutes.
3. Remove from the heat and stir in the walnuts and the pistachios. The compote will store well for weeks, covered, in the refrigerator. Can be served warm or cold.

Makes about 6 cups

Fruit and Nut Strudel

1 sheet frozen puff pastry, defrosted according to package
    instructions
2 cups (about) fruit compote (above)
1 egg, lightly beaten with 2 teaspoons water
Confectioners' sugar, for garnish

1. Preheat the oven to 400° F. On a floured board, roll out the pastry sheet into a rectangle approximately 12 × 16 inches.

2. With the long side in front of you, spoon the compote across the lower third of the pastry sheet, to within 1 inch of the short edges and the edge closest to you.

3. Starting with the edge closest to you, roll up the filled sheet, tucking in the short edges as you roll. Place the rolled pastry, seam side down, on an ungreased baking sheet.

4. Lightly brush the egg wash all over the pastry. With a sharp knife, cut 3 or 4 slashes in the top of the roll.

5. Bake the roll for about 20–25 minutes, until crisp and richly browned. Let cool, then dust with confectioners' sugar. Cut into slices with a sharp serrated knife.

Makes one 14-inch strudel (6–8 slices)

Fruity Bread Pudding

Like so many other cuisines that turn leftover or stale grain and starch products into hearty sweets, English tradition made good use of stale bread, sweetened, spiced, garnished with fruit, and enriched with milk, cream, and eggs, to fashion the puddings that are so dear to the English palate. Bread pudding has become somewhat fashionable in recent years, but its origins lie in the substantial appetites of thrifty, hardworking people.

2 cups milk

1 cup light cream

2 tablespoons butter

1/2 cup plus 2 tablespoons sugar

1 teaspoon grated orange zest

5–6 slices stale firm white bread, cut in coarse cubes
    (about 4–4 1/2 cups)—no need to trim crusts

1 large apple, peeled, cored, and diced

1 large pear, peeled, cored, and diced

1/2 cup raisins

2 teaspoons cinnamon

1/4 teaspoon grated nutmeg

1 tablespoon orange juice

1 tablespoon fresh lemon juice

2 eggs

1 teaspoon vanilla extract

1. In a heavy saucepan, combine the milk, the cream, and the butter. Heat until very hot, but do not boil. Stir in the 1/2 cup of sugar and the orange zest, mix well, and remove from the heat.

2. Place the bread cubes in a large bowl. Pour the milk mixture over them, mix well, then let stand at room temperature for 1/2 hour.

3. Combine the diced fruit, the raisins, the 2 tablespoons of sugar, the cinnamon, the nutmeg, the orange juice, and the lemon juice. Mix well.

4. Preheat the oven to 325° F. Generously butter a deep 2-quart baking dish or casserole.

5. Whisk the eggs thoroughly, then stir in the vanilla. Stir the eggs into the bread mixture, then add the fruit and mix well.

6. Turn the mixture into the casserole and bake for 55–60 minutes, until the pudding is puffed and very lightly browned. I like this best served warm, with ice cream, but it can also be served cold with heavy cream.

Serves 6–8

Cinnamon Apple Spoonbread

Sweetened puddings and spoonbreads made from cornmeal were a staple of the colonial American kitchen, where they satisfied not only the robust appetites of hardworking farmers and frontiersmen but also the notorious Anglo-American sweet tooth. Spoonbread is simply a cornmeal mush enriched with milk and fat, lightened with eggs, and, in this case, sweetened and layered with apples. It is a very hearty dish, best eaten warm with heavy cream or vanilla ice cream.

3 tart crisp apples (Granny Smith, Jonathan, Winesap),
    peeled, cored, and diced (about 2 cups diced)
2 tablespoons plus ½ cup sugar
2 teaspoons cinnamon
1 teaspoon fresh lemon juice
2 cups milk
2 tablespoons butter
½ teaspoon salt
1 cup stoneground cornmeal
3 extra-large eggs
1 teaspoon vanilla
¼ teaspoon grated nutmeg
2 teaspoons grated lemon zest

(continued)

1. Combine the diced apples, the 2 tablespoons of sugar, the cinnamon, and the lemon juice. Mix well and set aside.

2. In a medium saucepan, combine the milk, the ½ cup sugar, the butter, and the salt. Heat over moderate heat until small bubbles appear around the edges of the pot. Gradually stir the cornmeal into the hot milk, whisking as you add it to remove any lumps. When all the cornmeal has been added in, continue to cook, stirring, until the mixture is smooth and thick. Remove from the heat and let cool for 10–15 minutes. Preheat the oven to 350° F.

3. Whisk the eggs thoroughly with the vanilla, the nutmeg, and the lemon zest. Stir the beaten eggs into the cooled cornmeal mixture, mixing vigorously until they are thoroughly incorporated.

4. Spoon half of the cornmeal mixture into a well-buttered 2-quart casserole. Spoon the apple mixture over the cornmeal. Top the apple layer with the remaining cornmeal.

5. Bake the spoonbread for about 55–60 minutes, or until it is firmly set and lightly browned. Serve it hot or warm, with heavy cream or ice cream.

Serves 6–8

Orange Blossom Rice Pudding

Though in recent years ice cream has emerged as a universally popular sweet, the more traditional choice may well be rice pudding, a dish that appears in cuisines all over the world. The Chinese make theirs without milk or dairy products but garnish it lavishly with the "eight treasures," a variety of costly fruits and nuts. The French prepare an extravagant version called "riz à l'impératrice," with glacéed fruit, kirsch, currant jelly, and heavy cream. Rice and milk are two of the most valued foods in Indian cuisine, and rice pudding, called "kheer," is a festive and esteemed dish frequently garnished with gold or silver leaf. Here in America, we all grew up with the Horn and Hardart variety, scented with cinnamon and studded with plump raisins. Any rice can be used for rice pudding, but Arborio or other short-grained varieties produce a thicker, creamier mixture, because of their higher starch content. Orange-flower water, available in Middle Eastern and Indian groceries, adds a flowery perfume and a delicate flavor.

1 cup Arborio or other short-grain rice
2 cups water
½ cup sugar
3 cups milk
¼ teaspoon salt
6 cardamom pods
1 tablespoon julienned orange zest
½ cup light cream
½ teaspoon vanilla extract
2 teaspoons orange-flower water
Ground cinnamon or orange-blossom honey, for garnish
  (optional)

1. Cook the rice in 2 cups simmering water, covered, for about 15–20 minutes, until all the water is absorbed.

2. To the cooked rice add the sugar, the milk, the salt, the cardamom pods, and the orange zest. Bring to the simmer, then cook, uncovered, over low heat for about 25–30 minutes, until it is very thick. Stir the pudding frequently as it cooks, especially toward the end, when it is becoming thick.

3. Remove from the heat and stir in the cream, the vanilla, and the orange-flower water. Let cool, stirring occasionally. Fish out and discard the cardamom pods.

4. Spoon the pudding into small individual serving dishes. Dust lightly with cinnamon, if desired, or pass orange-blossom honey to drizzle on as desired.

Serves 6–8

Lemon Curd Cheesecake

I grew up believing that cheesecake was an American original, created in a fabled New York restaurant called Lindy's. Well, New York, you often take the cake—but not this time! Cheesecake, in one form or another, both savory and sweet, is an ancient dish with a venerable tradition in many cultures that produce fresh cheeses. The ancient Greeks and Romans made cheesecake, sweetened with honey and garnished with nuts, and a traditional favorite sweet in India is spiced cheese balls soaked in sugar syrup. The following cheesecake approaches the limits of excess, combining two incredibly rich substances in one voluptuous, indulgent cake.

12–16 gingersnaps, finely crushed
3–4 tablespoons unsalted butter, melted
1½ pounds cream cheese, softened
5 eggs
1½ cups sugar
1 teaspoon vanilla extract
1 cup lemon curd (half the recipe on page 354)
Fresh raspberries or sliced fresh strawberries, for garnish

1. Butter the bottom and sides of an 8- or 9-inch springform pan. Combine the crushed gingersnaps and melted butter and mix well. Press the crumb mixture evenly into the bottom of the pan. Preheat the oven to 350° F.
2. In a food processor, combine the cream cheese, eggs, sugar, and vanilla (do it in several batches if necessary). Puree until smooth. Pour the cream-cheese filling over the crust.
3. Drop the lemon curd in large spoonfuls over the top of the cheese. With the dull side of a table knife, carefully swirl the lemon curd into the cheese mixture, being careful not to cut down into the crust.
4. Bake the cake for about 60 minutes, or until it is puffed and lightly browned. Remove from the oven and let cool completely. The cake will shrink as it cools, but do not despair; this ensures the dense, velvety texture that is important to the finished cake.
5. Chill the cake thoroughly, then serve garnished with some fresh berries. Cut in thin slices to serve.

Serves 8–10

Hazelnut Crème Brûlée with Dried Sour Cherries

In the hands of the French, the egg achieved immortality in a number of forms; surely one of those is the crème brûlée, an outrageously rich and voluptuous dessert that makes an ordinary custard bow its head in shame. In this version, crushed hazelnuts, hazelnut liqueur, and dried sour cherries dress up the basic crème, which doesn't need dressing up at all, but, well, why not? I do the crème in a baking dish, but it can also be baked in small individual custard cups or ramekins.

½ cup dried pitted sour cherries

2 tablespoons Frangelico (hazelnut liqueur)

3 cups heavy cream

½ cup sugar

6 egg yolks

1 teaspoon vanilla extract

½ cup lightly packed light-brown sugar

¼ cup very finely chopped skinned hazelnuts

1. Combine the dried cherries and the hazelnut liqueur; let stand for at least ½ hour.

2. In a heavy saucepan, heat the cream over low to moderate heat until it is very hot, just coming to the simmer. Stir in the sugar and mix well, then remove from the heat.

3. In a large bowl, whisk the egg yolks until they are very thick. Slowly pour the cream into the eggs, whisking constantly until the mixture is very well blended. Stir in the vanilla and the liqueur from the cherries. Preheat the oven to 350° F.

4. Sprinkle the drained cherries on the bottom of a shallow 8- or 9-inch casserole or baking dish. Strain the custard mixture into the dish.

5. Set the custard dish into a larger container or baking tin, then carefully pour boiling water into the larger container so that the water comes about halfway up the sides of the smaller baking dish.

6. Carefully place the double casserole on the middle rack of the oven. Bake for about 40–45 minutes, until the crème is just lightly set.

(continued)

7. Remove the crème from the hot-water bath and cool for at least 1 hour.

8. Combine the brown sugar and the chopped nuts and mix thoroughly. Sprinkle the mixture evenly over the top of the cooled crème.

9. Place the crème under the broiler and watch carefully until the sugar melts and begins to bubble—it takes only a few seconds. (Professional chefs use a propylethylene torch to caramelize the topping.)

10. Let the crème cool, then chill thoroughly.

Serves 6–8

Strawberry Soufflé

The soufflé is the egg at its most ethereal—airy, hot, melt-in-the-mouth flavor. Many years ago, making the requisite first "grand tour" of Europe, I was taken to the great three-star restaurant La Pérouse, where I ate my first strawberry soufflé. I have been trying to duplicate it ever since. Here is one version. It is important to use small, ripe, flavorful berries, not the gargantuan, mealy monsters that appeal for reasons of size rather than flavor.

1 pint small ripe strawberries
½ cup sugar
2 tablespoons fresh lemon juice
3 tablespoons cornstarch
3 egg yolks
1 teaspoon vanilla extract
6 egg whites
Pinch salt
Lightly sweetened whipped cream, for garnish

1. In a medium saucepan, mash or crush the berries with a potato masher or the back of a heavy spoon, or process them coarsely in a food processor. You want a mash, not a puree.

2. Add the sugar, the lemon juice, and the cornstarch to the berries and cook, stirring constantly, over moderate heat until the mixture comes to the boil and becomes thickened and clear. Remove from the heat and let cool slightly.

3. Generously butter and sugar a 6–8-cup soufflé dish or a deep straight-sided casserole (or use 6–8 3-to-4-ounce individual soufflé dishes). Preheat the oven to 375° F.

4. Beat the egg yolks into the strawberry mixture and blend thoroughly, then stir in the vanilla.

5. Beat the egg whites with a pinch of salt until they are stiff but not dry, just until they hold firm peaks.

6. Gently fold the egg whites into the strawberries. Spoon the mixture into the prepared soufflé dish(es). Bake for 30–40 minutes (about 15 minutes for small ones), until puffed and very lightly browned.

7. Serve immediately, garnished with a dollop of whipped cream.

Serves 6–8

Biscuit Tortoni

"I scream, you scream, we all scream for ice cream!" As well we should, for it is only in this century, with the advent of widespread commercial refrigeration, that the sweet, cold, creamy treat has become available to everyone, in a staggering variety of flavors, from Chunky Monkey to Bubble Gum Chip. Frozen confections have a long history, however, and Italy has a centuries-old tradition of icy extravagances—gelati, sorbetti, granite, semifreddi—expensive indulgences created for the elite and cooled with imported ice. The tortoni are a part of this tradition, frozen creams into which cake or cookie crumbs are incorporated. Biscuit tortoni, made with almond-cookie crumbs, was one of two desserts served in the Italian restaurants of my childhood; it was a rare and supreme treat that I learned could be more cheaply and more frequently satisfied with a Good Humor Toasted Almond Bar.

2 egg yolks

⅓ cup sugar

2 tablespoons rum

½ teaspoon vanilla extract

½ teaspoon almond extract

⅓ cup (about) fine amaretti crumbs (macaroon or other
   almond-flavored biscotti crumbs can be substituted)

1 cup heavy cream

1. In the top of a double boiler, combine the egg yolks, the sugar, and the rum and whisk to blend thoroughly. Cook the mixture over gently simmering water, whisking constantly, for 4–5 minutes, until it is thick and pale. (Don't overcook or you'll get scrambled eggs.) Remove from the heat and stir in the extracts and 2 tablespoons of the amaretti crumbs. Set aside to cool.

2. Whip the cream until stiff. Fold the whipped cream into the egg mixture.

3. Spoon the tortoni lightly into small fluted paper cups, or cupcake tins lined with paper or foil cups, or small individual 3-to-4-ounce soufflé cups. Lightly smooth the top of the tortoni, then sprinkle each with a teaspoon or so of amaretti crumbs. The whole top should be covered with a layer of crumbs. (Biscuit tortoni is traditionally garnished with a maraschino cherry, but since I don't like maraschino cherries I have omitted them.)

4. Cover the tortoni with plastic wrap and freeze. Remove from the freezer about 10 minutes before serving.

Makes 6–8 cups

Cranberry Fool

The English have bequeathed us a legacy of sweet treats and a wealth of whimsical names to describe them—trifle, flummery, tipsy cake, and fool. The fool is a simple but delectable concoction of stewed pureed fruit mixed with whipped cream—really, a simple mousse. It was traditionally made with gooseberries, an English favorite, but cranberries make an excellent alternative, their unique tart flavor enhanced with a bit of Grand Marnier. The fool should be served chilled in small goblets or glasses, but small teacups or custard cups will do as well.

1½ cups fresh cranberries
¼ cup orange juice
½ cup plus 2 tablespoons sugar
2 tablespoons Grand Marnier
1½ cups heavy cream
½ teaspoon vanilla extract
Fresh mint sprigs, for garnish

1. In a small saucepan, combine the cranberries, the orange juice, and the ½ cup of sugar. Bring to the simmer, then cook, uncovered, over moderate heat, stirring occasionally, for about 10–15 minutes. The mixture should be soft and thick. Remove from the heat and let cool.

(continued)

2. Puree the cranberry mixture with the Grand Marnier in a blender or food processor.

3. Whip the cream with the vanilla and the 2 tablespoons of sugar until stiff. Fold the whipped cream gently but thoroughly into the cranberry puree.

4. Spoon the mixture into individual serving glasses or cups. Chill thoroughly. Garnish each cup with a sprig of mint.

Serves 6–8

Karidopita

(Greek Walnut Cake)

Nuts, both cultivated and wild, have been an important and valuable food for humans throughout history, and wherever resources permitted were sweetened with sugar or honey and combined with fruits and other costly ingredients to produce luxurious sweets and confections. The walnut has been a favorite in Greece from ancient times, and appears as the central ingredient in this traditional cake flavored with cinnamon, lemon, and olive oil.

$2\frac{1}{2}$ cups sugar

$\frac{1}{2}$ cup olive oil (preferably a fruity Greek variety)

2 eggs

2 cups flour

1 teaspoon baking powder

1 teaspoon baking soda

$\frac{1}{4}$ teaspoon salt

2 teaspoons cinnamon

$\frac{2}{3}$ cup buttermilk or sour milk (see Note)

$1\frac{1}{2}$ cups finely chopped freshly toasted walnuts

1 teaspoon grated lemon zest

1 cup water

1. In a large mixing bowl, combine 1 cup of the sugar with the oil and blend thoroughly. Beat in the eggs one at a time and mix until creamy. Preheat the oven to 350° F.

2. Combine the flour, baking powder, baking soda, salt, and cinnamon. Add the flour mixture to the batter alternately in thirds with the buttermilk, mixing well after each addition.

3. Stir in the walnuts and the lemon zest and mix thoroughly.

4. Spread the batter evenly in a buttered 13 × 9 × 2-inch baking pan or 12-inch round baking pan. Bake for about 30 minutes, until the cake is lightly browned and firm to the touch.

5. While the cake is baking, combine the remaining 1½ cups sugar with 1 cup water in a small saucepan. Bring to the boil, then simmer uncovered over low heat for about 10 minutes.

6. When the cake is done, remove it from the oven and turn off the oven heat. Pour the warm syrup slowly all over the hot cake, then return the cake to the oven for 5 minutes. Remove the cake from the oven and let cool completely. Cut into small pieces to serve.

Makes one 13 × 9 × 2-inch cake or one 12-inch round cake

NOTE: To make sour milk: Put 2 teaspoons of vinegar in a measuring cup. Add in enough milk to make ⅔ cup. Let stand at room temperature without stirring for ½ hour.

Fruited Almond Tea Loaf

Dried and preserved fruits have been appreciated for many generations as a costly and extravagant addition to sweets and cakes; they were esteemed in ancient Egypt, contribute heavily to the sweet tradition of China, and are widely used throughout the Middle East and Europe. So entrenched is the Christmas fruitcake that it has become a seasonal joke, the gift that no one wants. And who would, with its burden of bitter citron and hunks of nasty candied peels, all overwhelmed by a heavy dose of molasses and brandy? Here is a fruitcake I can relate to, with some really good dried fruits, bright almond flavor, and a dense buttery texture.

½ cup dried cranberries

½ cup dried blueberries

¼ cup Amaretto or other almond liqueur

1 cup (½ pound) unsalted butter, softened

1 cup sugar

2 extra-large eggs

½ cup sour cream

½ teaspoon almond extract

2 cups flour

¾ cup coarsely chopped blanched almonds

1. Combine the cranberries, the blueberries, and the amaretto and let stand for about ½ hour.

2. Cream the butter and the sugar together until fluffy and pale; add the eggs one at a time, beating well after each addition.

3. Stir in the sour cream and the almond extract and mix well. Preheat the oven to 350° F.

4. Add the flour to the batter and stir it in until it is just well blended. Add the almonds and the fruit mixture and mix well.

5. Butter a 9 × 5-inch or 12 × 4-inch loaf pan. Spoon the batter into the pan; even it out with the back of a spoon.

6. Bake the cake for 45–50 minutes, until it is lightly browned and a straw inserted in the middle comes out clean.

7. Let the cake cool on a rack for 20–30 minutes, then run a sharp knife around the edge of the pan and unmold the loaf. Let the cake cool completely, then cut into thin slices to serve.

Makes one loaf cake

Applesauce Cake with Mixed Nut–Honey Topping

The inspiration for the topping for this moist, spicy applesauce cake comes from the Near and Middle East, with its long tradition of honeyed nut pastries and confections. It makes a festive presentation, particularly for an autumn dinner or harvest celebration.

1 cup vegetable oil

1 cup sugar

2 extra-large eggs

2 cups applesauce

2 cups flour

1½ teaspoons baking soda

2 teaspoons cinnamon

1 teaspoon ground ginger

½ teaspoon ground allspice

½ teaspoon salt

½ cup honey

2 tablespoons fresh lemon juice

1–1¼ cups pecan halves

½ cup sliced almonds

⅓ cup coarsely chopped walnuts

2 tablespoons pine nuts

1 tablespoon finely chopped pistachios

1. In a large mixing bowl, beat the oil with the sugar, then add in the eggs one at a time, beating well after each addition. Stir in the applesauce and mix well. Preheat the oven to 350° F.

(continued)

2. Combine the flour, the baking soda, the spices, and the salt. Add the dry ingredients to the batter and mix until just well blended.

3. Spread the batter evenly in a buttered 12-inch round cake pan. Bake for 30–35 minutes, until it is nicely browned and firm to the touch. Let the cake cool on a rack for 30 minutes, then unmold onto a serving plate (or leave in the pan, if desired). Let cool completely.

4. In a small saucepan, combine the honey and the lemon juice. Heat, stirring, until it is liquid and smooth.

5. Brush the top of the cooled cake lightly but thoroughly with the honey mixture. Place the pecan halves, touching, in a ring around the outer rim of the cake.

6. Sprinkle the almond slices in a 1-inch-diameter ring inside the pecan ring. Sprinkle the chopped walnuts in a 1-inch-diameter ring inside the almond ring. Sprinkle the pine nuts in a ring inside the walnut ring; sprinkle the pistachios in the center.

7. Carefully spoon the remaining honey all over the nuts.

Makes one 12-inch cake; serves 10

Sweet Starts

The taste for sweetness has always been with us, but the means to satisfy it have not always been so readily available. The primary sweetener of the ancient world was honey, a syrupy sweet liquid manufactured by bees as food for the hive. It was sought out as a special, coveted treat by our prehistoric ancestors, and its great value and appeal led ultimately to the nearly worldwide occupation of beekeeping. So precious was honey that it figures as a primal food in the myths and legends of many cultures, a metaphor for the sweetest and therefore the best. Sweetness was also provided by a number of fruits with a high sugar content: dates, figs, and grapes were all used to produce syrups that gave other foods that all-important sweet taste. North American natives collected the sap from the sugar maple and boiled it to make a sweet syrup; the color and unique flavor of maple syrup come from impurities in the tree bark. Refined cane sugar seems to have originated in India some thousands of years ago; the English word "candy" is thought to derive from the Sanskrit term for raw sugar, *khanda*. It was not until the European conquest of the New World, however, that cane sugar became available as a cheap food for the masses. The islands of the Caribbean were ideal for the growing of sugar cane, and sugar plantations, worked by slaves from Africa, provided the world with enough refined sugar to satisfy its sweet tooth, but at a human cost that cannot be reckoned. Shakespeare, as he so often did, summed it up best: "Things sweet to taste prove in digestion sour."

Almond Raspberry Cake

The almond is an ancient native of the Near East; almonds and pistachios are the only nuts mentioned by name in the Old Testament. The Arab world has long valued almonds sweetened with sugar or honey in a variety of pastries and confections, and the tradition traveled to Europe with the Greeks and later the Romans. The paste of ground almonds and sugar known as marzipan, or "marchpane" in Elizabethan England, was considered an esteemed luxury, colored and shaped into a variety of decorative forms and presented to royalty or to honored guests. This rich little torte is very similar to many old recipes for almond cakes, except, of course, for the chocolate bits in the cookie crust.

For the crust

⅓ cup brown sugar, firmly packed

¾ cup flour

½ cup quick oats

½ cup chocolate mini-morsels

½ cup (4 ounces) unsalted cold butter, cut into small pieces

For the cake

½ cup (4 ounces) unsalted butter, at room temperature

½ cup sugar

3 eggs

1 cup very finely chopped blanched almonds

¼ teaspoon salt

½ teaspoon almond extract

½ cup seedless raspberry preserves

Confectioners' sugar and shaved chocolate curls,
    for garnish

1. Make the crust: In a medium bowl, combine the brown sugar, the flour, the oats, and the chocolate bits and mix well. With a pastry cutter, two knives, or your fingers, work the cold butter into the dry ingredients until the mixture resembles a coarse meal.

2. Pat the crumb mixture evenly into the bottom of a lightly buttered 9-inch springform pan.

3. Make the cake: In a mixing bowl, cream the room-temperature butter with the sugar until it is smooth and creamy. Add the eggs one at a time, beating well after each addition. Preheat the oven to 350° F.

4. Stir the almonds, the salt, and the almond extract into the batter and mix thoroughly.

5. Spread the preserves evenly over the bottom crust, to within about ½ inch of the sides. (You may have to heat the jam slightly in order to spread it easily.)

6. Spread the almond batter evenly over the preserves. Bake the cake for about 40 minutes, until it is nicely browned and just set. Remove it from the oven and let cool completely.

7. When the cake is cool, run a sharp knife around the edge and unmold onto a serving plate. Decorate with a light dusting of confectioners' sugar and some chocolate curls. Chill thoroughly before serving. Cut into small wedges to serve.

Makes one 9-inch cake; serves 8–10

Harvest Vegetable Spice Cake

For Europeans, from Roman times on, the allure of the "fabled East" lay largely in its wealth of spices and seasonings, primarily black pepper, which was quite literally worth its weight in gold. Also coveted were the sweet aromatic spices—cinnamon, nutmeg, ginger, cloves—that gave wonderful fragrance and flavor to both sweet and savory foods. These spices have been retained as an intrinsic part of the savory tradition in Asia and the Middle East but have largely dropped out in Europe, where they function primarily as flavoring for sweet foods—cookies, cakes, and sweet breads. The French *pain d'épices* and the English gingerbread are examples of this now venerable tradition of European spiced sweets, one that came to America and evolved into a new complex of spice cakes and quick breads. In this cake, the traditional aromatic spices enhance a vegetable mixture of carrot, zucchini, and yellow squash, which give it a moist, dense texture, attractive color, delicate flavor, and a good supply of valuable nutrients.

    1 cup olive or vegetable oil
    2 cups sugar
    4 eggs
    2 cups flour
    ½ teaspoon salt
    2 teaspoons baking soda
    2 teaspoons cinnamon
    1 teaspoon ground ginger
    ½ teaspoon ground allspice
    ¼ teaspoon grated nutmeg
    2 teaspoons grated orange rind
    1 teaspoon vanilla extract
    2 carrots, grated
    2 small-to-medium zucchini, grated
    2 small-to-medium yellow summer squash, seeded and
        grated (you should have a total of about 4 cups grated
        vegetables)

1 cup coarsely chopped walnuts

Confectioners' sugar, for garnish

1. In a large mixing bowl, combine the oil and sugar and mix well.

2. Add the eggs one at a time, beating well after each addition.

3. Combine the flour with the salt, baking soda, cinnamon, ginger, allspice, and nutmeg. Add these dry ingredients to the wet and mix until thoroughly blended. Preheat the oven to 350° F.

4. Add the orange rind, the vanilla, the grated vegetables, and the nuts to the batter and mix well. Pour the mixture into a well-buttered 10-inch bundt pan and bake for 50–60 minutes, until a straw inserted in the middle comes out clean.

5. Let the cake cool on a rack for 20 minutes, then unmold onto a plate. Let cool completely, then dust with confectioners' sugar.

Makes one 10-inch cake; serves 10–12

Flourless Chocolate Cake with Praline Whipped Cream

Since the introduction of relatively inexpensive confectionary, eating, and baking chocolate to a wide market at the end of the nineteenth century, Americans have set themselves the goal of producing the deepest, darkest, densest chocolate cakes imaginable; in that endeavor they have employed a variety of somewhat bizarre ingredients, including sauerkraut, mashed potatoes, mayonnaise, and condensed tomato soup. Only in the last couple of decades did someone figure out that what you leave out might be more important than what you put in—in this case, the flour. There are a host of variations on the theme; in this one, the cake is baked in a water bath, which makes for a more even and delicate texture.

8 ounces semisweet or bittersweet baking chocolate
  (not chips)
4 ounces (½ cup) unsalted butter
¼ cup sugar
4 eggs, separated
1½ teaspoons vanilla extract
¼ teaspoon salt
2 tablespoons brown sugar
1 cup heavy cream
2–3 tablespoons finely chopped freshly toasted pecans

1. In a medium saucepan, combine the chocolate and the butter and cook, stirring, over low heat until the mixture is melted and smooth.

2. Stir in the sugar and mix until well blended. Remove from the heat and let cool slightly. Preheat the oven to 350° F.

3. When the chocolate mixture has cooled slightly, add the egg yolks, one at a time, mixing well after each addition. When all the yolks have been incorporated, stir in 1 teaspoon of the vanilla.

4. Add the salt to the egg whites and beat until foamy. Add 1 tablespoon of the brown sugar and continue to beat until the whites form soft peaks.

5. Carefully but thoroughly fold the beaten egg whites into the chocolate mixture.

6. Butter the bottom and sides of a 9-inch cake pan. Carefully spread the batter evenly into the pan, then set the pan into a larger pan. Pour boiling water into the larger pan so that it comes about halfway up the sides of the smaller pan.

7. Bake the cake for about 35 minutes, until the center feels firm when gently pressed.

8. Remove the cake from the water bath; let cool completely.

9. Whip the cream with the remaining 1 tablespoon brown sugar and ½ teaspoon of vanilla until stiff. Cut the cake into small wedges to serve; garnish each serving with whipped cream and the chopped pecans.

Serves 8

Chocolate-Glazed Shortbread Squares

Cookies! They are among the most familiar and popular of the world's sweets, bite-sized morsels of sugary fun in a multitude of forms, for special occasions and holidays, or just a quick fix for an aching sweet tooth. Our word "cookie" comes from the Dutch *koekje*, "little cake," but our cookies come from everywhere, and who can choose among them—the plump little French madeleines, the buttery Scottish shortbread, the rich Chinese almond cakes, the crisp Italian biscotti, the sugar-drenched Greek kourabiethes, and the classic American chocolate-chip? Here's one more for the cookie jar.

1 cup (8 ounces) plus 2 tablespoons unsalted butter,
    softened
1 cup sugar
2 egg yolks
½ teaspoon vanilla extract
2 cups flour
4 ounces semisweet or bittersweet chocolate
3 tablespoons finely chopped pistachios (any other nut
    can be substituted, but pistachios look very pretty)

1. Cream the 1 cup of softened butter with the sugar until it is smooth. Add the egg yolks and the vanilla and blend in well.
2. Add the flour and mix it in until it is thoroughly blended. The batter will be fairly stiff. Preheat the oven to 300° F.
3. Generously butter a rimmed 15 × 10-inch baking sheet. Spread the batter evenly in the pan, using a small spatula or broad knife, or use your hands and a sheet of waxed paper. It is important to spread the batter in as even a layer as possible, so that it bakes evenly.
4. Bake the sheet for 30–40 minutes, until lightly and evenly browned.
5. While the cake is baking, combine the chocolate with the remaining 2 tablespoons of butter. Cook over low heat, stirring, until the mixture is melted and smooth.
6. As soon as the cake is done, remove it from the oven and care-

fully spread the chocolate mixture evenly over the top. Sprinkle the chopped nuts over the chocolate.

7. While the cake is still hot, cut it into small squares or rectangles, making sure that the knife cuts all the way through the shortbread. After cutting, let the cookies cool completely in the pan.

Makes about 40 cookies

Yellowjacket Tart

A high point of the English and Scottish sweet tradition is lemon curd, a rich and delicious concoction of lemon, sugar, butter, and eggs. Though the English use it as a spread for toast or scones, I prefer it as an ingredient in pies and cakes, like this tart, named for its colors, which so closely mimic those of the plump little yellowjacket bee. The recipe makes two cups of lemon curd; save the second cup for the cheesecake on page 334.

For the crust

1½ cups flour
3 tablespoons sugar
½ teaspoon cinnamon
Good pinch salt
9 tablespoons (1 stick plus 1 tablespoon) cold unsalted
    butter, cut into small pieces
2 egg yolks
½ teaspoon vanilla extract

For the lemon curd

3 whole eggs
1 egg yolk
1 cup sugar
2 tablespoons grated lemon zest
6 ounces fresh lemon juice
½ cup (1 stick) unsalted butter

1 small fresh flower (marigold, nasturtium, etc.), for
    decoration
1 pint fresh blackberries

1. Make the crust: In a bowl, combine the flour, the sugar, the cinnamon, and the salt. Mix well.
2. Add the butter pieces and cut them into the flour with a pastry

cutter or your fingers until the mixture has the consistency of a coarse meal.

3. Add the egg yolks and the vanilla and mix until well blended. Preheat the oven to 300° F.

4. Pat the mixture evenly and firmly into the bottom, not up the sides, of an 11-inch tart pan with a removable bottom. Bake for 25–30 minutes, until the crust is lightly browned. Remove from the oven and let cool.

5. Make the lemon curd: In the top of a double boiler, combine the eggs, the egg yolk, and the sugar, and mix thoroughly. Stir in the lemon zest, the juice, and the butter.

6. Cook over lightly boiling water, stirring constantly, for about 10 minutes, or until the mixture is thickened and smooth. Remove from the heat and let cool completely.

7. To assemble: Remove the tart crust from the ring and place on a serving plate. Spread the crust evenly with 1 cup of the lemon curd. Place the flower in the center of the tart. Place the berries in a 1-inch ring around the outside of the tart; then place the remaining berries in a ring around the flower.

Makes one 11-inch tart; serves 6–8

NOTE: The lemon curd will keep for several weeks in a tightly covered jar in the refrigerator. It can be frozen for longer storage.

Toasted Coconut–Banana Cream Pie

The coconut is an ancient native of the Asian tropics, where it has long functioned as a critical ingredient in both sweet and savory dishes. In this recipe, its unique flavor joins hands with a Western tradition of sweets based on dairy products and eggs and spooned into pie crusts and pastry shells. Coconut not only flavors the pastry cream but forms the shell for the pie.

2 cups plus 2 tablespoons flaked sweetened coconut
4 tablespoons unsalted butter, melted
1 cup milk
1 cup unsweetened coconut milk
2 tablespoons unsalted butter
½ cup sugar
3 tablespoons cornstarch
¼ teaspoon salt
2 eggs
½ teaspoon vanilla extract
1 cup heavy cream
2 medium bananas

1. Preheat the oven to 400° F. Combine the 2 cups of sweetened coconut with the melted butter and mix thoroughly.

2. Lightly butter a 9-inch pie plate with a rim at least 2 inches high. With a spoon, press the buttered coconut evenly over the bottom and sides of the pie plate to form a shell (it does not need to go all the way to the top).

3. Bake the shell for 5–7 minutes, or until the coconut is lightly browned (the edge will brown faster than the bottom; remove the crust from the oven when the edge is browned or it will burn). Set aside to cool.

4. While the shell is baking, spread the remaining 2 tablespoons of coconut on a pan or baking sheet and place in the oven to brown. It will take only 2–3 minutes; watch carefully and remove it as soon as it is browned. Set aside to cool.

5. In a medium saucepan, combine the milk, the coconut milk, and the 2 tablespoons of butter. Over moderate heat, bring just to the scald without stirring.

6. Combine the sugar, cornstarch, and salt, and mix well.

7. Whisk the eggs until thoroughly blended, then whisk the sugar mixture into the eggs and blend very well.

8. Slowly add a little of the scalded milk to the egg mixture, beating or whisking as you add it. Add a little more, continuously beating, until the egg mixture is warm.

9. Add the egg mixture to the milk in the pot, stirring as you add it. When all the egg mixture has been added, cook over moderate heat, stirring constantly, for about 5 minutes, until the mixture becomes smooth and thickened. Remove from the heat, stir in the vanilla, then let cool thoroughly.

10. Whip the cream until stiff, then fold it into the cooled coconut cream.

11. Slice the bananas about ¼ inch thick and layer the slices evenly over the bottom of the coconut crust. Spoon the cream mixture over the bananas. Chill the pie thoroughly.

12. Just before serving, garnish the top of the pie with the reserved toasted coconut.

Serves 6–8

Pear Tart with Hazelnut Praline Topping

A tart is a layer of dough or a pastry shell spread or filled with all sorts of things, savory or sweet. The dough layer is frequently made from short crust or pastry dough but can also be made from a softer cake batter, with a slightly spongy texture, as in this tart, that contrasts nicely with the crunchy praline topping.

½ cup plus 3 tablespoons unsalted butter, softened
½ cup sugar
3 eggs
½ teaspoon vanilla extract
1 cup flour
4 medium pears, ripe but firm
½ cup brown sugar, firmly packed
2 tablespoons heavy cream
½ cup finely chopped hazelnuts

1. Cream the ½ cup of butter with the white sugar until smooth. Beat in the eggs, one at a time, and when they are fully incorporated, stir in the vanilla. Add the flour and blend in thoroughly.

2. Cut the pears in quarters, then peel and core. Cut each quarter into 3 slices lengthwise. Preheat the oven to 375° F.

3. Butter the bottom and sides of an 11-inch tart pan with a removable bottom. Spread the batter evenly in the bottom of the pan.

4. Starting at the outer edge, place the pear slices in a ring around the dough; use the remaining slices for the inside.

5. In a small saucepan, combine the remaining 3 tablespoons of butter with the brown sugar and blend until smooth. Cook over low heat, stirring, until the mixture is melted and smooth. Stir in the cream, then the hazelnuts, and mix well.

6. Spoon the topping over the pears, then spread carefully so that the topping covers as much of the tart as possible.

7. Bake the tart for 30 minutes, until the cake layer is firm and the topping is bubbly. Remove the tart from the oven and allow to cool thoroughly. Remove the tart from the tart ring (but leave the removable bottom) and place on a serving plate.

Serves 6–8

A Spoonful of Sugar

Mary Poppins knew of what she sang, but she may not have known why. In its early history in the West, refined sugar was regarded more as medicine than as food; it was not sold in food shops but dispensed in apothecaries and used as a remedy for a variety of ills, thought to soothe sore throats and quiet digestive upsets. Its reputation as a curative may have arisen from the fact that it was rare and costly and, in its most refined state as a pure white crystal, resembled drugs and other valuable substances. It was sometimes mixed with other precious ingredients, like powdered pearls, and used as a remedy for eye infections. Ouch! It was not until refined sugar became widely available as a cheap and accessible commodity that its value as a medication declined, but the tradition of sweets as remedies persists in such preparations as hot toddies, tea with honey, and sweetened cough syrups.

Blueberry Spice Pie with Whipped Ginger Cream

Sweetened fruit baked in pastry crusts or shells came to America from England, and we have made the most of a good thing. Not only has the repertoire of fruit expanded, but the toppings, the garnishes, and the shells have been elaborated into a multitude of delicious new varieties, as in this blueberry pie in a gingersnap crust. The flavor of the crust is echoed in the ginger-flavored whipped cream.

20 gingersnaps, crushed into fine crumbs
    (about 1½–1⅓ cups)
3 tablespoons butter, melted
2 quarts fresh blueberries
1 cup plus 1 tablespoon sugar
¼ cup cornstarch
2 tablespoons fresh lemon juice
1 teaspoon cinnamon
1 cup heavy cream
½ teaspoon vanilla extract
2 tablespoons ginger liqueur

1. Preheat the oven to 400° F. Lightly butter a deep 9-inch pie plate. Mix the crumbs with the melted butter, then spread the mixture evenly on the bottom and sides of the pie plate. Bake for 7–10 minutes, or until just lightly browned. Remove from the oven and let cool.

2. In a medium saucepan, combine 1 quart of the blueberries with the 1 cup of sugar, the cornstarch, the lemon juice, and the cinnamon. Cook over moderate heat, stirring constantly, until the mixture comes to the boil and becomes thickened and clear. Remove from the heat and let cool slightly.

3. Add the remaining 1 quart of blueberries to the cooked, cooled mixture and mix them in gently but thoroughly.

4. Whip the cream with the 1 tablespoon of sugar and the vanilla. When the cream is becoming thick, add the ginger liqueur and continue beating until the cream is stiff.

5. Mound the blueberry mixture into the reserved crust. Spoon the whipped cream in mounds around the edge. Chill the pie before serving.

Serves 6–8

Layered Apple Crisp Torte

A sweet, spicy apple filling is layered between apricot-glazed flour tortillas, which provide an easy and texturally interesting pastry layer. Like all layered dishes, this involves some time in the assembly but can be done ahead to be baked at the last minute. Though the crunchy crumb topping will lose its crispness if left to stand overnight, it can be restored by reheating in the oven.

5–6 large Granny Smith apples, peeled and thinly sliced
    (8 cups sliced)
¾ cup (about) sugar
1 tablespoon cinnamon
¼ cup plus 1 tablespoon flour
1 tablespoon fresh lemon juice
1 cup sour cream
½ teaspoon vanilla extract
¼ cup quick oats
¼ cup brown sugar, firmly packed
4 tablespoons cold butter, cut into small pieces
3 large (10-inch, burrito-size) flour tortillas
⅓ cup apricot preserves

1. In a large bowl, combine the sliced apples, ⅓ cup of the sugar, the cinnamon, the 1 tablespoon of flour, and the lemon juice. Mix well and set aside.

2. Combine the sour cream, 1 tablespoon of the sugar, and the vanilla. Mix well and set aside.

(continued)

3. Combine the ¼ cup of flour, the oats, the brown sugar, and ¼ cup of the granulated sugar. Mix well, then cut in the butter pieces with a pastry blender or your fingers until the mixture has the consistency of a coarse meal. Preheat the oven to 375° F.

4. Generously butter the bottom and sides of a 10-inch springform pan. Fit one of the tortillas into the bottom of the pan, pressing it so that the edges come up slightly onto the inside edges of the pan. Spoon about 2 tablespoons of the preserves evenly over the tortilla.

5. Spoon a third of the apples evenly over the tortilla. Spread another tortilla with 2 tablespoons of the preserves, then place it over the apples. Spoon another third of the apples evenly over the tortilla, then spoon the sour-cream mixture over the apples, to within ½ inch of the edges.

6. Spread the remaining tortilla with the remaining preserves, then place the tortilla in the pan. Spoon the remaining apples over the tortilla, and sprinkle the crumb mixture evenly over the apples.

7. Place the torte on a baking sheet and bake for 45–50 minutes, until it is bubbly and the topping is nicely browned. Remove from the oven and let cool for at least ½ hour.

8. Run a sharp knife around the edge of the pan, then unmold the torte onto a serving plate. Use a sharp serrated knife to cut into wedges. The torte is good warm or at room temperature; serve with ice cream, if desired.

Serves 6–8

Afterword

We began our story with simple chunks of meat sizzling over a fire, and we ended with a raft of elaborate constructions made from many ingredients manipulated with complex and sophisticated techniques. But the end of a book is not the end of the story, for with our endless curiosity and quest for novelty, we humans have always looked for new ways to go. What we see in the universal kitchen is an unfolding, a realization, of that which has been a part of our essential nature from the very beginning—the urge, the inclination, to transform raw foodstuffs into something wholly different. In some real way, an enchilada casserole or a strawberry soufflé existed as possibilities in our brains and in our hands long before the ingredients and the equipment necessary for their production became available. And on the other side of the coin, we still hugely enjoy those fire-charred kabobs and simple flatbreads that satisfied our remote ancestors so many generations ago.

In undertaking our destiny as the cooking animal, we have traveled along very similar paths, responding to new choices and new opportunities in ways that are remarkably alike. And in that enterprise, crucial to all our kind, we have occasionally produced art, for there are and have always been those few among us who have the genius, the special talent, to make us see things in a new way, to bring us to heightened levels of understanding and awareness. But it is to that which is already in us, a fundamental and defining part of our humanness, that the artist appeals, evoking the pleasure and gratification in well-cooked food that is in all of us.

It is, then, all the cooks we celebrate, the simple, the anonymous, the amateur, the rustic, as well as the artists and the professionals, who have always given us what is apparently necessary for a meaningful and fulfilled existence.

Index of
Ethnic Recipes

(*Denotes meatless dishes)

*Mediterranean Layered Salad
  Mussel Soup Avgolemono
*Olive, Walnut, and Garlic Pesto
  Stifatho of Duck with Onions and Mushrooms
  Tapenade with Tomatoes
  Taverna Shrimp
  Turkish Mussel Pilaf
*Turkish-style salsa
  Turkish Swordfish Kabobs
*Turkish Tarator
*Turkish White Bean Salad

India

  Ceylonese Chicken Korma
  Chicken Biryani
  Chicken Tikka
*Curried Vegetable Bake
*Fresh Mint and Coriander Chutney
*Ginger Coconut Raita
*Himalayan Hot Sauce
*Indian Potato-Stuffed Peppers
*Indian salsa
  Keema Curry
*Onion Kulcha
*Spiced Chickpeas and Potatoes
*Vegetable Pilau
*Vegetable Samosas

Italy

*Baked Vegetable Lasagne
  Braised Veal Shanks with Mixed Exotic Mushrooms
  Creamy Asparagus Risotto
  Herbed Polenta with Seared Portobello Mushrooms
  Italian Escarole Soup
*Mixed Vegetable Antipasto Salad
*Mixed Vegetable Caponata
*Mushroom and Artichoke Frittata
*Rosemary Focaccia with Olives, Garlic, and Pepper

Sicilian Sausage Sauce with Fennel and Peppers
Spaghetti with Anchovy and Garlic Cream
*Spinach and Mushroom Salad with Pine Nuts

Japan

Fresh Salmon Teriyaki
*Japanese Eggplant and Double Ginger Salad
Japanese Oyster Consommé
Norimake with Smoked Salmon
Salt-Grilled Mackerel
*Sesame-Ginger Spinach Salad

Korea

Korean Braised Chicken with Mushrooms and Cucumbers
Korean Crab and Vegetable Pancake
Korean-Style Barbecued Lamb
*Sesame Beansprout Salad

Latin America–Caribbean

Costa Rican Chicken-Tortilla Nuggets
Creole Chicken and Shrimp in Coconut-Cashew Curry
Curried Cream of Plantain Soup
Hot and Smoky Jerked Chicken
Pastel de Camarones (Creole Shrimp and Corn Pie)
Piccadillo

Mexico

Chile-Grilled Salmon Kabobs
*Enchilada Casserole with Green Chile–Tomatillo Sauce
Fresh Chorizo
Green Chile Rice with Crab
Mayan Turkey Kabobs
Mexican Carnitas
Panuchos
Pollo Almendrado (Chicken with Garlic-Almond Sauce)
Scrambled Eggs with Chorizo and Pepper Strips
Sopa de Tortilla (Mexican Chicken and Vegetable Soup)
*Sopa Seca de Tortilla (Tortilla Casserole with Chiles and Cheese)

*A Trio of Salsas
Veracruz Snapper Soup

Middle East and Central Asia
  Afghani Lamb and Onion Stew
*Afghani Leek Dumplings with Minted Yogurt
  Afghani Meat and Noodle Casserole
  Armenian Meat Sauce
  Armenian Shish Kabob
  Braised Spiced Lamb Shanks
  Central Asian Spiced Meat and Lentil Sauce
*Fattoush
*Hilbeh (Yemeni Fenugreek and Coriander Sauce)
*Iraqi Barley, Lentil, and Vegetable Stew
  Lahmajun (Armenian Meat Pies)
*Lebanese Eggs with Squash and Tomato
*Middle Eastern Tomato and Cucumber Salad
  Peppers Stuffed with Chicken, Rice, and Walnuts
*Persian Green Vegetable Cake
  Spiced Chicken-Falafel Croquettes
*Spiced Eggplant Wrapped in Phyllo
*Spiced Rhubarb Sauce
  Toasted Orzo Pilaf
*Tomato Bulgur and Toasted Noodle Pilaf

North Africa
  Egyptian Lentil and Chickpea Soup
*Moroccan Eggplant Salad
*Spiced Lentil and Golden Orzo Salad
*Spiced Vegetable Couscous

Northern Europe
  Cock-a-Leekie with Vegetables and Barley
  Coulibiac of Fresh Salmon with Leeks and Dill
  Creamy Bisque of Smoked Herring and Potato
*Russian Mixed Vegetable Salad
  Scandinavian-Style Veal and Mushroom Sauce
*Tangy Beet and Horseradish Relish

Index